P9-DOF-549

SEP 2000

The Tree & Shrub Finder

CHOOSING THE BEST PLANTS FOR YOUR YARD

ROBERT KOURIK

The Taunton Press

ST. THOMAS PUBLIC LIBRARY

*To my father, John Kourik, whose never-ending appreciation and support
have always nurtured my writing career and personal life.*

Publisher: *Jim Childs*
Acquisitions Editor: *Anne Halpin*
Assistant Editor: *Jennifer Renjilian*
Copy Editor: *Marjorie Wexler*
Cover and Interior Designer: *Lynne Phillips*
Layout Artist: *Lynne Phillips*
Illustrator: *Dolores R. Santoliquido*
Icon Illustrator: *Rosalie Vaccaro*
Indexer: *Catherine Goddard*

Taunton
BOOKS & VIDEOS
for fellow enthusiasts

Text © 2000 by Robert Kourik
Illustrations © 2000 by The Taunton Press, Inc.

All rights reserved.

Printed in the United States of America
10 9 8 7 6 5 4 3 2 1

The Taunton Press, Inc., 63 South Main Street, PO Box 5506, Newtown, CT 06470-5506
e-mail: tp@taunton.com

Distributed by Publishers Group West

Library of Congress Cataloging-in-Publication Data
Kourik, Robert.
The tree and shrub finder : choosing the best plants for your yard / Robert Kourik.
p.   cm.
ISBN 1-56158-258-1
1. Ornamental trees. 2. Ornamental shrubs. I. Title
SB435.K733   2000
635.9'77—dc21   99-053376

Acknowledgments

This book would not have been possible without the vast practical wisdom of the following experts from eight different regions of the country. Each person reviewed all the Plant Finders from the perspective of his or her unique experiences of climate, herbarium specimens, and reference books—a vital and intricate task.

Ron Brightman, horticulturist, provided valuable perspective for the Pacific Northwest region. Barrie Coate, consulting horticulturist, is one of the foremost experts in native and exotic plants growing in the middle coastal range of California, as well as elsewhere in the West. Donald R. Hodel, Landscape Advisor at the University of California Cooperative Extension, supplied detailed input for Southern California. Mary Irish, at the Desert Botanical Garden in Phoenix, Arizona, proved an able consultant for the arid zones of the Southwest. Several people at the Morton Arboretum in Lisle, Illinois, provided ideas about which cultivars are superior for the region. Those people are Tim Boland, Curator of Horticulture Collections; Doris Taylor, Plant Information Specialist; and Dr. Gary W. Watson, Root System Research Biologist. Mike Ruggiero, of The New York Botanic Gardens, used his vast knowledge coupled with library research and herbarium specimens to, in particular, authenticate the most up-to-the-minute names (both scientific and common) of all the plants from his region in the Plant Finders. Dr. Ken Tilt, from the Department of Agriculture at Auburn University, provided knowledgeable advice on the southeast region of the country. Chip Tynan, from the Missouri Botanical Garden, added his encyclopedic knowledge of the performance of trees and shrubs in the middle portion of the greater Midwest. (To contact any of these experts, see the listing in Resources on p. 180-181.)

Many thanks to the following people who provided invaluable help in making this book accurate and factual:

Victor D. Merullo, Attorney, Columbus, Ohio, for the care and time he took to explain the tangled web of the law as it pertains to tree and property ownership.

Barbara Barton, author of *Gardening by Mail: A Source Book,* 5th edition (Boston: Houghton Mifflin, 1997), who kindly lent me numerous books from her extensive collection to use for reference.

Marilyn Davis, of the Native Species Network (NSN), for insight into the ongoing discussion of pet and feral cats and their impact on wildlife and wild birds.

Many thanks also for the bountiful and selfless personal support I received while working on this project from the following friends and associates:

Chester Aaron, Suzanne and Roger Adams, Elvin and Cara Bishop, Ron and Patsy Chamberlain, Jan Coello, Michael Eschenbach, Sandy Farkas, Don Ketman, Kandis Kozolanka, Sandra Kazanjian, Marshia Loar and Clayton Ward (for providing such a beautiful, tranquil place to live), Mimi Luebbermann, Bernie Moss, Jan Mettler, Martha Metzger, Linda Parker, Winnie Piccolo, Salli Rasberry, "Sooz" Reeder, Owen Shirwo, Jim Sullivan, and Betsy Timm.

At Taunton Press, there were many helpful people without whom the book would have never even reached infancy:

Helen Albert (associate publisher), who started the process by considering my first proposal; Lynne Phillips, who designed and laid out the book; and Dolores Santoliquido, who created the illustrations.

A special thanks to two patient, understanding, and professional people at Taunton Press for nursing this book to fruition: Jennifer Renjilian (my editor) and Anne Halpin (garden books acquisitions editor). My hat is off to these two thoughtful and kind women.

Contents

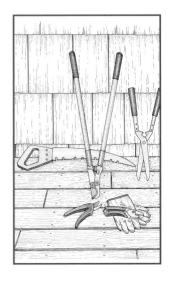

Introduction

This solitary Tree! a living thing

Produced too slowly ever to decay;

Of form and aspect too magnificent

To be destroyed.

"Yew Trees"—William Wordsworth

Artists have long celebrated trees. In poetry, fiction, and song, in painting and sculpture, trees stand for fertility, sturdiness, longevity, strength, and renewal. Much as a poet may use the tree to represent deep-rootedness and an ability to weather any storm, gardeners have added much mystical significance to these stately creatures of the forest. To gardeners, trees—and shrubs as well—seem to grow everywhere and appear so sturdy as to be nearly indestructible. Trees and woody shrubs are ubiquitous and thrive in almost every American environment and climate. Only the highest windswept peaks, the harshest saline desserts, and the deepest waters forgo their company.

Trees and woody shrubs are amazingly hardy, tenacious plants. Even surrounded by an asphalt jungle, some will prosper and hang on to dear life for decades. They exhibit a remarkable resilience for life and grow in the most apparently abysmal conditions, from vacant lots to deserts and swamps. On the other hand, they can appear to be delicate and vulnerable in the home setting, much to a gardener's dismay.

The solution is to plant the proper tree for the soil, the climate, and its intended function. Choosing the right trees and shrubs for your needs and growing conditions is the key to success. Choose wisely and your trees and shrubs will reward you with years of pleasure and few, if any, problems.

It is often tempting to select a plant for superficial reasons. We are drawn to them the way a shiny red tomato attracts us at the supermarket in the dead of winter. The allure of the form or color of the tomato can make an impression on a shopper. But when the tomato is eaten, it turns out to be a disappointment.

Similarly, many homeowners choose trees and shrubs because of their beautiful foliage, dramatic color, spectacular flowers, or impressively textured bark. They forget to consider whether the plant, and its root system, is suited to their yard's soil and climate. A few years after planting, the homeowner realizes the tree or shrub isn't growing well, doesn't produce many of those spectacular flowers, or succumbs to pest or disease problems because it is weak. But such disappointments needn't happen.

This book will guide you toward choosing just the right tree or shrub for your needs. It will assist you in making a decision that incorporates function along with beauty. For example, many people enjoy the natural majestic pyramidal shape of a liquidambar, or sweet gum, tree *(Liquidambar styraciflua)* and its blaze of orange, red, or yellow fall color. This glorious tree

can tolerate the compact soils found near many homes, but not all gardeners know or consider that its roots play havoc with driveways, sidewalks, and patios. A tree like this is best placed in the further reaches of the yard where it is easily seen from the house.

There need not be any conflict between beauty and function when it comes to selecting long-lived plants for

your yard. Woody shrubs and trees can serve a variety of functions. They can provide privacy screens, windbreaks to cut heating bills in the winter, and cooling summer shade. There are trees that tolerate the extremes of water and nutrients found in a well-tended lawn, trees that can support a cozy treehouse, trees that attract birds and butterflies, and even trees that are ideal to plant as a legacy for one's grandchildren.

Some forethought is required and perhaps a bit more searching at your local nurseries or tree farms to find the best tree or shrub for the job. But all

these practical uses can be merged with growing needs, and you will discover attractive, functional trees and shrubs for every region in the country.

Part 1 of this book covers many of the functions shrubs and trees can offer the gardener, the home, and its landscape. The goal is to help you weave together the best of utility with form, color, texture, and beauty. A well-functioning yard need not be bleakly utilitarian; it can be useful *and* gorgeous. This book attempts to incorporate a wide range of aesthetics, realizing that one person's "beautiful" may be another's "mediocre," and vice versa.

Each chapter focuses on one of these utilitarian or aesthetic features. You'll find the information you need to choose the tree or shrub based on the function you want it to perform. You will find the top plants for each purpose in plant finders (see p. 6 on how to use these guides). But you will also find out the background information you need to know before you choose your plants. For instance, you'll need to determine how high your hedge needs to be before you decide what to plant.

The second part of the book tells you how to care for your chosen trees or shrubs. This book gathers together the best, most up-to-date information for the "cradle-to-grave" care for ornamental and fruiting shrubs and trees for the contemporary gardener. It would be a waste of precious money and time to purchase a tree and then proceed to plant it in a fashion that encumbers its natural growth and well-being. To nurture a shrub or tree wisely, you first must realize what commonly held misconceptions might currently be among your gardening "commandments." Gardeners wrapped in a cloak of old-fashioned fables are only stumbling on myth—and their trees and shrubs will suffer.

Sometimes we create a yard by removing the forest. Other times we add trees where only a wild meadow has been. But the forest is *the* primordial model for what we do with trees in our yards. Sometimes our perception of the forest is full of grandiose wishes, other times we're making false assumptions, and sometimes we just invent the truth. So much of our intentions with trees and shrubs have really been just hit or myth. The little-questioned assumptions about how trees and shrubs grow, the amount of water and fertilizer they require for healthy growth, and how to care for them are often more shrouded in mythology than fact. But all this is about to change with this book.

The new attitudes begin with buying the trees and shrubs we want to plant. The old guideline of "bigger is better" is slowly fading. Observant

gardeners have begun to notice that smaller plants often grow quickly, readily catching up with larger transplants, and they are hardier to drought, ice, snow, and wind because they have healthier root systems. And research has confirmed these observations. Equally important, smaller transplants cost considerably less money. These new ideas provide the plant *and* the gardener with a win-win situation.

Quietly, over the past 20 years, a revolution in the way we look at tree and shrub growth and how we care for trees has occurred. The careful research of dedicated scientists has uncovered many radical new guidelines for home gardeners. In most cases, these new guidelines are completely contrary to what we've always been told—even by our own grandparents! My grandfather

didn't lie when he said, "Dig as deep a hole as possible, fill it with plenty of good loose soil, and plant." He was just reflecting one of the popular assumptions of the day.

Science and good observation have since revealed that planting in *completely* unamended native soil—using the proper rootstock—is far more effective and is likely to produce much greater, healthier growth. (This is fully explained in Chapter 10.)

Part of a healthy approach begins with adequate amounts of water and fertility. My relatives in the country watered young shade trees only if the summer was really dry. Routinely, they placed the sprinkler next to the trunk to "give the roots a deep watering." Now we know that watering beyond the crown (past the drip line of the foliage) and using drip irrigation

results in healthier, more rapid or productive growth.

Another good example of following nature's lead is making sure the compacted subsoil left by the building contractor gets inoculated with naturally occurring mycorrhizal fungi. These often-ignored fungi—which act like living feeding tubes to extend a tree or shrub's root system—are found in every undisturbed forest. The reintroduction of these beneficial fungi into a highly disturbed or sterile soil can increase the growth of potted or transplanted trees by as much as 1,500 percent. Such an approach, along with modern planting techniques, can allow the gardener to skip fertilizing most trees and shrubs altogether.

Once a tree or shrub is planted, it may require occasional pruning. Once in a while, some bit of old-time wisdom disappears only to resurface decades later and be well supported by modern scientific scrutiny. A perfect example is my grandmother Tevis's advice, "You can't prune fruit trees in the summer; that's only for late winter (dormant) pruning."

After heeding this advice for over 20 years, I found an original copy of Edward Wickson's 1919 book entitled *California Fruits.* This was the first time I had heard about the value of pruning fruit trees in summer—and it applies to most ornamental trees and shrubs as well. At the same time, the

research of intensive orchard techniques by state cooperative extension services and universities around the country was recertifying this important pruning strategy as valid and safe. The concept has come full circle.

After World War II, many people firmly believed in the science of gardening—that is, using chemical pesticides to eliminate pests. Each spring, many homeowners would routinely powder the base of the home's foundation with a white powder containing DDT, chlordane, or lindane to prevent ants from entering. All of these are persistent chemical pesticides that kill many good as well as bad insects that come in contact with the powder. All three also linger in the environment and are a potential health hazard to people, especially young children.

These days, more and more people are aware that the healthiest way to deal with pests is to wait until they show up, use the least toxic compound (whether chemically or organically derived), and target only the pest— trying to avoid harming the natural predators of the pest. All these earth-friendly principles, and more, will be discussed in Chapter 13.

As poetic as trees remain, one practicality is litigation when things go awry across property lines. Trees, sadly, have legal ramifications. Mix

trees, property lines, and wind or ice storms, and legal troubles can lift their Medusa-like head. Fortunately, there are some good guidelines for communication between neighbors without the cost of legal counsel. These are outlined in Appendix 2. If a dispute comes to an impasse, there is help from lawyers who specialize in the legal "standing" of trees or how to mediate disputes with regard to the damage done by (or to) trees. How to find these special lawyers is also described in Appendix 2.

The science and practice of trees and shrubs entails relentless exploration and constant evolution. In the coming years and decades, much will be learned, and it may outdate whole chapters in this book. Then I'll write an updated book for you!

How to Use the Plant Finders

In each chapter you'll find one or more "Plant Finders"—the core of the book's reference material. These are lists of special plants from around the country and world that have unique attributes to the chapter's topic. The plants are listed alphabetically by their Latin name, but the most frequently used common name is also provided.

The approximate height and width of each plant is given, along with the United States Department of Agriculture's (USDA) recommended range of zones in which the plant will thrive. For most plants, icons are provided indicating, for example, that

the tree or shrub resists being eaten by deer, provides food for birds, resists strong winds, tolerates drought, withstands clayey soils, or tolerates sandy (low-nutrient) soils (more about these icons later).

All plants are not all good. Therefore, after each plant's initial listing there appears a short notation of the special attributes and pertinent limitations of the tree or shrub. For example, some beautiful or practical trees are well behaved in one climate but "escape" to be rampant weeds in other parts of the country. Some of these exotic intruders have been excluded from the book altogether;

others have a detailed description of where they should be grown or *not* grown. If a highly useful tree or shrub is suited for more than one purpose, it will be described in full in one Plant Finder and then cross-referenced in other Plant Finders.

The plants in each Plant Finder are only a basic starter list. Nature offers a much greater variety and complexity than any chart can reflect. Also, elevation, latitude, and many other factors will influence the type of climate from one part of a zone to another. Be observant and learn what thrives in your town and neighborhood. Check with local

Plant Finders

Latin name
COMMON NAME

USDA ZONES:
SIZE:

COMMENTS:

Latin name
COMMON NAME

USDA ZONES:
SIZE:

COMMENTS:

Latin name
COMMON NAME

USDA ZONES:
SIZE:

COMMENTS:

nurseries and with your nearest cooperative extension and/or Master Gardeners group for other options.

Sometimes, experts from around the country offered different judgments. Whenever, for example, one regional expert listed a plant as resistant to deer browsing but others listed the same plant as being susceptible, I took the conservative route and did not give the plant a deer icon. Always double-check with local experts if you have any concerns about the appropriateness of a plant in this book. Any error with regard to entering or combining the regional experts' input is solely my responsibility.

Here's what the icons mean:

 DEER indicates some degree of resistance to deer eating the foliage. However, this is affected by many factors, such as weather and the deer population (cold winters and over-crowding make deer less choosy). I've used several national references to double-check this information, but when in doubt you should check with your local experts.

 BIRDS means the tree or shrub supplies fruits, berries, nuts, or seeds for all birds except hummingbirds (which are in a separate list on p. 90). Almost all trees and shrubs are attractive to birds for shelter, roost-ing, and nest-building, but the icon focuses on food supply. Bird feeding will vary considerably from place to place, so observe your local bird activity or consult a birder.

 WIND indicates a tree or shrub inherently resistant to wind, snow, or ice dam-age if properly planted.

 DROUGHT is a rela-tive concept. In the Midwest, 3 weeks without rain in July is a drought. In the arid West, virtually rainless summers can stretch out to 5 or 6 months. When a plant is marked with an icon to denote drought resistance, it usually pertains to the worst-case scenarios of summer-dry California. If the plant survives such a drought with little or no irrigation, then it *may* thrive in other climates with rainier summers. (However, too much rain can cause root rots, mildew, and fungus, which

may disfigure or kill certain drought-resistant plants. Be sure to check with local resources for details pertaining to your climate.)

 CLAY refers to heavy clay (also called gumbo), which is tough on the roots of most plants. A finely tex-tured soil (clay, but not gumbo) is more forgiving and may have plenty of nutrients, but it's hard for water to penetrate it (once the soil is moist, however, it holds moisture for a long time). Any plants marked with this icon will grow decently in heavy clay soils but will thrive with better drainage.

 SANDY indicates the plant can grow in a sandy soil that provides rapid drainage, is low in fertility (added fertilizer is easily washed away), is rather deep (not sitting on top of heavy clay), and has little humus. Plants marked with this icon have roots systems that can support them in this looser soil.

Choosing the Best Plants

CHAPTER ONE

Privacy

ALL OF US VALUE PRIVACY, but it can be hard to come by in many neighborhoods, where homes are often built close together. Some privacy issues are obvious. For instance, you may be tired of the neighbors looking in your bathroom window from their living room. But other privacy needs are more subtle. Maybe you're sick of having the neighbors' megawatt porch light shining through your bedroom curtains. The good news is that privacy usually can be created, even on small suburban or city lots, with well-planned hedges and screens. For those with larger yards, hedgerows offer privacy, as well as bird and butterfly habitat and energy-conserving advantages. In essence, the plants become "living fences" for personal sanctuary.

This hedge defines the line between public and private spaces.

aspects of a hedgerow means you'll have more comfortable time to enjoy the yard and its "living privacy." Because of their size, hedgerows are composed of trees and shrubs that remain unclipped and grow unencumbered. All three privacy options are planted with evergreen shrubs or trees so your family's privacy is protected year-round.

A hedge often defines a space and creates a sense of seclusion, even though some hedges are short enough to look over when you're standing. Other hedges create rooms in the garden with "walls" tall enough to block the view of passing cars and people. Screens are taller still, quite useful when obscuring a nearby house or neighbors on a hill. Screens are often long and narrow and may be clipped like hedges.

If you need more than just a hedge or a few trees to provide privacy, a hedgerow may be the solution. Frequently composed of both trees and shrubs, hedgerows are wider, and often longer, than normal hedges. But a well-designed hedgerow (also called a windbreak) is placed with enough distance from the home—on larger properties—to shelter the house from cold winds in the winter or desiccating summer winds. Using the windbreak

This long hedgerow of spruce trees (*Picea* spp.) was planted mostly perpendicular to the cold winter winds to make it easier to heat the home.

The species form of the American arborvitae (*Thuja occidentalis*) can grow to 60 ft., but the cultivar 'Fastigiata' (shown here) stays below 25 ft. when mature.

Determining the Plant Size You Need

Unlike fences, plants are alive and ever changing, so when using them as barriers, you must consider short-term versus long-term growth. A shrub or tree that quickly grows to 5 ft. tall will probably continue to grow just as rapidly to 15 ft. or 20 ft., or even higher. Conversely, a plant that is 5 ft. tall at maturity may take a *long* time—possibly a decade or more—to reach its full size.

Many cultivars of hedge plants grow considerably shorter than the original species of the plant from which they were bred. For example, the typical American arborvitae (*Thuja occidentalis*) can grow as tall as 60 ft., but there are many cultivars that are much shorter and more compact. The cultivar 'Fastigiata' reaches only 25 ft. at maturity, while 'Nana' stays below 2 ft. In many plants, cultivars have been bred for special traits not present in the original species of the plant. The cultivar 'Greenspire' has a more uniform branching form and a stronger central leader than the species form of the deciduous littleleaf linden (*Tilia cordata*).

It can be tempting to plant a fast-growing hedge to get quick results. But if the plant is too assertive, it may require frequent pruning. A good hedge requires some care, but it should not make outrageous demands on your time. On average, a plant can be kept at about 20 to 25 percent of its normal mature height without an excessive investment of time and effort. For example, the evergreen Japanese yew (*Taxus cuspidata*)

Before planting, determine how high and wide a sheared hedge will be allowed to grow to provide the desired privacy.

normally grows to 40 ft. tall, but it can be sheared back to 8 ft. to 10 ft. without a lot of work.

Matching the plant's growth rate to the amount of time you have available for pruning is important. In another scenario, while an evergreen tree like the southern magnolia (*Magnolia grandiflora*) grows 80 ft. to 100 ft. tall if left alone, it can be kept to 8 ft. tall—but only with considerable skill and effort.

While compact cultivars require less work, it will take considerably longer for a hedge composed of them to reach its mature height. For example, an English holly (*Ilex aquifolium*) naturally grows slowly to about 40 ft., but the holly cultivar Gold Coast grows to no more than 6 ft. to 8 ft. tall. Both take up to 10 years to reach their mature height. While the Gold Coast holly might fit your ultimate goal of 8 ft., it will leave the view unscreened for more years than the clipped species. The species form may reach the 8-ft. level in about 2 years—as much as 7 to 8 years sooner than 'Gold Coast'. It's often better to plant the faster-growing plant and clip or shear the top as the plant nears its mature height.

When you begin your search for a hedge plant for your soil and climate, you'll need to know where in the yard to plant the hedge to screen the undesirable view(s). It's also important to consider how high and wide you need the mature plants to be so they give privacy.

Where to plant

You must make sure the site is compatible with the size of plant you need. The best place for a hedge, screen, or hedgerow to block unwanted views depends greatly on the size, width, and depth of your yard. The common tendency is to place the hedge along the property line to keep the lawn or yard as open as possible. This can create a problem.

Many courts have declared trees or shrubs planted directly on a boundary line to be jointly owned by both homeowners. With less-than-friendly homeowners, this can lead to considerable difficulties if the two sides cannot agree on how to care for or trim the hedge. Courts have generally ruled that your neighbors have the right to trim or shear as they see fit, any portion of any shrub or tree planted on your property but overhanging their yard. (For more details, see Appendix 2 on p. 177.) The prudent approach is to plant your hedge, screen, or hedgerow so the mature width of the foliage doesn't overhang the property line.

Also, be sure to check your deed for any utility or other form of easement—such as roads, public paths, parklands, or rights of passage. Utilities both above and below the

The Japanese yew (*Taxus cuspidata*) 'Capitata,' above, is clipped closer to its mature height of 40 ft. The same cultivar is sheared as a 4-ft. hedge on the left.

Measuring Changes in Elevation

IF THE ELEVATION YOU'RE MEASUR-ING is on your neighbor's property, you'll need his permission to use this technique. To measure the elevation, you'll need to take several small measurements. It takes a bit of effort, but it's pretty simple. You'll need a 10-ft. 2x4, a carpenter's level, some string, and a tape measure.

Place one end of the 2x4 at ground level where the ground starts to rise or drop off. Tie the level to the top of the 2x4, and keep it and the 2x4 level. Measure the distance to the ground (shown below) and record this measurement. Place one end of the 2x4 on the ground at the point you just measured to, hold it level, measure

down to the ground again, and add this number to your list.

Keep moving the 2x4 down or up the hill in 10-ft. increments. After spanning the distance of the slope, total all the individual measurements and you will have the total change in elevation.

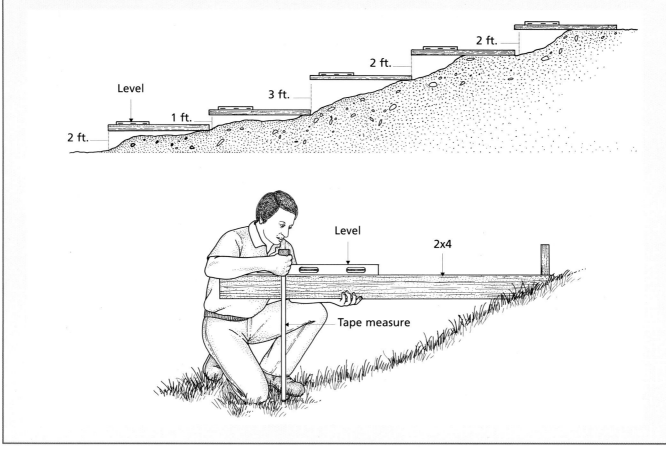

Level

2 ft.

1 ft.

3 ft.

2 ft.

2 ft.

2 ft.

Level

2x4

Tape measure

ground are often granted easements, which allow the utility company to control or remove plants as deemed necessary for the construction, maintenance, or improvement of the utility. This means a mature hedge can be ripped out without notice if, for example, a new pipe needs to be installed by a local water and sewage authority. On the other hand, some courts have awarded the homeowner money for the value of the trees or shrubs removed by utility companies or government agencies.

Predicting growth

When planning a privacy hedge, screen, or hedgerow, especially in tight or hilly situations, there's a simple way to ballpark its appropriate location and height. There's also a slightly more complicated method that allows you to experiment with various sizes and locations on paper.

For the simple approach, all you need is a 20-ft.-tall pole or 2x4, some spray paint, a wooden stake, and a hammer. Mark the pole with spray paint at 1-ft. intervals. Station one person in the house at the window that needs screening, while another person walks around the yard and stands the pole vertically at potential planting locations. The person in the house will quickly be able to see, by looking at the marks on the pole, what height will be required at each location to screen out undesired views or viewers. Make a note of the minimum height and pound a stake into the ground at the place where the pole was located.

To chart many options at once (including trees), the procedure is more complicated. You will need a pencil, a ruler, and some graph paper (four squares to the inch works well, with each small square on the graph paper equaling 1 ft. on your chart). For this example, imagine that you're viewing the yard from the north. The left side of the graph paper represents the east, so the west is on the right side, where a neighbor's house stands.

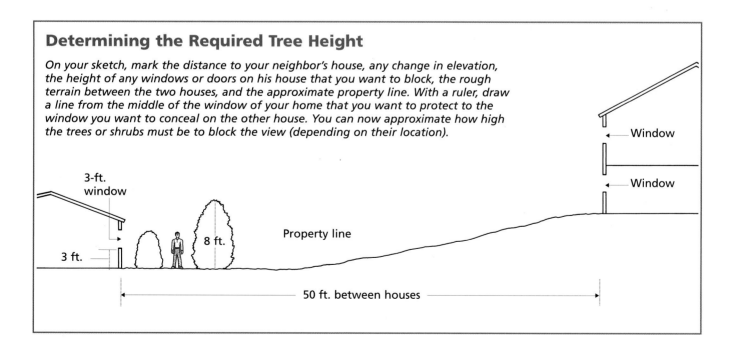

Determining the Required Tree Height

On your sketch, mark the distance to your neighbor's house, any change in elevation, the height of any windows or doors on his house that you want to block, the rough terrain between the two houses, and the approximate property line. With a ruler, draw a line from the middle of the window of your home that you want to protect to the window you want to conceal on the other house. You can now approximate how high the trees or shrubs must be to block the view (depending on their location).

3-ft. window

3 ft.

8 ft.

Property line

Window

Window

50 ft. between houses

(You'll need to choose the appropriate direction from which to view your own property.) Near the center of the left side of the graph paper, mark a horizontal line representing the floor of your home. Sketch in a vertical line for the wall—usually 8 ft. to 10 ft. tall—facing your neighbor's house. Be sure to note the lower and upper edges of the window with the view to be protected with horizontal hash marks.

If your neighbor's house has a lower or higher elevation than yours, try to estimate the change in elevation. If you want to measure it more accurately, try the technique shown in Measuring Changes in Elevation on p. 14.

Now, roughly sketch in the terrain between the two houses and be sure to mark the approximate property line (see p. 15). If your neighbor gives permission, measure the actual distance between the two houses. Otherwise, take your best guess. Mark the distance and any change in elevation for the neighbor's house on the right side of the paper. Be sure to measure or guess the height of any windows or other portion of their house that you want to block with your hedge. With the ruler, draw a line from the middle of the window on your home that you want to protect, to the window or other portion you want to conceal on your

Hedgerow Length

To protect the house from wind eddies coming around the ends of a hedgerow, the hedgerow should extend at least 50 ft. on both sides of the house.

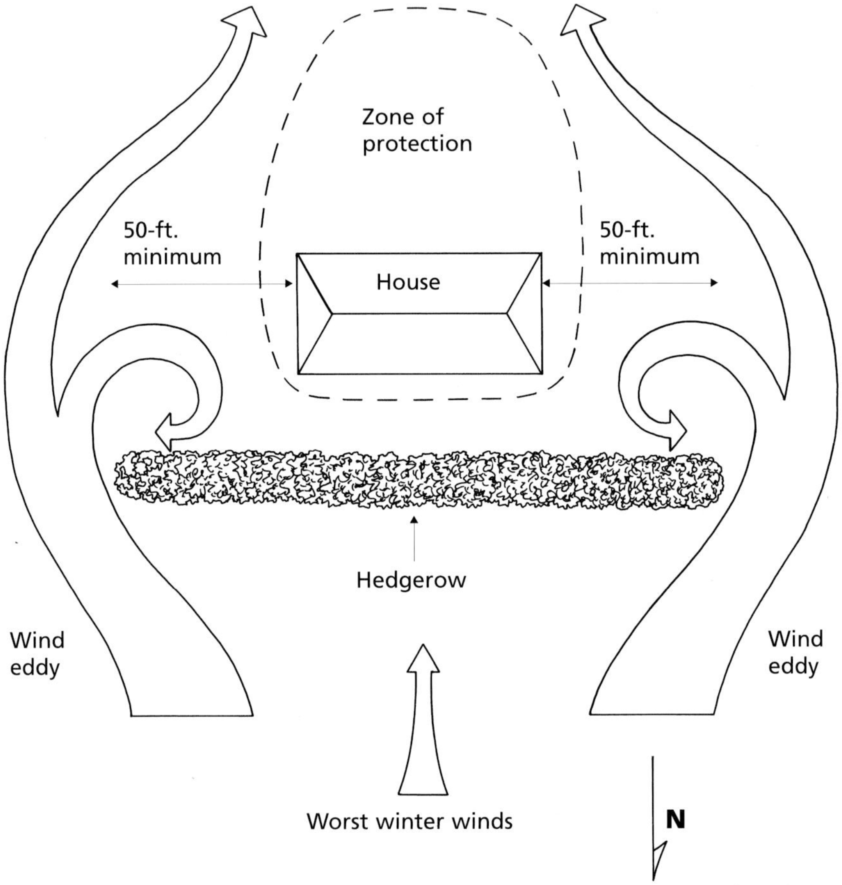

Zone of protection

50-ft. minimum

House

50-ft. minimum

Hedgerow

Wind eddy

Wind eddy

Worst winter winds

N

neighbor's house. This line represents the minimal required height of a hedge or screen to block the view.

Charting out the potential mature height is an important step, especially for trees. Unlike shrubs, which

usually remain fairly low even when full grown, trees on the south side of a house may wind up blocking winter sunlight along with the undesired view. Planning for both privacy and full winter sunlight is tricky but achievable. Begin by charting on graph paper in much the same way as you do for evergreen hedges (see p. 15). Because this plotting is more relevant to how trees can block the winter's sunshine from your home's south-facing windows, it is discussed in detail in Chapter 2, beginning on p. 27.

Simple math for an effective hedgerow

It's easy to site a hedgerow when privacy is its only purpose (see p. 15), for then its length may not be very important. But to moderate the climate (particularly the winds), you'll need more space for a longer hedgerow. It should extend at least 50 ft. beyond the sides of the house or the area to be protected (see the facing page), so that speeded-up eddies of wind don't come whizzing around the ends, making the yard more uncomfortable than it was before.

With proper planning and an appropriately shaped piece of property, effective wind protection can be created on as little as half an acre of land. Most important, for a mature hedgerow to be effective as a windbreak there must be a certain proportion between its height and its distance from the house or area to be protected.

A hedgerow can reduce the wind's speed by 50 percent for a distance beyond the break of 10 to 20 times its height. The best area of protection, however, usually extends from the leeward (protected) side of a hedgerow to a distance of about 5 to 10 times its height (shown below). This means that a planting of 20-ft.-tall shrubs, such as the common juniper (*Juniperus communis*), protects the yard to some degree for up to 400 ft. to its leeward side, but it offers

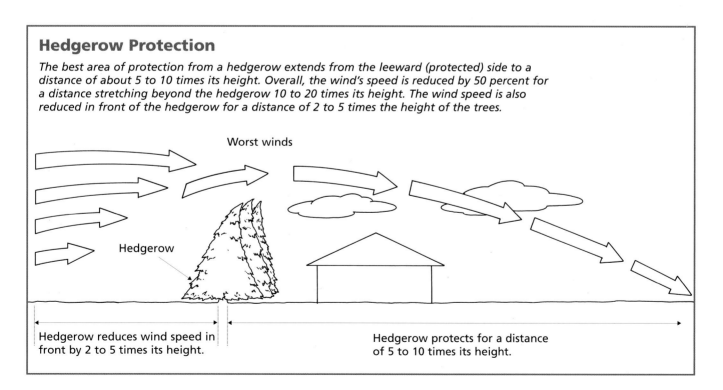

Hedgerow Protection

The best area of protection from a hedgerow extends from the leeward (protected) side to a distance of about 5 to 10 times its height. Overall, the wind's speed is reduced by 50 percent for a distance stretching beyond the hedgerow 10 to 20 times its height. The wind speed is also reduced in front of the hedgerow for a distance of 2 to 5 times the height of the trees.

Worst winds

Hedgerow

Hedgerow reduces wind speed in front by 2 to 5 times its height.

Hedgerow protects for a distance of 5 to 10 times its height.

the most shelter in a zone 100 ft. to 200 ft. from the hedgerow.

Another way to look at this formula is that a hedgerow's height should measure one-fifth to one-twentieth of the distance to be protected. The wind speed is also reduced in front of the hedgerow—the windward side—for a distance of 2 to 5 times the height of the trees. This is a good place to plant young tree seedlings, which will grow to be sturdy, well-rooted trees because of the continual "exercise" provided by the wind. Plan your hedgerow so that the mature size of the trees is appropriate to the area you wish to protect.

A hedgerow also works best when its length is perpendicular to the prevailing or worst winds. One or two rows of the right trees and shrubs are much more effective than wide, multirow plantings. Vertical, narrow hedgerows (rather than wide, angled, sloping ones) are usually the most effective in keeping winds lofted over a more extended area (shown below). You still get privacy as well as much more room to use within your yard.

A hedgerow should not be trained or trimmed into an impenetrable hedge, which could cause some of the

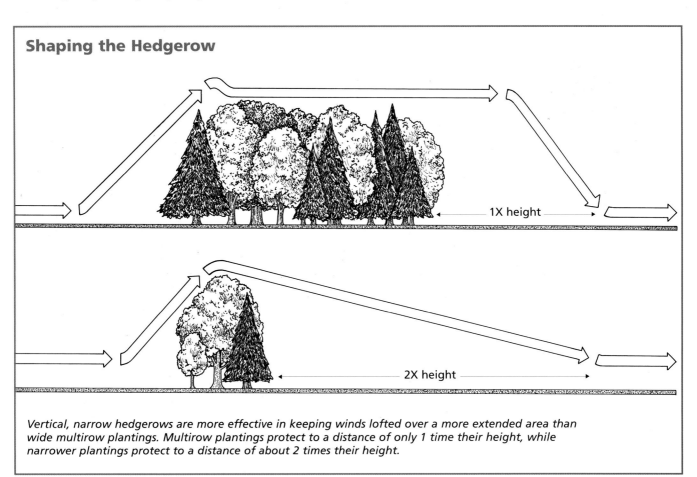

Shaping the Hedgerow

1X height

2X height

Vertical, narrow hedgerows are more effective in keeping winds lofted over a more extended area than wide multirow plantings. Multirow plantings protect to a distance of only 1 time their height, while narrower plantings protect to a distance of about 2 times their height.

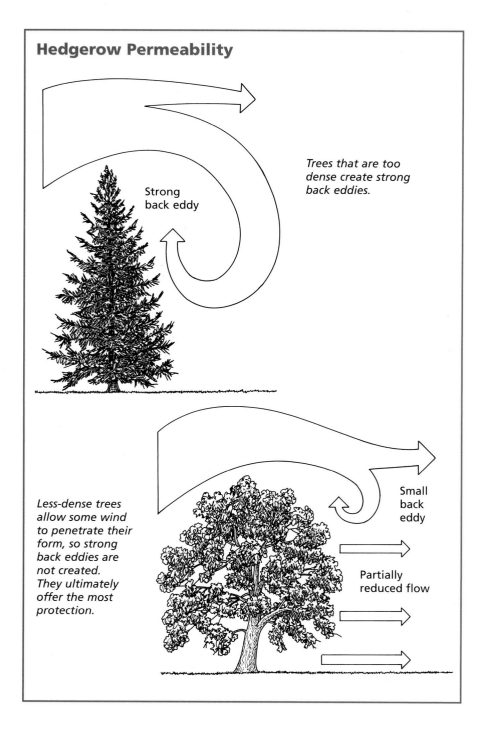

Hedgerow Permeability

Strong
back eddy

Trees that are too dense create strong back eddies.

Less-dense trees allow some wind to penetrate their form, so strong back eddies are not created. They ultimately offer the most protection.

Small
back
eddy

Partially
reduced flow

wind to whip up over the top and down again to create a blustery vortex—like a sideways tornado—on the very side you're trying to protect. If a hedgerow is partially permeable, some of the wind can slip through to form a gentle buffer of laminated air. This blanket of layered air helps to keep swift winds aloft for a much longer distance (after they pass over the top of the hedgerow) than will solid foliage. The most effective hedgerows are actually 50 percent penetrable—you should be able to see some small areas of sky through the foliage canopy (shown at left).

Although the hedgerow needs some permeability to keep wind lofted above the sheltered area, don't leave any large gaps. If you do, the wind will be funneled through such openings at a speed up to 20 percent greater than its normal velocity. You'll also compromise your privacy.

All the research and diagrams for hedgerows are based on flat land. Predicting the flow of the wind over complicated topography can't be done without complex technology, so homeowners with hilly property will have to observe wind patterns carefully. Place lots of little wind socks throughout the yard to determine where the wind flows.

This palo verde tree (*Cercidium* sp.) has a penetrable canopy, allowing some air currents through but keeping most of the wind lofted above the canopy. Avoid large holes in the hedgerow.

Selecting the Best Plants

Spend plenty of time choosing the best evergreen shrubs and trees for your hedge, screen, or hedgerow, because the choice is usually a final one. Most gardeners can't face removing a large plant. Be aware that some good unpruned screening shrubs and trees get so wide over time that they will engulf a good portion of any yard. Most plants can be controlled with periodic pruning, but keep in mind that this adds to your gardening time (or cost, if you hire an arborist). Another thing to consider is deer. A hedge favored by browsing deer will soon have its foliage eaten up to almost 6 ft. above the ground—which may be enough to reveal a clear view of the neighbors. If deer are a problem in your area, choose hedge plants resistant to their munching.

Hedge plants

Hedges—particularly of informally clipped shrubs or small trees—provide a soft, less conspicuous division of the land and can impart a natural feel to the linear nature of property lines and yards. (For those who prefer an exacting, angular style, most hedges can be clipped periodically into a formal look.) If you need to keep out marauding pets, these border plantings can be used to enclose, hide, or soften a more substantial barrier.

Hedges are usually not a top priority for weekly gardening care, so maintenance is an important consideration in your choice of plants. You'll need a plant that is well adapted to your climate and soil, that grows well without additional fertilizer, that is tolerant of weather

Even hedges planted along the property line will look more natural if they are not pruned too often and are clipped, not sheared.

Evergreens for Hedges

Cotoneaster lacteus
PARNEY COTONEASTER

USDA ZONES: 7 to 9

SIZE: 6 ft. to 20 ft. tall; 6 ft. to 20 ft. wide

COMMENTS: Graceful arching limbs make an excellent informal hedge, but can be shaped with some effort. Dark green leaves, white flowers from early to midsummer, and plentiful long-hanging red berries that last well into winter. Good plant for sculptural effect or seaside planting. Deer- and drought-resistant in some areas.

Ilex crenata
JAPANESE HOLLY

USDA ZONES: (5, 6) 7 to 9

SIZE: 8 ft. tall; 12 ft. wide

COMMENTS: Attractive, deep green, shiny, dense foliage. Compact cultivars vary from 2 ft. to 6 ft. Tolerates some shade. Deer-resistant in some areas. 'Convexa' is best choice for central Midwest. 'Glory' is tolerant of Zone 6 in Kentucky.

Other evergreens for hedges include: *Arbutus unedo* (strawberry tree) (p. 23), *Buxus sempervirens* (common boxwood) (p. 23), *Camellia japonica* (common camellia) (p. 61), and *Juniperus communis* (common juniper) (p. 23).

Juniperus virginiana 'Grey Owl'
GREY OWL EASTERN RED CEDAR or HYBRID EASTERN RED CEDAR

USDA ZONES: 3 to 9

SIZE: 2 ft. to 4 ft. tall; 3 ft. to 6 ft. wide

COMMENTS: Much smaller than the species form. Has delightful silver-gray foliage with limbs sweeping toward the ground. Not for formal hedges. Naturally grows a taproot and is sensitive to soil compaction. Resists deer and tolerates wind and clay soils in some areas. 'Grey Owl' shows good resistance to cedar apple and other rusts and twig blight, as does 'Burkii'. 'Burkii' is bluish, narrower, and more upright—a good barrier plant. The cultivar 'Canaertii' is better for the northern portion of the Midwest.

Picea omorika
SERBIAN SPRUCE

USDA ZONES: 4 to 7

SIZE: 50 ft. to 60 ft. tall; 20 ft. to 25 ft. wide

COMMENTS: An excellent tall hedge for the central Midwest. Although it grows very tall when left unpruned, it can easily be kept to about 12 ft. tall and 5 ft. wide. Good as a barrier plant, as a plant for narrow spaces, and as a specimen or accent plant. Tolerates wind and clay soils in some areas. 'Nana' and 'Pendula' are good ornamental cultivars.

Tsuga canadensis
EASTERN or CANADIAN HEMLOCK

USDA ZONES: 3 to 8

SIZE: 70 ft. tall; 25 ft. to 35 ft. wide

COMMENTS: Native to the eastern U.S. May grow several trunks with branches drooping gracefully toward the ground. To keep this tall plant within hedge height and width, prune early in its life and frequently thereafter. Doesn't like dry or urban air. Tolerates part shade, preferring at least some shade in hot, dry climates. Shallow, wide, fibrous root system. Mulch roots in the southern regions. Few major pest infestations. Sometimes gets bagworms, hemlock borer, hemlock sawfly, scale, and mites. Good as barrier plant, formal hedge, or specimen plant. Tolerates clay and sandy soils in some areas.

Viburnum cinnamomifolium
CINNAMON VIBURNUM

USDA ZONES: 7 to 9

SIZE: 15 ft. tall; 15 ft. wide

COMMENTS: Elegant evergreen with a well-behaved pyramidal form and large, oval, rich green leaves. Star-shaped white flowers in early summer are followed by small oval and blue fruits. Tolerates wind and clay in some areas.

Formal hedges add a sense of symmetry, dignity, and order. Shear the top of the hedge narrower than the bottom for good sunlight exposure.

extremes, that can be sheared to a neat regular shape if desired, and that remains relatively pest and disease free. This may seem like a tall order, but for every region of the country there are tried-and-true top performers that, if properly pruned, maintain their foliage from the ground up. Unfortunately, the colder the area, the less choice you have in plants, but there are options for most North American regions.

Many plants make excellent formal hedges, providing they are sheared properly to a slight pyramidal shape so the sunlight can reach all the foliage. You may also look for hedge plants that produce flowers to add another aspect of beauty to your yard. Bear in mind, though, that hedges requiring frequent shearing may not bloom well.

If you can't find a shrub that is as dense as you'd like, don't despair. You may be able to prune one of your choices to be denser. Clipping or shearing usually produces two new shoots just below each cut, which increases the leafiness of the hedge and helps increase the privacy it

Considerations for Formal Hedges

THE USE OF A FORMAL, SHEARED HEDGE is mostly an aesthetic choice because it requires more effort and time than an informal, irregular planting. Some people love the geometric form and the way the sheared shape can match or mimic the house's architecture. Formally pruned hedges can also be squeezed into smaller spaces to give more room to the adjacent yard.

Formal hedges require periodic shearing of the tips of new growth, which doubles the number of side shoots with each pruning, making the foliage thicker and more lush. You can shear a plant's tip buds with hand by-pass clippers, hand-operated hedge clippers, or

electric hedge clippers. Using by-pass clippers is more time-consuming than using hedge clippers, but it creates a nicer look on large-leafed evergreen plants like English laurel (*Prunus laurocerasus*), Japanese privet (*Ligustrum japonicum*), or wintergreen barberry (*Berberis julianae*).

Either the hand- or electric-powered type of hedge clippers can leave the foliage slightly coarse and is best reserved for those evergreen shrubs with small leaves and tight foliage, such as boxleaf hebe (*Hebe buxifolia*), Japanese boxwood (*Buxus microphylla* var. *japonica*), or tea tree (*Leptospermum rotundifolium*).

Evergreens for Screens

Arbutus unedo
STRAWBERRY TREE or STRAWBERRY MADRONE

USDA Zones: 7 to 10

Size: 20 ft. to 25 ft. tall; 20 ft. to 25 ft. wide

Comments: Attractive, deep green foliage, pink-white flowers, brown bark, and red fruits. Can be trained as a sculptural element or informal espalier. Often pest free, although can get greenhouse thrips in California. Tolerates partial shade and ocean winds. May grow as a multitrunk. Attracts birds in some areas. Cultivars 'Elfin King' and 'Compacta' can be easily kept to only 3 ft. to 4 ft. tall.

Buxus sempervirens
COMMON or ENGLISH BOXWOOD

USDA Zones: 5 to 9

Size: 12 ft. to 20 ft. tall; 12 ft. to 20 ft. wide

Comments: Shiny, dark green leaves. Can be trained as a sculptural element or informal espalier. Tolerates some light shade. May get scale and mites. Tolerates wind in some areas, as well as clay and sandy soils. More ornamental cultivars are 'Salicifolia', 'Suffruticosa', and 'Vardar Valley'. 'Glencoe' is a good selection for the northern Midwest, but only gets 3 ft. tall and wide.

Ilex opaca
AMERICAN HOLLY

USDA Zones: (5) 6 to 9

Size: 35 ft. to 50 ft. tall; 12 ft. to 30 ft. wide

Comments: Native to the eastern U.S. Good display of red berries and dark green foliage. Resistant to oak root fungus, but susceptible to leaf miners. Needs slightly acidic and well-drained soil. Can be kept to 8 ft. to 10 ft. tall with periodic pruning. Only female plants bear fruit.

Juniperus communis
COMMON JUNIPER

USDA Zones: 2 to 8

Size: 5 ft. to 10 ft. tall; 8 ft. to 12 ft. wide

Comments: Native to New England. Grows to irregular forms. May be used as a barrier plant or accent element, or trained as an informal espalier or sculptural element. Turns brownish each winter, but recovers in the spring. Thrives in rocky soil and prefers colder climates. Wind-tolerant in some areas. 'Repanda' is a good cultivar for the northern Midwest.

Pinus contorta var. contorta
BEACH or SHORE PINE

USDA Zones: (6) 7 to 8

Size: 20 ft. to 35 ft. tall; 12 ft. to 15 ft. wide

Comments: Can be used for a windbreak, an informal espalier, accent point, or sculptural element. Fairly fast grower. Naturally grows in coastal areas, wet soil, and bog conditions. Dislikes hot, dry places and pollution. Watch for aphids and mites.

Pinus coulteri
BIG-CONE or COULTER PINE

USDA Zones: 7 to 9

Size: 80 ft. tall; 35 ft. to 60 ft. wide

Comments: Moderate to fast grower that may form an oak tree-like shape. As with all pines, watch for aphids and mites. Big cones falling near the house are a hazard. Tolerates clay and sandy soils in some areas.

Other evergrees for screens includes: *Camellia japonica* (common camellia) (p. 61), *Cotoneaster lacteus* (parney cotoneaster) (p. 21), *Garrya elliptica* 'James Roof' (James Roof silktassel) (p. 79), *Juniperus chinensis* 'Columnaris' (blue Chinese column juniper) (p. 25), *Myrica pensylvanica* (northern bayberry) (p. 61), and *Osmanthus fragrans* (sweet osmanthus, sweet olive) (p. 87).

gives. You'll usually get a denser hedge with more frequent shearing or pruning.

Screen and hedgerow plants

Evergreen trees grow considerably taller and wider than many shrubs used for hedges. Their height and width usually mean that a tree will ultimately block an unwanted view more effectively than most shrubs. However, the time it takes an evergreen tree to obscure a view can be measured in years, requiring some degree of patience.

When purchasing an evergreen tree for privacy, always make sure its limbs originate near the ground and that it does not lose its lower limbs with age. You may have to shop around to find naturally low-limbed trees, but they are a must for view-blocking. For example, the California redwood (*Sequoia sempervirens*) normally loses its lower limbs as it gets older, but the cultivar 'Soquel' does not. Likewise, the hardy white spruce (*Picea glauca*) maintains descending, drooping limbs that sweep the ground and even hide its trunk throughout its life.

On some evergreen trees, the lower limbs may naturally begin to droop toward the ground as the tree gets older. For large yards, you can

The giant sequoia (*Sequoiadendron giganteum*) is a classic example of a majestic tree with limbs sweeping toward the ground.

consider pendulous trees like deodar and atlas cedar (*Cedrus deodara, C. atlantica*), Himalayan spruce (*Picea smithiana*), big-cone pine (*Pinus coulteri*), eastern hemlock (*Tsuga canadensis*), bald cypress (*Taxodium distichum*), and California redwood (*Sequoia sempervirens*). But for smaller yards, avoid such expansive and sweeping limbs.

Many coniferous trees have a single trunk, although there are exceptions like the hardy Japanese red pine (*Pinus densiflora*), which naturally develops multiple trunks. Many broadleaf evergreen species, on the other hand, can develop in either single or multitrunk forms. Purchasing a multitrunked tree will often make it easier to maintain hedgelike foliage all the way to the ground.

No tree is worth planting for privacy unless it's hardy, adapted to the soil and climate, and generally free of pests and diseases. The same guidelines apply for choosing trees as for selecting plants for use in evergreen hedges (see p. 21). The most important thing is to get to

know your soil, and then choose only those types of trees with roots that will adapt well to that soil type.

Consider a worst-case situation where in order to block a view, trees need to be planted near a creek. In this situation, roots tolerant of moisture and poor drainage are important, because you can't possibly mound up or improve enough soil to make drainage for the natural extent

Evergreens for Hedgerows

Juniperus chinensis
CHINESE or PYRAMIDAL JUNIPER

USDA ZONES: (3, 4) 5 to 9

SIZE: 40 ft. to 50 ft. tall; 15 ft. to 20 ft. wide

COMMENTS: Common, reliable tree. Dark green, aromatic foliage. The species form may be hard to find in the nursery, but there are many named varieties to choose from with smaller habits and different shades of foliage. Resistance to rust disease makes this species superior to *J. virginiana* in the central Midwest. Attracts birds and tolerates clay in some areas. Good cultivars are 'Keteleeri' and 'Hetzii Columnaris'.

Picea abies
NORWAY SPRUCE

USDA ZONES: (2) 3 to 8

SIZE: 40 ft. to 60 ft. tall; 20 ft. to 35 ft. wide

COMMENTS: Hardy, common landscape conifer that also makes a dramatic focal point in the yard. The older limbs droop toward the ground. Prefers slightly acidic, well-drained soil with some moisture. Does not like high heat. Tolerates sandy soils in some areas.

Pinus cembra
SWISS STONE PINE

USDA ZONES: 4 to 7 (8)

SIZE: 30 ft. to 40 ft. tall; 15 ft. to 25 ft. wide

COMMENTS: Needs well-drained soil that is loamy (not clayey) and slightly acidic. Produces well-behaved, dense, columnar growth with a rich green needle color when young. When mature and untended, has a loose, more open canopy. Grows slowly. Tolerates sandy soils in some areas.

Pinus nigra subsp. *nigra*
AUSTRIAN PINE

USDA ZONES: (4) 5 to 7

SIZE: 50 ft. to 60 ft. tall; 20 ft. to 40 ft. wide

COMMENTS: Favored in the lower Midwest and East for its dense pyramidal form and dark green needles. Before planting, make sure the area isn't troubled with pine nematodes or a disease called sphaeropsis. Tolerates alkaline soil. Not recommended in the upper Midwest.

Other evergreens for hedgerows include: *Picea pungens* forma *glauca* (blue spruce) (p. 62), *Picea omorika* (Serbian spruce) (p. 21), *Pinus pinea* (Italian stone pine, umbrella pine) (p. 34), and *Pinus sylvestris* (Scotch pine) (p. 105).

Quercus ilex
HOLM or HOLLY OAK

USDA ZONES: 7 to 9 (10)

SIZE: 30 ft. to 70 ft. tall; 25 ft. to 70 ft. wide

COMMENTS: Dark, rich green upper leaf with silvery or yellow underside. Fills in like a hedge or screen with regular pruning. Attracts sapsuckers and woodpeckers, but can reseed heavily. Tolerates ocean winds and salt, but constant wind keeps size down considerably. Plant with other wind-tolerant trees. Heaves pavement, so keep it to the perimeter of the yard as a hedgerow plant.

Thuja occidentalis 'Pyrimidalis' or 'Douglasii Pyrimidalis'
PYRIMIDALIS or DOUGLASII PYRIMIDALIS AMERICAN ARBORVITAE

USDA ZONES: (2) 3 to 7 (8)

SIZE: 20 ft. tall; 3 ft. wide

COMMENTS: Adaptable, fast growing, and sturdy. No pruning needed to maintain a good-looking shape. Grows shallow, wide roots. Tolerates medium-coarse, fine, wet, and rocky soil. Few pest and disease problems, but watch for bagworms. Attracts birds and tolerates wind, drought, and clay soils in some areas. *T. plicata* seems more deer resistant in the upper Midwest.

Manzanita shrubs (*Arctostaphylos* spp.) have attractive multitrunks that work well in a mixed hedgerow.

of their roots. There are few evergreen trees appropriate for riparian (creekside) areas and wet soils, so the selection is quite limited: balsam fir (*Abies balsamea*), black spruce (*Picea mariana*), bald cypress (*Taxodium distichum*), California bay laurel (*Umbellularia californica*), and

American arborvitae (*Thuja occidentalis*). There are many deciduous examples of good riparian trees, but they will fail to obscure the view during the winter.

Mixing Trees and Shrubs in a Hedgerow

The combining of shrubs and trees should start as soon as you begin to plant your hedgerow. First, you can plant larger-sized shrubs to act as wind buffers for seedling trees planted in and around them. Start with healthy-sized, 5-gallon shrubs (or the equivalent balled-and-burlapped stock) and small tube-grown tree seedlings.

A shrub will protect on both its windward and leeward sides, and it will allow the wind to buffet the seedlings (but not blow them over) as they grow, thus building up thicker, sturdier trunks and robust roots for the mature trees. The shrubs act as a "nurse crop"—a plant grown solely to assist another plant's growth to maturity. It's the best way to grow a permanent hedgerow without ever having to stake the trees. The trees' foliage will then grow together in

5 years or so and cause the shrubs to wither from overshading.

Sometimes the best tree for your soil and climate will be one with naturally upturned or even somewhat vertical limbs. Many species of conifers—pines, cypresses, junipers, and arborvitae, to name a few—produce limbs that grow above the horizontal, especially when the trees are young.

If trees with this limb configuration are planted side by side, there may be keyhole-like gaps at the ground level between them. The wind will whistle through such holes at high speeds, and they are much too big to provide the beneficial permeability that makes a hedgerow perform well. At the same time, your yard's intimacy will not be protected.

In this case, you can plant shrubs to the windward side of the hedgerow, either in a row or equidistant between the trees, making sure to plant them far enough away that the mature tree foliage won't shade them out. Although a hedgerow loses its effectiveness if many rows of trees are planted, this simple planting of two rows of plants can be as effective as a single vertical hedgerow.

CHAPTER TWO

Shade & Sun

The sun advances through the seasons by arcing through different positions in the sky in relation to the home. Deciduous or evergreen trees overhanging the home can reduce the sweltering heat of midsummer when the sun is directly overhead. During the same season, evergreen shrubs and small trees near the west- and east-facing walls will help prevent overheating in the early to midmorning and the mid to late afternoon, when sunlight might be shining beneath the taller shade trees directly onto the walls. Of course, shade trees also provide a wonderful respite in the yard.

Deciduous trees can also allow sunlight through to help warm the home in the depths of winter. Evergreen trees provide the added advantage of insulating the home's

Once trees along both sides of a street begin to mature and their canopy shades the pavement, the neighborhood will not only feel cooler but it will also have a sense of elegance.

northern side from winter's cold and chilling winds.

To take advantage of all of these benefits, you'll need to learn where to place each tree. You'll also need to know what type of shade is cast by trees in both summer and winter. As the sun migrates low in the southern sky each winter, only deciduous trees along the south side of the home can allow sunlight through the canopy.

Summer Cooling

When you visit older neighborhoods on a hot summer day—where streets are named Maple, Oak, and Walnut for their shade trees—something

amazing happens. A cool, fresh air bathes your sweaty skin. While the arching canopy of shade trees may reduce the temperature by just 3°F to 9°F, there's a noticeable respite from the onerous heat. It's a difference you can feel, and it's a difference reflected in the savings on the homeowners' cooling bills. Homeowners in these neighborhoods are saving 30 to 75 percent on their cooling bills.

From California to Utah to Florida, studies have proven that shade trees can significantly reduce energy costs. The U.S. Department of Energy recommends using strategically placed landscape materials to help lower home utility

bills. In fact, a well-positioned shade tree is more effective at cooling a house than plastic window films, adjustable blinds, or glass with reflective coatings.

Tree and shrub location

Many people assume protecting the most south-facing portion of their house with shade trees is the most important aspect to summer comfort. Yet, for much of the summer, the sun moves directly overhead, not shining directly into south-facing windows. (South-facing windows receive plenty of sunlight during warm Indian summer days, but blinds and curtains can help moderate these few exceptions.)

How to Shape the Wind for a Cooler Garden

THE SAME HEDGEROW DYNAMICS mentioned on p. 16 can be applied in reverse to help cool your garden in the summer. Instead of fending off the wind, a pair of hedgerows can be used to funnel afternoon breezes toward the patio.

Make the hedge portion of the hedgerows at least as tall as the house's walls. Place the hedgerows nearly parallel to the prevailing summer air currents, and make the distance between them wider away from the house and narrower near the home. Your "wind tunnel" will increase the breezes by up to 20 percent. The bigger the difference between the wider opening at the far end and the narrow opening near the patio, the greater the speed of the wind and the cooling effect.

In arid climates, the air can be made to feel even cooler if it passes over a moist-brick patio or wet shrubs. The channeled breezes pick up moisture, acting like a swamp cooler to chill the air with evaporative cooling.

So to moderate summer's heat, you'll want to shade the east and west sides of the house as well as the roof.

Especially in hot-summer areas, the sun shines for hours through an east-facing window in the morning before the eave casts its cooling shade, and through a west-facing window for hours in the afternoon after the eaves' prevailing shade is gone. A Mesa, Arizona, study showed that the west-facing wall was 6 times more important than the south-facing side, and the east-facing wall was *14.5 times* more significant than the southern wall and almost *2.5 times* more critical than the west-facing wall. Of course, not all houses are oriented with their length exactly east-west, but all homes have windows that partially face west and east and benefit proportionally.

It's also important to protect the southwest corner from the late afternoon heat of late summer and Indian summer. To determine where to plant along this corner, first figure out when you typically experience the hottest summer days. To do this, check over old utility bills from a number of previous years and

A deciduous maple tree provides pleasant cooling for the home during the summer and allows some sunshine through during the winter.

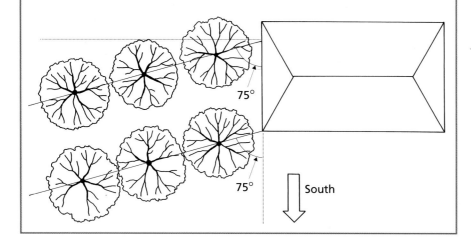

Shading the Critical NW and SW Corners

Afternoon sunlight increases the need to cool the house in the summer. Placing shrubs and small trees on an angle from the western corners of the house casts shade on the western wall, reducing the load on your air conditioner. The example shown here is to accommodate the 75-degree angle of the sun during the hottest part of summer in St. Louis, Missouri.

75°

75°

South

determine which month consistently has the highest air-conditioning costs.

Next, find the angle of the sun in the midafternoon (from 2 to 4 P.M.) during the time you have the hottest weather. You can find this angle on sun charts at the local library, your utility company's energy conservation office, or the local university cooperative extension office. This angle determines where to plant your trees and shrubs to give protection from the sun at its hottest time. For example, the hottest period in St. Louis, Missouri, is usually the last week of July when the midafternoon

sun is 75 degrees high in the sky (this number will vary from city to city). Thus, all trees west of the southwestern corner of the house, in this example, should be planted along a line 75 degrees west of the solar south axis. Use the same angle to protect the northwestern corner of the home.

To shade just the eastern and western walls, place smaller deciduous or evergreen trees so the mature form allows a 5-ft. gap between the branches and the walls. Place shrubs so that within 4 years their limbs come within 1 ft. of the walls. This requires an educated

guess based on the natural growth of the plant, the soil fertility, and how often you water and fertilize. Ask a local nurseryperson or landscaper for advice. Mature evergreen shrubs along a southern wall help insulate it during the winter if placed within 3 ft. of the wall, but they shouldn't be allowed to block light from the windows in the winter. Smaller shrubs are well suited for this role. Similarly, locate deciduous trees or shrubs on east or west walls away from windows.

In all cases, plant the shrubs so that the limbs facing the wall can be trimmed back far enough so you can repaint the walls as needed without ruining the form of the shrub. Use those shrubs that can regenerate new shoots from bare branches and limbs such as the common lilac (*Syringa vulgaris*), boxwood (*Buxus* spp.), hydrangea (*Hydrangea* spp.), all deciduous fruit trees, and firethorn or pyracantha (*Pyracantha* spp.). Avoid cedar, cypress, fir, juniper, pine, and spruce trees. If the tree or shrub is prone to losing its lower limbs with age, plant an understory of shade-tolerant shrubs to fill the gaps.

To further the energy-conservation effect, shade ground-mounted air conditioners with trees that have crowns that will cover the area over the unit within 5 years (make sure no limbs touch the air conditioner). This

Locating deciduous trees to the west and east of the house's windows and solar-heating devices will allow the most warming sunlight in during the winter.

single planting will increase the efficiency of the air conditioner by approximately 10 percent.

Trees that overhang the roof during the summer's heat need to be planted fairly close to the foundation. Be sure to choose a tree with a root system that will not heave the foundation (see pp. 108-109). Also prune the lower branches and limbs on the side of the tree near the house—called crown lifting or forming a "standard" or "limbing up" the canopy—so the siding, paint, or roofing is not damaged (see Deciduous Trees for Shading the

Roof on p. 32). Note that in wildfire-prone areas of the arid West and Southwest, deciduous trees should *not* overhang roofs. Technically, there should be no trees or shrubs within 40 ft. of the house on level land in wildland zones—and nothing planted under the eaves.

Trees close to the house come with several warnings. Black carpenter ants are found in the cooler sections of the Pacific Northwest and New England and are good at tunneling through and destroying wood. They often nest in the decayed wood of shade trees and then send out scouting parties to find new homes in

stacks of firewood and wood debris outside the home's walls. From there, it's just a few bites into the house. Make sure you inspect your shade trees for dead and decaying wood, remove it, and hire a pest control specialist if required.

Also, trees that overhang the roof can potentially damage it. Always inspect the limbs of your shade trees near the house during a rain or ice storm. Look for limbs that are moving or weighted down enough to damage roofing material and eaves. Wind further increases the likelihood of damage. (See the pruning guidelines in Chapter 12, beginning on p. 153.)

Shade trees on the west side of the house help cool it in the summer. Don't let limbs touch the roof or gutters.

Deciduous Trees for Shading the Roof

Celtis occidentalis
COMMON HACKBERRY

USDA Zones: 2 to 9

Size: 40 ft. to 50 ft. tall; 50 ft. to 75 ft. wide

Comments: In some areas, this tree develops deep roots, making it a good choice for near pavement or for in a lawn. However, in other areas shallow roots develop and cause heaving, so check with local experts before planting. Not planted in the Northeast or Southeast. Tolerates desert heat and alkalinity. Foliage gets nipple gall. Can develop witches' broom. Deer-resistant in some areas. 'Prairie Pride' does not develop gall or witches' broom and has reduced fruiting.

Koelreuteria paniculata
GOLDEN RAIN TREE

USDA Zones: 6 to 9

Size: 20 ft. to 35 ft. tall; 20 ft. to 30 ft. wide

Comments: Young irregular growth changes to round, uniform shape when mature. Dramatic hot-yellow flower clusters. Tolerates alkaline soils. Roots not invasive, so a good tree near pavement or in lawns. An excellent choice for near the ocean. Seeds naturalize in some areas; double-check with local nurseries before planting.

Malus × moerlandsii 'Profusion'
PROFUSION HYBRID CRABAPPLE

USDA Zones: 4 to 7 (8)

Size: 15 ft. to 20 ft. tall; 20 ft. to 30 ft. wide

Comments: Loaded with red-violet spring blossoms. Reddish-purple foliage changes to a bronze-green in summer, golden-amber in fall. Deep red fruits. Good resistance to scab except in Pacific Northwest. Tent caterpillars, aphids, codling moth (in fruits), spider mites, fireblight, and scale can cause problems. Tolerates acid, alkaline, clay loam, and rocky soil. Tolerates drought in some areas. 'Prairie Fire' is excellent for cold zones in the upper Midwest.

Quercus rubra
RED OAK, NORTHERN RED OAK

USDA Zones: 4 to 8

Size: 60 ft. to 90 ft. tall; 60 ft. to 75 ft. wide

Comments: Pleasing large, spreading limbs. New spring foliage has soft ruddy red color. Easier to garden under than other oaks and tolerates lawns. Needs deep, fertile soil and ample moisture. Fairly easy to transplant. Deer-resistant and drought-tolerant in areas with periodic rains.

Sophora japonica
CHINESE SCHOLAR or JAPANESE PAGODA TREE

USDA Zones: (5) 6 to 10

Size: 40 ft. to 70 ft. tall; 50 ft. to 75 ft. wide

Comments: A good choice for shading a patio or lawn, but spent flowers can stain pavement yellow. Soapy seedpods can make pavement slippery. Tolerates drought in areas with periodic rains and rocky soil. Requires a large area to thrive. Disease- and pest-resistant. Prone to ice, snow, and wind damage. Tolerates sandy soils in some areas.

Ulmus parvifolia
CHINESE or LACEBARK ELM

USDA Zones: 5 to 9

Size: 40 ft. to 50 ft. tall; 40 ft. to 50 ft. wide

Comments: Has the look of an American elm tree but with a beautiful multicolored exfoliating (shedding) bark. This species is a durable street tree, resistant to Dutch elm disease and most insects and diseases. Good patio tree. Grows well near the ocean. Attracts birds in some areas.

Other trees for shading the roof include: *Cercis canadensis* (eastern redbud) (p. 82), *Fraxinus americana* (white ash) (p. 34), *Ginkgo biloba* (ginkgo, maidenhair tree) (p. 71), *Nyssa sylvatica* (black tupelo, black gum) (p. 71), and *Platanus × acerifolia* (London plane tree) (p. 55).

The black walnut (*Juglans nigra*) is an excellent example of a tree that forms a beautifully shaped canopy without pruning.

drawing to sketch to scale the mature size of an intended shade tree in relation to the house.

Selecting a good shade tree

Choosing the right shade tree from the hundreds of possibilities can be daunting, but some are better than others. One easy way to surmise a good tree is to canvass your neighborhood or town. Those trees that are tall, wide, vital, and doing their shady best after decades "on the job" are prime candidates for your yard as well. By viewing other homes cloaked

Planning for your mature shade tree

Anticipating the mature size of a shade tree is important when deciding where to plant. Most shade trees grow quite large. The homeowner plants a 4-ft.- to 5-ft.-tall tree and settles into life's routines. Then 10 to 20 years go by and "all of a sudden" the tree is crowding the walls, tearing up the roof or heaving the patio. Before you plant, find out the tree's mature size, and make sure you give it enough space to reach its full size without crowding the home and its foundation.

As described in Chapter 1, use cross sections of your home drawn to scale on paper as a guide (see p. 15). Use tracing paper laid over your scale

A Chinese flame tree (*Koelreuteria bipinnata*) does not need pruning to produce a well-rounded crown. It makes a good street tree.

Shade Trees and Shrubs for the Yard

Catalpa speciosa
WESTERN or NORTHERN CATALPA

USDA Zones: (4) 5 to 9

Size: 40 ft. to 50 ft. tall; 20 ft. to 50 ft. wide

Comments: Bold, large, light green leaves and attractive clusters of white, tubular flowers make this tree attractive throughout the spring and summer. The long skinny fruits (up to 15 in. long) give rise to another name for the tree—Indian bean. This deciduous tree is adaptable to many soils but prefers a fertile, moist, and deep one. May develop leaf spot, blights, wilts, and stem dieback; may be host to catalpa midge and sphinx moth.

Celtis australis
EUROPEAN HACKBERRY

USDA Zones: 6 to 9

Size: 40 ft. to 50 ft. tall; 50 ft. to 75 ft. wide

Comments: Similar to elm tree in looks. Sharply pointed dark green leaves; flowers are hardly noticeable. Prefers well-drained, fertile soil. Produces small purple-black fruits before leaf-fall. Spreading, oval habit. Can grow in a lawn or near a foundation. Most likely pest is aphids. Also gets some galls from insects. Deer-resistant in some areas.

Chilopsis linearis
DESERT WILLOW

USDA Zones: 7 to 10

Size: 12 ft. to 20 ft. tall; 12 ft. to 20 ft. wide

Comments: Flowers range from white to pink to rose and even lavender and a deep red-purple. Many bloom all summer. Can be pruned to a beautiful form. Willow-like deciduous foliage. Tolerates very high summer heat. Can be used as a summer screen plant.

Fraxinus americana
WHITE ASH

USDA Zones: 3 to 9

Size: 50 ft. to 80 ft. tall; 50 ft. to 75 ft. wide

Comments: As long as it's healthy, it's an attractive addition to a large yard or property. Prefers the deep, moist, and fertile soils of the Midwest, but will grow in poor, rocky soil. Tolerates clay soils in some areas. Can be plagued by borers and scale. Not planted in the Northeast because of blight concerns. 'Autumn Purple' has great fall color and 'Tures' is wind resistant.

Other shade trees and shrubs include: *Carpinus caroliniana* (American hornbeam) (p. 105), *Cercis canadensis* (eastern redbud) (p. 82), *Ginkgo biloba* (ginkgo, maidenhair tree) (p. 71), *Jacaranda mimosifolia* (jacaranda) (p. 82), and *Magnolia × soulangiana* (saucer magnolia) (p. 61).

Pinus pinea
ITALIAN STONE PINE, UMBRELLA PINE

USDA Zones: 9 to 10

Size: 40 ft. to 80 ft. tall; 40 ft. to 80 ft. wide

Comments: The word "umbrella" hints at the unique, well-formed wide and rounded or ovoid shape of the mature crown of this pine. Needles range from bright green to grayish. Tolerates plenty of dryness and heat, so a good choice for the Southwest. An excellent choice for ocean-side plantings. It's the source of the expensive pignolas (pine nuts). Deer-resistant in some areas.

Pinus strobus
WHITE PINE

USDA Zones: 3 to 8

Size: 50 ft. to 80 ft. tall; 20 ft. to 40 ft. wide

Comments: Well-behaved, spreading, asymmetrical crown with horizontal branches. Needles are light green to slightly blue-green. Also good for hedges or screens. Alkaline soils in the Midwest cause yellowing foliage. In the Northeast, watch for tip dieback due to moths. Can burn or turn reddish brown in cold, windy areas but will recover in the spring. Can get blister rust in the West. Deer-resistant in some areas.

Quercus coccinea
SCARLET OAK

USDA Zones: 5 to 8 (9)

Size: 70 ft. to 75 ft. tall; 40 ft. to 75 ft. wide

Comments: Don't confuse this with the pin oak (*Quercus palustris*) that is often mislabeled as a scarlet oak. Absolutely spectacular display of rich, luminous red fall foliage when planted in full sun. Plant as small trees. Difficult to transplant, but the prospect of a gorgeous tree makes it worth the gamble. Tolerates many soils but favors an acidic, moist, well-drained one. Wind-tolerant in some areas.

Quercus douglasii
BLUE OAK

USDA Zones: 7 to 10

Size: 35 ft. to 50 ft. tall; 50 ft. to 75 ft. wide

Comments: Develops a sculptural form that makes an impressive focal point or accent. Large-lobed leaves with a delightful pale bluish green hue. Tolerates hot summer weather. Native to the foothills of the Sierra Mountains near California's central valley, but sometimes trees grow within a few miles of the coastline. Tolerates clay and sandy soil in some areas.

Quercus robur
ENGLISH OAK

USDA Zones: 3 to 7

Size: 40 ft. to 80 ft. tall; 40 ft. to 80 ft. wide

Comments: Attractive crown with a round, wide form that makes an impressive focal point or accent. Also a good street tree. Green foliage with some blue overtones. The brown leaves last into the winter. Requires plenty of space. Watch for leaf mildew, and spray with a fungicide. Tolerates clay soils in some areas. The subspecies form *Q. robur* var. *fastigiata* (also called the cultivar 'Fastigiata') is much more columnar but is also prone to mildew.

Tilia cordata
LITTLELEAF LINDEN

USDA Zones: 3 to 10

Size: 60 ft. to 70 ft. tall; 50 ft. to 75 ft. wide

Comments: A good shade tree for lawns in cooler summer climates where the clear droppings of the aphid, and the subsequent sooty mold, aren't a problem. Makes a good hedge or barrier plant when clipped, a good street tree, or an accent or focal point; also suited to formal gardens. Sometimes bothered by Japanese beetles. Trunk susceptible to sunscald. Tolerates acidic and alkaline soils. Tolerates wind, drought, and sandy soils in some areas.

in a protective summer shade, you'll be able to visualize how the tree might look shielding your home from the hot sun. (Don't forget to keep an eye out for the best evergreen trees for the north side of the house.) Also, ask neighbors which trees failed to grow in your area.

In general, the best shade trees are the following:

- *Trees whose natural growth provides a well-defined, pleasingly shaped canopy without pruning.*
- *Trees whose limbs have sturdy attachments to the main trunk.*
- *Trees that do not have brittle branches.*
- *Trees with reasonably well-behaved root systems.*
- *Trees that are well anchored by the roots against winds and loads of ice and snow.*

Not all trees cast the same amount of shade in the summer. The range can be dramatic. For example, the honey locust tree (*Gleditsia triacanthos*) has an open, airy crown that lets 40 percent of the sunlight pass through to heat the roof. It's the right amount of shade if you want to be able to garden below. Choosing trees with a lower percentage of shade allows more choices in what you can plant beneath the canopy, but there are ornamental plants that will flourish even in dense shade. Strictly for cooling the house, though, choose trees with a high percentage of shade.

The structure of the branches of a honey locust tree (*Gleditsia triacanthos*) is revealed as fall approaches. This tree allows 40% of the summer's sunlight through, which can overheat the home.

The weeping mulberry (*Morus alba* 'Pendula') grows a few feet above the graft and then cascades down to or onto the ground—depending on how you prune the limbs.

One often-overlooked option for shading east-facing and west-facing walls is the unusual weeping form of more common trees. For example, the weeping mulberry (*Morus alba* 'Pendula') has attractive drooping limbs and dramatic yellow leaves in the fall. The weeping mulberry grows only a few feet above the point at which it is grafted onto a regular mulberry rootstock. This form also makes considerably less messy fruit than a regular, full-sized mulberry tree.

Other weeping specimens fountain much higher and cascade onto the ground like a pool of running water or a ground cover, but these branches can be trimmed back with summer pruning. Weeping forms are often grafted at the 5-ft. to 6-ft. level on a standard rootstock for the sake of easy production and shipping. If you plant an ordinary rootstock and then graft, you can choose to graft much lower or higher to suit the needs of your wall. But be warned: Trees that naturally weep without being grafted, such as the common Babylon weeping willow (*Salix babylonica*), grow quite tall (in this case, 30 ft. to 40 ft.).

Winter Warming

In the summer we want shade to keep our homes more comfortable, but in winter we welcome the sun. Deciduous trees and shrubs allow us to fill both needs, but they have to be located carefully. To take the best

Deciduous Shrubs for Shading Summer Walls

Calycanthus floridus
HYBRID CAROLINA ALLSPICE or COMMON SWEETSHRUB

USDA ZONES: 5 to 9

SIZE: 6 ft. to 12 ft. tall; 6 ft. to 12 ft. wide

COMMENTS: Spinach green leaves have a rich luster and gray-green undersides. The maroon flowers in early summer offer a delightful fragrance reminiscent of a complex mixture of fruits. Seeds also have a marvelous fragrance when crushed. Tolerates wind, and clay and sandy soils in some areas. The cultivar 'Michael Lindsey' is good for the Northeast.

Chaenomeles speciosa
COMMON FLOWERING QUINCE

USDA ZONES: 4 to 9

SIZE: 6 ft. to 12 ft. tall; 6 ft. to 12 ft. wide

COMMENTS: Very reliable in most areas. Many flower colors: white, pink, peach, salmon, orange, and red. Shiny green foliage. Most varieties have thorns. Buds can swell during winter warm spells, leading to brown, cold-damaged petals. The mass of multi-stems requires semiannual pruning. Will get chlorosis (yellow leaves) in alkaline pH soils. Deer-resistant in some areas.

Deutziav × kalmiiflora
KALMIA DEUTZIA

USDA ZONES: 5 to 8

SIZE: 4 ft. to 5 ft. tall; 4 ft. to 5 ft. wide

COMMENTS: Dramatic dense flowers in a pink to pinkish purple range, depending on the cultivar. Flowers are fragrant and more apparent than other species and crosses. Cold hardy. Can withstand neglect, but for best results prune those stems that have flowered. Drought-sensitive even in the upper Midwest. Needs mulch. Wind-tolerant in some areas.

Kerria japonica 'Pleniflora'
PLENIFLORA JAPANESE KERRIA

USDA ZONES: (4) 5 to 9

SIZE: 6 ft. to 8 ft. tall; 8+ ft. wide

COMMENTS: Sturdy plant with impressive masses of butter yellow double flowers in April and May and bright green stems in the winter. This cultivar can spread easily because of rampant suckers. Best flowers bloom in partial shade. Prefers porous, fertile soil. Deer-resistant in some areas.

Other shrubs for shading walls include: *Chilopsis linearis* (desert willow) (p. 34), *Cornus sanguinea* (bloodtwig dogwood) (p. 55), *Hydrangea macrophylla* (bigleaf hydrangea) (p. 86), *Lindera benzoin* (spicebush) (p. 79), and *Syringa vulgaris* (common lilac) (p. 79).

Morus alba 'Chaparral' or 'Pendula'
WEEPING MULBERRY

USDA ZONES: 4 to 9

SIZE: 6 ft. to 8 ft. tall; 8 ft. to 10 ft. wide

COMMENTS: The cultivar 'Pendula' is a fast-growing weeping form of the white mulberry. Shiny, dark green foliage. Leaves in the fall are a strong yellow. However, 'Pendula' produces insipid black fruits, which can stain pavement or patios. 'Chaparral' grows much like 'Pendula' but is fruitless and has deeply cut leaves. Both cultivars tolerate clay and sandy soils in some areas.

Viburnum carlesii
KOREANSPICE VIBURNUM

USDA ZONES: 4 to 8

SIZE: 3 ft. to 8 ft. tall; 6 ft. to 12 ft. wide

COMMENTS: Its exquisite spicy and sweet fragrance is familiar to gardeners. Blooms from mid-May to early June. Fall color is red to wine red. Prefers shade during the summer and sunlight during the winter and spring (near the southeast corner of the house). Can be trimmed to a hedge. Wind-tolerant in some areas. In the colder zones of the Midwest, plant *V. x juddii*.

Percentage of Shade Cast by Deciduous Trees in the Summer

The shade of these trees has been measured with light meters to determine their average percentage of shade. The higher the number, the greater the amount of shade cast. Choose a plant with the most shade for the most cooling comfort in the lawn or near your home.

Latin Name	Common Name	% Shade
Celtis australis	European hackberry	90
Juglans nigra	Black walnut	90
Liriodendron tulipifera	Tulip tree	90
Platanus racemosa	California sycamore	90
Koelreuteria bipinnata	Chinese flame tree	90
Tilia cordata	Littleleaf linden	88
Pistachia chinensis	Ornamental pistache	85
Platanus × acerifolia	London plane tree	84
Betula pendula	European birch	83
Liquidambar styraciflua	Sweet gum, liquidambar	82
Ginkgo biloba	Ginkgo	81
Quercus robur	English oak	81
Fraxinus holotricha 'Moraine'	Moraine ash	78
Sophora japonica	Japanese pagoda tree, Chinese scholar	78
Catalpa speciosa	Western catalpa	76
Gleditsia triacanthos	Honey locust	60

advantage of winter sunlight, it's best to keep a zone on the south side free.

Because most winter sunlight comes from the south, most people assume winter warmth from sunlight is combined with summer cooling from shade trees, so plant a bunch of deciduous trees along the south side of the house. However, the sunshine pouring through the leafless crown of the trees in the winter is deceiving. Trees on the south side of the home can often actually *increase* the home's energy bills, because they cast much unnoticed shade from their bare shoots, branches, and limbs. A study for Sacramento, California, determined that all homes, both solar and conventional, would pay *more* for energy year-round if deciduous and evergreen shade trees were planted along the south side of the house. Some varieties of trees can even double the energy costs.

Another factor is distance from the house: In many cases, the closer to the house the shade trees are located, the higher the yearly utility bills. Not surprisingly, houses with solar hot water systems were the most severely impacted by shade trees near the south wall.

The reason for this apparent contradiction is that the shade cast by the smaller twigs and stems isn't directly seen on the ground, unlike the shadows cast by the trunk and larger limbs. The shade cast by the smaller-diameter wood of the deciduous tree terminates before it reaches the ground but still contributes to a general background of overall light reduction. Thus, a camera light meter—not the naked eye—is the only accurate way to discern the difference between sunshine in an open lawn and the reduced light beneath a deciduous tree's crown in the midst of winter.

Instead of using a light meter, you can follow this general guideline: The total amount of sunlight reaching the windows is reduced from 25 to 50 percent because of the tree. (See the graph on p. 40 for the more specific numbers of some shade trees.) This has a significant negative impact on the quantity of light that illuminates south-facing windows because the winter sun, unlike the summer sun, is low in the sky, rising in the southeast and setting in the southwest. Of course, this effect is most prominent with houses having their length running east-west. But a similar effect occurs with houses oriented at various angles to the south.

Some deciduous trees have so many branches and limbs that up to 78 percent of the winter sunlight is blocked. If your landscape calls for a large tree on the south side, choose trees with as low a winter shade percentage as possible. The ideal is to find

Even when deciduous trees lose all their foliage, the shoots, branches, and limbs can block a considerable amount of the winter sunlight—up to 78%.

a tree that lets in plenty of winter sunlight but also provides dense shade in summer. English oak (*Quercus robur*) fills the bill by letting in plenty of sunlight in the winter—83 percent— yet providing a good amount of shade in the summer—81 percent.

The simple approach to getting maximum winter sunlight into your home is to plant no large evergreen or deciduous shade trees or shrubs along the south-facing side of the home. The formula for determining this "no-tree zone" is easily charted on the master scale drawing of your yard. Using a compass, draw a line due south from both the eastern-most and

the western-most sides or corners of the house (two examples are shown on p. 41). Next, use a simple protractor to trace a line with a 45-degree angle east of the line on the eastern corner of the house, and one 45 degrees west of the western corner. The zone between these two outer lines defines the area *not* to be planted.

Using Existing Trees

Many people inherit large, mature shade trees already thriving in the no-tree zone on the southern side of the home. An advantage of leaving

Percentage of Shade Cast by Deciduous Trees in Winter

The following chart is a collection of studies from around the country using light meters to determine the percentage of shade cast by deciduous trees in the winter. Select deciduous trees that block less sunlight (cast a lower percentage of shade) during the winter. If, for example, a sweet gum fits your needs as well as a ginkgo tree, choosing the sweet gum will allow more sunlight through the canopy (27 percent shade, compared with 37 percent shade for the ginkgo).

Latin Name	Common Name	% Shade	Latin Name	Common Name	% Shade
Quercus robur	English oak	17	*Tilia cordata*	Littleleaf linden	41-58
Fraxinus spp.	Ash (young)	19	*Morus alba*	Ornamental mulberry	42
Liquidambar styraciflua	Sweet gum, liquidambar	27	*Sassafras albidum*	Sassafras	45
Liriodendron tulipifera	Tulip tree	27	*Platanus racemosa*	California sycamore	48
Koelreuteria paniculata	Golden rain tree	30-40	*Celtis australis*	European hackberry	50
Betula pendula	European birch	32	*Fraxinus holotricha* 'Moraine'	Moraine ash	50
Catalpa speciosa	Western catalpa	32	*Platanus* × *acerifolia*	London plane tree	55-57
Carya illinoensis	Pecan	33	*Fraxinus velutina* 'Modesto'	Modesto ash (mature)	62
Gleditsia triacanthos	Honey locust	33-40	*Sophora japonica*	Japanese pagoda tree, Chinese scholar tree	65
Quercus velutina	Southern black oak	35	*Prunus armeniaca*	Fruiting apricot	67
Pistachia chinensis	Ornamental pistache	36-62	*Ulmus parvifolia*	Chinese elm	67
Ginkgo biloba	Ginkgo	37	*Prunus* spp.	Fruiting plums	78
Juglans nigra	Black walnut	37			
Alnus rhombifolia	White alder	38			

these trees in place is that they will protect the southern portion of the home's roof from heat during late summer or Indian summer.

However, you can shade the southern roof in summer *and* let in sun in winter by carefully pruning trees located near the southern walls of the home. The solution is more complicated to chart, but it offers you the greatest measure of comfort throughout the year and saves the most on your utility bills.

Having both summer shade and winter sunlight along a southern wall

requires figuring out which lower limbs to remove on a fairly mature deciduous or evergreen tree in the no-tree zone south of the home. This is more easily explained with an example about how to prune an existing tree. You'll need that scale drawing of either the east or west side of your home. Use the top of the highest window as your reference point. Figure out your latitude on a map (see p. 43). Use the latitude to determine the sun's altitude at noon during the period from September 21 through March 22—an average

Using light meters, it has been shown that English oak (*Quercus robur*) allows up to 83% of winter sunlight through the canopy, yet blocks 81% of the summer's light—a good combination.

The No-Tree Zone

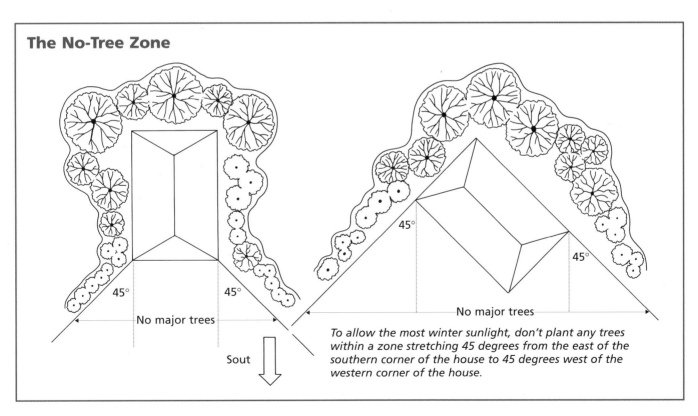

45°   45°

No major trees

Sout

45°   45°

No major trees

To allow the most winter sunlight, don't plant any trees within a zone stretching 45 degrees from the east of the southern corner of the house to 45 degrees west of the western corner of the house.

Alnus rhombifolia
WHITE ALDER, SIERRA ALDER, or CALIFORNIA ALDER

USDA ZONES: 5 to 10

SIZE: 35 ft. to 50 ft. tall; 20 ft. to 35 ft. wide

COMMENTS: Dark green leaves, coarsely toothed on branches that droop at the tips. The underside of the leaf is an attractive pale green, which is noticeable in a breeze or wind. Not planted in the Northeast. Grows quite fast, especially in narrow spaces and near the coast. Watch for alder beetles, tent caterpillars, aphids, and mistletoe. Tolerates heat, wind, and sandy soils in some areas.

Carya illinoensis
PECAN

USDA ZONES: 5 to 9

SIZE: 70 ft. to 100 ft. tall; 20 ft. to 40 ft. wide

COMMENTS: Huge deciduous tree with richly colored dark olive-green leaves. Difficult to transplant but worth the effort. Plant in a spot far enough from the house to ensure the falling, messy nuts are not a problem. If foliage overhangs the roof, be sure to cover gutters with protective screening. Requires a moist, deep soil with good drainage and fertility. Not planted in the Northeast. Deer- and drought-resistant in some areas.

Juglans nigra
EASTERN or BLACK WALNUT

USDA ZONES: 4 to 10

SIZE: 50 ft. to 75 ft. tall; 50 ft. to 75 ft. wide

COMMENTS: This deciduous tree makes tasty nuts that are hard to crack and shell. Dark green lustrous leaves. Don't plant near pavement because the fallen rotting husks easily stain. Can spread and naturalize, so remove unwanted seedlings when still young. Deer-resistant in some areas.

Morus alba 'Mapleleaf' *and* 'Stribling'
MAPLELEAF AND STRIBLING FRUITLESS ORNAMENTAL MULBERRY

USDA ZONES: 4 to 9 (10)

SIZE: 30 ft. to 40 ft. tall; 30 ft. to 40 ft. wide

COMMENTS: Round-headed canopy with large-lobed leaves that turn an attractive yellow each fall. Fast-growing but brittle wood, so plant away from the roof. Tolerates many soils: dry, saline, fertile, and alkaline. Tolerates clay soil in some areas. More susceptible to disease in the South. Watch for leaf spots, mildews, cankers, and bacterial blight. Spider mites and scales are two possible pests.

Quercus velutina
SOUTHERN or BLACK OAK

USDA ZONES: (5) 6 to 9

SIZE: 80 ft. to 100 ft. tall; 80 ft. to 100 ft. wide

COMMENTS: Leaves are large, lobed, and glossy green. Buds and new growth are velvety. Brownish red fall color is not very attractive. Frequently gets cankers, rust, leaf blister, oak wilt, and twig blight, as well as scales and leaf miner. Tolerates clay soils in some areas. In the upper Midwest, substitute *Q. ellipsoidalis*.

Sassafras albidum
SASSAFRAS

USDA ZONES: 4 to 10

SIZE: 35 ft. to 50 ft. tall; 25 ft. to 40 ft. wide

COMMENTS: Glorious hot red, rich orange, or golden-yellow colors in the fall. Rarely gets mildew, leaf spots, or Japanese beetles. Ice or wind can easily snap branches. Naturalizes. Don't plant near foundations. Resists deer, attracts birds, and tolerates drought and sandy soils in some areas.

Other trees and shrubs for winter sunlight include: *Catalpa speciosa* (western catalpa, northern catalpa) (p. 34), *Fraxinus pennsylvanica* (green ash) (p. 92), *Ginkgo biloba* (ginkgo, maidenhair tree) (p. 71), *Liquidambar styraciflua* (sweet gum, liquidambar) (p. 71), and *Pistachia chinensis* (Chinese pistache) (p. 71).

Determining the Sun's Angle

FIND YOUR LATITUDE ON THE MAP, then use the chart to determine the angle of the sun at your latitude.

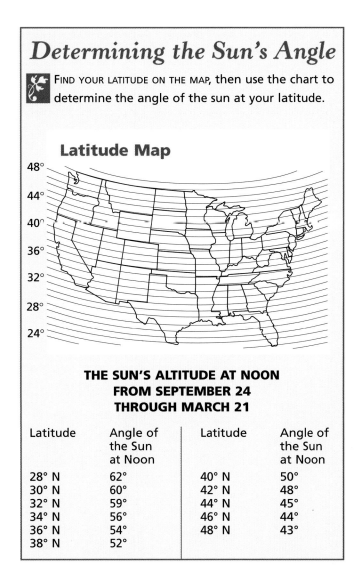

Latitude Map

**THE SUN'S ALTITUDE AT NOON
FROM SEPTEMBER 24
THROUGH MARCH 21**

Latitude	Angle of the Sun at Noon	Latitude	Angle of the Sun at Noon
28° N	62°	40° N	50°
30° N	60°	42° N	48°
32° N	59°	44° N	45°
34° N	56°	46° N	44°
36° N	54°	48° N	43°
38° N	52°		

Pruning Existing Trees for Maximum Winter Sun

Once you determine the angle of the sun during winter, you can apply it to your scale drawing to determine where to trim your tree so the most light gets in. The two lines coming from the window show the span of sunlight that will pass along the floor or onto furniture that might fade in direct sunlight.

To determine how far the sunshine will penetrate into the room, use only the line that cuts across top of the window.

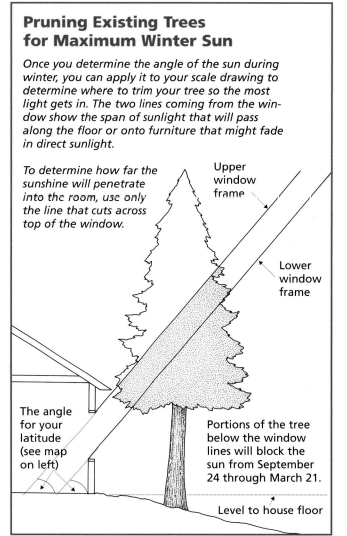

Upper window frame

Lower window frame

The angle for your latitude (see map on left)

Portions of the tree below the window lines will block the sun from September 24 through March 21.

Level to house floor

---

heating season. This angle will help you determine where to prune your trees to allow the most sunlight in your windows.

On your scale drawing, draw a line from the top of the window to the floor, based on the angle for your latitude. Then draw the angle from the interior of the home out through the crown of the tree. During the fall and winter, the sun will always be lower than the altitude line (the sun moves higher in the sky after March 22). The limbs that hang below the line you've marked will obscure the winter's warming sunshine. Remove these offending limbs with summer pruning cuts.

CHAPTER THREE

Within Lawns

IN MANY NATURAL ECOSYSTEMS, there is a fascinating mosaic of tall trees, lower shrubs, herbaceous perennials, and various grasses randomly enclosed in pools of light within the forest and in scattered meadows. These rich layers of canopies add texture and diversity to the unconstrained forest. Where forests predominate, grasses don't often cover huge expanses: They sprout more as bunches than as an even carpet of lawn. Our domesticated lawn grasses, grown over large portions of the yard, are an anomaly for many areas of the country.

Yet, in the grand scheme of gardening, lawn care actually doesn't take that much time. That means most homes will have lawns. Lawns serve many purposes—sports arena, backyard campground, picnic area, tanning salon. But the lawn can seem empty without trees and shrubs to break up the expanse and shade some areas. While incorporating trees and shrubs creates an attractive look, it can be tricky. Tree and shrub root systems aren't always compatible with lawns. It's essential to understand the root system before you plant trees and shrubs in the lawn. Fortunately, there are some steps you can take to ensure successful in-lawn plantings. These steps involve planting habits as much as the actual tree you choose to plant.

Understanding Root Growth

Root patterns are often wrongly portrayed under a pointy pine tree with roots exactly as wide as the width of the crown, and a deep triangular root system to match the shape of the top. Often these simplified drawings show trees with a deep taproot, which is more often the exception rather than the rule.

In reality, most trees and shrubs have what is called a fibrous root system. In tree parlance, fibrous doesn't mean a very fine, hairy root system such as that found on an azalea, heather, or fern. It simply means not taprooted. Fibrous tree and shrub roots are distinguished by many major horizontal roots originating at the base of the trunk (also called the crown of the root system). Most of these horizontal roots are within the top 1 ft. to 2 ft. of the soil. Also, there are numerous vertical roots, called sinkers, which arise anywhere along the horizontal roots and mostly serve to anchor the shrub or tree (shown below). Most of the nutrient uptake happens in the top 2 ft. of soil, regardless of the type of root system.

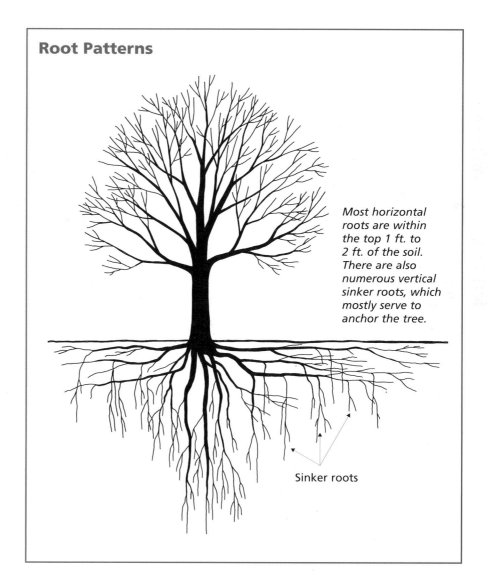

Root Patterns

Most horizontal roots are within the top 1 ft. to 2 ft. of the soil. There are also numerous vertical sinker roots, which mostly serve to anchor the tree.

Sinker roots

Taproots

A taproot tree is one with a single, large root growing down from below the trunk to "tap" into deep soil and moisture. From the taproot grow many, much smaller horizontal roots, called lateral roots. Taprooted plants often have very few, if any, large horizontal or lateral roots. A taprooted tree fit the old mirror-image view of roots—sort of. But two things are wrong with this idealized picture.

First, the roots of any tree, even one with a taproot, still have most of their feeding roots near the soil's surface, within the top 2 ft. And these roots roam far beyond the canopy's drip line to seek food and water. This roaming around for food can take the roots as much as three or more times wider than the drip line. And in shallow soils with clay, calcium hardpans, and bedrock, the roots can extend up to five or more times wider than the crown.

Second, very few of the trees most of us grow are actually taprooted. Most members of the nut tree family—walnut, pecan, hickory, and butternut, for example—are true taproot trees. (Hazelnuts and almonds are not taprooted.) Also, many trees and shrubs in desert climates use taproots as a partial survival strategy. Other examples of taprooted trees include many oak trees (*Quercus* spp.), but only when they're young, and redbuds (*Cercis* spp.).

But even these trees are not taprooted under all circumstances. In fact, taprooted trees can form healthy taproots only when grown in the landscape from seed. Taproots develop only if the soil is a good, loose texture and very deep—deep enough to accommodate a typical taproot. Otherwise, any obstruction in the soil, such as a shallow hardpan or shelf of rock, will deform the taproot to grow horizontally, or effectively stop its growth. When trees are dug from nursery fields to be sold in containerized or bare-root form, the taproot is almost certainly damaged or destroyed.

Interestingly, some trees start out with a taproot that naturally withers away. Examples include many members of the Californian and western oak trees (*Quercus* spp.). When the young seedling of some California oaks is a mere 3 in. high, the taproot extends below the acorn for as much as 36 in. After many years, the taproot rots away and many large horizontal roots with short vertical roots everywhere—which have been forming all along—take over as stabilizers, as the bulk of the root's storage place for nutrients, and as places from which to launch new feeding roots.

Scientists think the young taproot gives the vulnerable seedling a com-

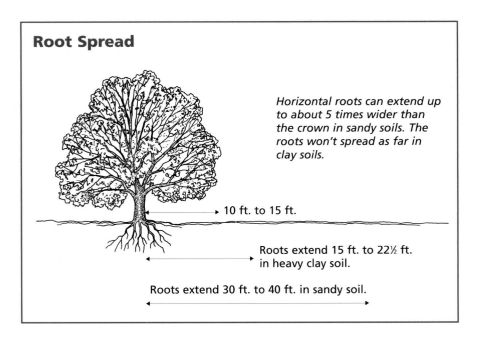

Root Spread

Horizontal roots can extend up to about 5 times wider than the crown in sandy soils. The roots won't spread as far in clay soils.

10 ft. to 15 ft.

Roots extend 15 ft. to 22½ ft. in heavy clay soil.

Roots extend 30 ft. to 40 ft. in sandy soil.

petitive advantage because it can find moisture before the rainless summer dries out the upper level of soil. The new root system that takes over on an oak tree after the taproot has disintegrated represents our most common type—the fibrous root system.

Fibrous roots

A fibrous root system, whether on trees or shrubs, is distinguished by many major horizontal roots originating at the base of the trunk (the crown of the root system). Most of these horizontal roots are within the top 1 ft. to 2 ft. of the soil, and numerous vertical sinker roots arise along the horizontal roots. These horizontal roots always grow wider than the foliage above ground. As in a maturing older oak without its taproot, the bulk of the roots are in the upper 1 ft. or 2 ft. of an ideal soil. If the yard has heavy clay 12 in. down or a calche (calcium-based) hardpan, then the *entire* root system will be in the upper 12 in.

Soil life, nutrients, and roots

To understand soil is to understand much about root growth. Soil is a teeming, living concoction of minerals, organic matter, animal and vegetable life, moisture, and various gases. The oxygen from the air promotes the health of all the critters, microbes, bacteria, fungi, and algae living in the soil, as well as the plant's slender, minute, feeding root hairs. The air-loving (aerobic) soil life liberates soil- and mineral-bound

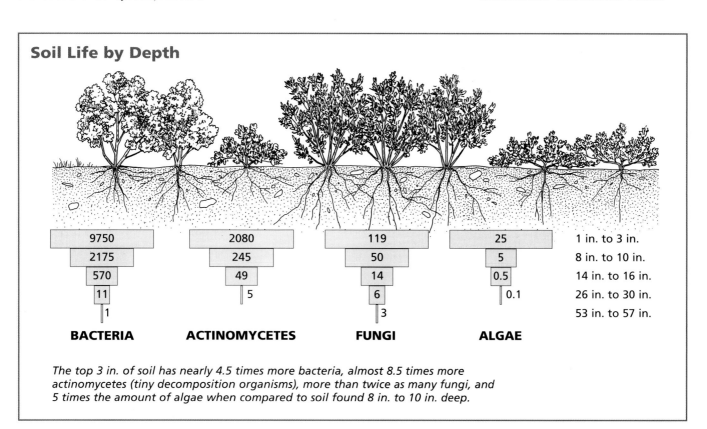

Soil Life by Depth

BACTERIA	ACTINOMYCETES	FUNGI	ALGAE	
9750	2080	119	25	1 in. to 3 in.
2175	245	50	5	8 in. to 10 in.
570	49	14	0.5	14 in. to 16 in.
11	5	6	0.1	26 in. to 30 in.
1		3		53 in. to 57 in.

The top 3 in. of soil has nearly 4.5 times more bacteria, almost 8.5 times more actinomycetes (tiny decomposition organisms), more than twice as many fungi, and 5 times the amount of algae when compared to soil found 8 in. to 10 in. deep.

nutrients into a soluble form easily absorbed by root hairs. The air flows through the tiny passages called the pore spaces, which are the natural water drainage and air "ducts" of a well-structured soil.

The very soil life that sustains plant growth also produces toxic gases. These gases, produced by microorganism and plant growth, must diffuse out of the soil. Shallow, loose soils quickly exchange the putrid waste gases with rejuvenating, fresh air. However, deep soils take a long time to "inhale" air and "exhale" harmful fumes.

Therefore, the soil close to the surface is always more aerobic than deeper soil. This is reflected in the fact that, compared to soil found 8 in. to 10 in. deep, the top 3 in. of soil has nearly 4½ times more bacteria, almost more than twice as many fungi, and 5 times the amount of algae. These are some of the bacteria and flora responsible for the decomposition of organic matter and the liberation of mineralized (unavailable) nutrients into a soluble form that the tree can absorb, and they live near the soil's surface because oxygen is required to fuel their activity. The aerobic soil life is found near the surface, and the feeding roots naturally colonize the same zone to feed on the nutrients released by the activity of these organisms.

In reality, most tree roots grow up—not down. These feeding roots are searching for and "mining" the most aerobic layers of a natural forest floor.

The depth of soil also shapes the root system. If your yard has only 6 in. of good loamy soil on top of a heavy clay soil or a rock-hard calche hardpan, then the tree's *entire* root system will be in the upper 6 in.

Turf and Tree Roots

Turf grows a dense mat of roots in the same zone of soil that tree roots prefer, creating competition. Learning about the potential competition helps you plan for what trees to use and how to plant them to minimize problems.

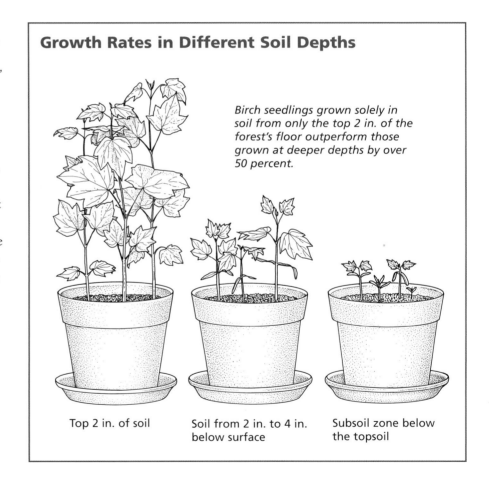

Growth Rates in Different Soil Depths

Birch seedlings grown solely in soil from only the top 2 in. of the forest's floor outperform those grown at deeper depths by over 50 percent.

Top 2 in. of soil

Soil from 2 in. to 4 in. below surface

Subsoil zone below the topsoil

Trees and lawns are often naturally incompatible for four reasons:

- *The turf grasses in our modern yards choke off the natural exchange of gases between the soil and the atmosphere, leading to a slight dwarfing or stunting of the tree.*
- *The forest floor has a deep litter of decomposing leaves, twigs, logs, and different size critters, which provides a welcome place above the soil for roots to forage for nutrients. Taking away this beneficial mulch (or duff) and replacing it with lawn both harms the tree and can leave the roots exposed. Thus, tree roots often appear to "surface" to be scalped by the lawnmower, a source of potentially debilitating wounds for the tree and frustration for the homeowner.*
- *Some trees are programmed by their genetic coding to have many, large surface roots.*
- *The fertility and irrigation required to keep a lawn happy is often more than a tree needs, causing pest and disease problems.*

Despite the inherent difficulties, most of us still want to have trees and shrubs in our lawns. To choose the best tree to be surrounded by turf, you need to address these four concerns. To help, we'll take a detailed look at each problem or dilemma, then look at the solutions (see pp. 52-55). As we explore these problems, keep in mind that many trees cast so much shade that is difficult to grow many types of lawn grasses below their drip line, especially near the trunk. The shading effect is, in a way, a defense mechanism of the tree or shrub against competition for moisture and nutrients. A continuous canopy of dense trees and shrubs greatly reduces the number of shorter plants below, favoring the growth of the trees and shrubs.

A thatched roof on the lawn's soil

The turf in most American lawns is a far cry from meadow or prairie grasses. Natural grasslands tend to be composed mostly of "bunch" grasses, which grow in patches or accidental clusters, not with stems of continuous coverage. As the term implies, bunch grasses don't form the mat of shoots formed by the stolons, or runner-roots, of some lawn grasses; instead, batches of root crowns bound forth from randomly spaced clumps. There is space between the bunches for dead grass stems and leaves to decompose and for gases to pass back and forth between the air and soil.

As mentioned earlier, well-textured soil has an enormous

These roots are growing in a shallow soil. The duff has been removed by foot traffic, and we are left with this unnatural view.

The lawn surrounding these fruiting cherry trees helps to control overly vigorous growth and brings the tree into bearing earlier in its life.

labyrinth of minute pore spaces (like the myriad pockets and channels permeating a good Swiss cheese) that allow debilitating gases to pass out of the earth and revitalizing air to seep into the soil. The buildup of thatch, undecomposed grass leaves, and roots in a lawn retards this important exchange of gases. If the thatch builds up and remains thick and undigested by soil microorganisms, it literally chokes off the absorption of air into the soil and stunts the growth of trees and shrubs.

Farmers in England have used this phenomenon to their advantage for hundreds of years. Long before there were dwarfing rootstocks for cherry trees, English orchardists seeded their cherry orchards with a grass cover (called a sward in the U.K.) to slightly dwarf the trees while encouraging them to bear earlier in life.

Some grasses, such as rye grass, produce a mild root excretion—called allelopathy by scientists—that chemically stunts the growth of nearby plants. Rye grass lawns can do the same to your trees. While the effect is mild, the rye grass works around the clock and you don't.

Root growth above the soil

The roots of any tree, even those with a taproot, still have most of their feeding roots near the soil's surface, usually within 1 ft. of the surface. The surface is defined as the top of the undigested, undecomposed leaf and twig litter (the duff) you'd find in a forest, *not* the top of the soil. Trees and shrubs can actually have an amazing number of roots above the soil (see Root Depth on the facing page). The roots feed in and on the decomposing litter without any trouble.

By planting a lawn beneath a tree, you're removing the natural, thick duff and replacing it with a thin layer of turf and thatch. The tree's roots, searching for the nutrients it would have gotten from the duff, rise above the soil and into the turf, only to be mangled by the lawnmower's blade.

Genetics

Some trees naturally have roots that tolerate or apparently thrive near or on the soil's surface. Many of these trees are originally from riparian (streamside) habitats, including alders (*Alnus* spp.), sycamores or plane trees (*Platanus* spp.), willows (*Salix* spp.), birches (*Betula* spp.), and the coastal redwood (*Sequoia sempervirens*). Along the bank of a stream, the roots of these trees are frequently exposed by bank erosion, or they may actually grow out into the water. Such trees are likely to have noticeable surface roots when irrigation is too shallow—mere inches or less. But even deeper irrigation won't completely override their genetic tendency toward surfacing roots.

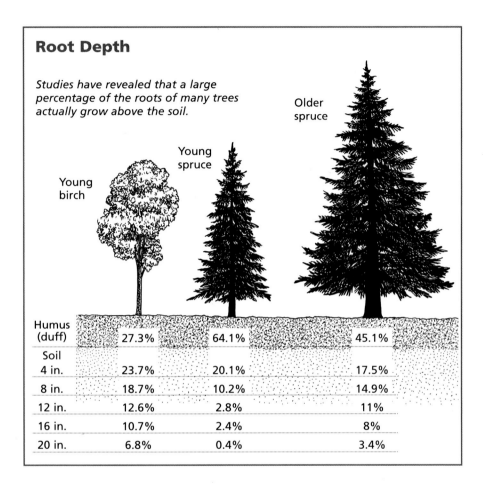

Root Depth

Studies have revealed that a large percentage of the roots of many trees actually grow above the soil.

Young birch
Young spruce
Older spruce

	Young birch	Young spruce	Older spruce
Humus (duff)	27.3%	64.1%	45.1%
Soil 4 in.	23.7%	20.1%	17.5%
8 in.	18.7%	10.2%	14.9%
12 in.	12.6%	2.8%	11%
16 in.	10.7%	2.4%	8%
20 in.	6.8%	0.4%	3.4%

Trees and shrubs that normally grow in riparian (creekside) habitats, such as these coastal redwoods (*Sequoia sempervirens*), have roots that will easily surface when grown in a lawn.

Other trees with surface roots, but not necessarily from riparian habitats, are the following:
- *Siberian elm (*Ulmus pumila*)*
- *Silver maple (*Acer saccharinum*)*
- *Mulberries (*Morus spp.*)*
- *Poplars (*Populus spp.*)*
- *Sweet gum (*Liquidambar styraciflua*)*
- *Ashes (*Fraxinus spp.*)*
- *Sumacs (*Rhus spp.*) (except the drought-resistant varieties from the western U.S.)*

Water and fertility

The water needs of a gorgeous green lawn exceed those of many trees and shrubs. The extra moisture forces growth, which can lead to problems with aphids, mildews, fungal

The sweet gum tree (shown here in fall color) has roots that may surface in a lawn even though they didn't originate in a riparian setting.

diseases, and bacterial blights. Also if too much water from lawn sprinklers hits the trunks of the shrubs and trees, it can cause crown rot of the upper root system.

Furthermore, many lawn grasses are so domesticated that they don't grow well or look appealing without consistent fertilizing. Most species of trees and shrubs thrive without any supplemental fertilizer. If properly chosen for your soil type and climate, no tree in the yard (except some fruit trees) should need added fertilizer or nutritious mulch—although perhaps just enough woody mulch to conserve some moisture and keep the soil cooler during hot summers.

Most grasses require a total yearly application of 1 lb. to 4 lb. of nitrogen per 1,000 sq. ft., but under a moderate scheme of fertilization, many people use far more. This amount is much greater than the 1 lb. of nitrogen per 1,000 sq. ft. that most landscape contractor guidelines advise for trees. (We'll see in Chapter 11 that even this small amount isn't usually necessary.) Only if the leaves of the shrub or tree turn yellow-green, indicating nitrogen deficiency, should nitrogen be added at the rate of 2 lb. per 1,000 sq. ft.

But, when you feed your lawn, the tree roots just below the surface will certainly grab as much as they can. The excess nitrogen causes many

trees in or near lawns to grow tall and somewhat spindly. This weak growth makes them prone to more damage from wind or ice storms and can also cause problems with aphids, mildews, fungal diseases, and bacterial blights.

Solutions for Lawn Plantings

Attempts to control the root systems of trees and shrubs by controlling fertilization and irrigation, or with root barriers, usually yield poor results. Nonetheless, with turf that needs little irrigation or fertilizer, and with the right tree, you *can* plant trees within a lawn. The trick is to choose those trees that are somewhat genetically "programmed" to have deeper lateral roots and not as many roots that would naturally grow into the forest's duff. (See Trees and Shrubs to Plant in a Lawn on the facing page for some good candidates for lawn planting. Also, for plants to avoid in a lawn, see p. 55.)

A skirt of loose mulch extending as far from the tree's trunk as is practical is often the best solution. Without thatch and the compaction of foot traffic and lawnmower, the soil's natural flora and fauna will keep the soil crumbly and well aerated.

The pragmatic way to reduce the conflict between lawns and shrubs and trees and to decrease your

Many species of maple (*Acer* spp.) naturally grow roots with more depth and can be planted within the lawn with less danger of surface roots being scalped by the lawnmower.

maintenance is to spatially separate these two elements of a landscape. A generic solution for many yards is to provide 2 in. to 4 in. of mulch at least out to the drip line, and to surround the mulch with a mowing strip or some other kind of border. This plan avoids conflict between the mower's

Trees and Shrubs to Plant in a Lawn

Acer × freemanii 'Autumn Blaze'
AUTUMN BLAZE HYBRID MAPLE

USDA ZONES: 5 to 9

SIZE: 40 ft. tall; 35 ft. wide

COMMENTS: Tolerates the watering a lawn gets. Seedless. Roots are aggressive near the soil's surface in clay soil, but deeper in aerobic sandier soils. Heavy shade from the tree keeps turf from growing well under the canopy, so be sure to mulch out to near the drip line. Sooty mold can develop on the aphid honeydew that drops from the tree onto the house and hardscape. Wind-tolerant in some areas. 'Royal Red' has attractive, glossy, dark red foliage.

Aesculus × carnea
RED HORSE CHESTNUT

USDA ZONES: 4 to 7

SIZE: 30 ft. to 40 ft. tall; 30 ft. to 40 ft. wide

COMMENTS: A cross between two native buckeye trees (*A. pavia* and *A. hippocastanum*). Has rich green foliage on a dense, rounded canopy. Rose-red flower clusters cover the tree each spring. Tolerates moisture as long as there is good drainage. Prefers deep soil. Birds may feed on the large nuts in some areas. Can get a blight that browns leaves in the late summer or early fall. Deciduous.

Juniperus chinensis 'Columnaris Glauca'
BLUE CHINESE COLUMN JUNIPER

USDA ZONES: 5 to 9

SIZE: 12 ft. to 25 ft. tall; 2 ft. to 8 ft. wide

COMMENTS: Some cultivars of this evergreen have an attractive blue-gray coloration. Tolerates high levels of moisture in a well-drained soil, but don't allow the roots to get overly wet. Relatively disease- and pest-free, but watch for blight on new shoots and for bagworms. Deer-resistant and wind-tolerent in some areas.

Magnolia stellata (*Magnolia kobus* var. *stellata*)
STAR MAGNOLIA

USDA ZONES: 4 to 10

SIZE: 15 ft. to 20 ft. tall; 10 ft. to 15 ft. wide

COMMENTS: A very attractive deciduous magnolia with fragrant 2-in.-long, narrow, pure white petals. Blooms early, so late freezes or rains can damage blossoms. Plant so it's sheltered from the winter sun to delay budding and flowering, to reduce late frost damage. It prefers an acidic soil high in organic matter. Even moisture is important. Don't plant on a western or southern exposure because it likes some shelter from hot sunlight. Resists deer and tolerates wind and clay soils in some areas.

Picea pungens 'Tomsen'
THOMSEN COLORADO BLUE SPRUCE

USDA ZONES: 3 to 6 (7)

SIZE: 30 ft. to 50 ft. tall; 10 ft. to 30 ft. wide

COMMENTS: One of the most dramatic cultivars of a popular spruce. A symmetrical evergreen tree with whitish blue to silver-blue foliage. Slow growing and prefers a cool spot. Watch for spruce aphid in Pacific Northwest and spruce gall aphid in the Northeast. Resists deer and tolerates drought, clay soils, and sandy soils in some areas.

Platycladus orientalis (*Thuja orientalis*)
ORIENTAL ARBORVITAE

USDA ZONES: 6 to 11

SIZE: 18 ft. to 25 ft. tall; 10 ft. to 15 ft. wide

COMMENTS: Usually sold as named cultivars, not just the species form. Naturally dense pyramidal evergreen shape. Adapts to some cold, heat, and all kinds of poor soil (except saturated soil). Discolors in cold weather.

Other trees that grow well in lawns include: *Acer griseum* (paperbark maple) (p. 74), *Cercis canadensis* (eastern redbud) (p. 82), *Platanus × acerifolia* (London plane tree) (p. 55), *Tilia cordata* (littleleaf linden) (p. 35), and *Ulmus parvifolia* (Chinese or lacebark elm) (p. 32).

A mulch beyond the drip line of shrubs and trees prevents the older roots from being an obstacle for a lawnmower and permits healthy woody root growth.

Safer Lawn Planting

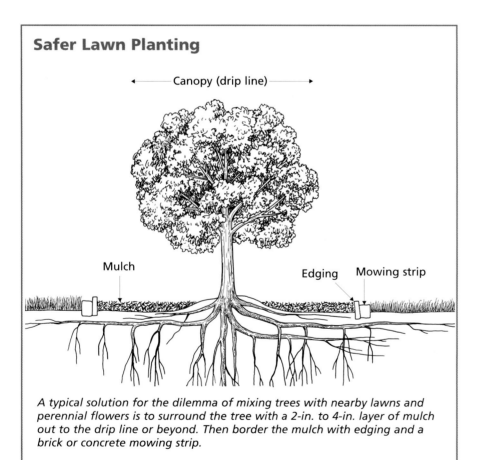

Canopy (drip line)

Mulch

Edging   Mowing strip

A typical solution for the dilemma of mixing trees with nearby lawns and perennial flowers is to surround the tree with a 2-in. to 4-in. layer of mulch out to the drip line or beyond. Then border the mulch with edging and a brick or concrete mowing strip.

Many shrubs and trees, such as this specimen of winterberry (*Ilex verticillata*), are healthiest when planted far from the lawn with a mulch wider than their canopy.

blade and protruding roots by giving individual trees or shrubs islands of protective mulch. Or, small groves can be planted where trees are clustered together within one large, irregularly shaped sea of mulch. It's often better to plant trees and shrubs grouped in groves like this than to plant them individually in the lawn.

Some trees near lawns prefer a mulch that extends well beyond the drip line. Such trees belong in their own section, like a miniature woodland in the further reaches of the yard. These trees are only for large yards with plenty of room where they can almost literally roam free. You should avoid them in smaller areas.

Trees and Shrubs Requiring a Wide Mulch

Acer saccharinum
SILVER MAPLE

USDA ZONES: 3 to 10

SIZE: 60 ft. to 75 ft. tall; 40 ft. to 50 ft. wide

COMMENTS: Most maples share the same traits as the silver maple, including surface-oriented roots. The tree evolved on flood plains and tolerates periodic flooding. The roots grow up into the more aerobic, upper levels of the soil. They are so invasive that this tree must be planted far from a lawn or foundation. Resists deer and attracts birds in some areas.

Cornus sanguinea
BLOODTWIG DOGWOOD

USDA ZONES: 4 to 7

SIZE: 6 ft. to 15 ft. tall; 6 ft. to 15 ft. wide

COMMENTS: Can be a large, floppy, spreading shrub, but some pruning will give it a better form. The beauty lies in the dramatic deciduous stem color during the winter; the young stems are blood red. Therefore many gardeners coppice the shrub, cutting it to the ground every spring to always force new shoots. Older stems turn a gray-green. The cultivar 'Viridissima' has green-yellow young stems. And 'Winter Flame' is yellow-orange stemmed. Tolerates clay soils in some areas.

Ilex verticillata 'Red Sprite'
COMMON WINTERBERRY

USDA ZONES: 3 to 9

SIZE: 3 ft. to 5 ft. tall; 3 ft. to 5 ft. wide

COMMENTS: This deciduous holly cultivar has bright red fruit up to ⅜ in. in diameter that lasts into December and even January. A round-shaped shrub with glossy dark green foliage. Grow in patches or clusters. Prefers acidic, moist, fertile, well-drained soils. Tolerates sandy soil in some areas.

Platanus × *acerifolia*
LONDON PLANE TREE

USDA ZONES: 5 to 10

SIZE: 60 ft. to 80 ft. tall; 40 ft. to 55 ft. wide

COMMENTS: Can be very dramatic in formal or grove-type plantings. Intriguing bark coloration. There is some dispute about this tree's rooting pattern. In many settings, the roots do not surface to cause a problem, but many cities have had to deal with sidewalks heaved by the older roots. Shallow irrigation leads to surfacing roots. While this tree can be grown in lawns with some success, it does drop plenty of fuzzy fruit. The dust from the fruit and underside of the leaves is irritating to some people. Tolerates almost any soil except the most clayey. This cross gets less of the debilitating anthracnose, which causes stem dieback.

Salix spp.
WILLOWS

USDA ZONES: 3 to 10

SIZE: 3 ft. to 50 ft. tall; 30 ft. to 40 ft. wide

COMMENTS: All species of this genus evolved on floodplains or near flowing water, so they tolerate periodic flooding. Pencil-diameter shoots jammed into the ground will often root if there is sufficient moisture. Tolerates clay soils in some areas.

Taxodium distichum
COMMON BALD CYPRESS

USDA ZONES: 4 to 10

SIZE: 50 ft. to 70 ft. tall; 20 ft. to 30 ft. wide

COMMENTS: This is a deciduous conifer with a well-behaved columnar to pyramidal shape. Rich green foliage in the summer. Often planted in groves where few other trees will thrive. In very wet soils or standing water, it will produce the famous cypress "knees," which protrude above the soil or water. Tolerates wind and sandy soil in some areas.

Other trees and shrubs that require a wide mulch include: *Carya illinoensis* (pecan) (p. 42), *Diospyrus virginiana* (common persimmon) (p. 92), *Juglans nigra* (eastern walnut, black walnut) (p. 42), *Liquidambar styraciflua* (sweet gum, liquidambar) (p. 71), *Picea abies* (Norway spruce) (p. 25), and *Sassafras albidum* (sassafras) (p. 42).

CHAPTER FOUR

Colorful Foliage & Bark

GARDENERS OFTEN FOCUS on floral display through the spring, summer, and fall. Flowering shrubs and trees can be quite impressive, yet some blossoms are so very fleeting. The backbone of many good garden designs falls back on the foliage color of both deciduous and evergreen trees and shrubs during various parts of the spring, summer, and fall. During the depths of winter, the foliage of evergreen shrubs and trees and the attractive bark on certain deciduous trees capture one's attention and provide the aesthetic "glue" for the yard.

Many selections of Japanese maples (*Acer palmatum*) have striking red, burgundy, or maroon foliage throughout the spring and summer. This is the cultivar 'Shaina'.

Sometimes seedlings with very different foliage from normal develop, giving us tree and shrub cultivars—such as this *Acer negundo* 'Flamingo', with a dramatic array of variegated foliage.

The variegated leaves of *Ilex × alta-clarensis* 'Golden King' provide a distinctive highlight to an otherwise simple, dark-green foliage.

Flowers are often focal points because of their strong, eye-catching color, whereas trees and shrubs, with more structure and form and less dramatic color, play an important role as fundamental, sometimes even imposing, elements of an overall design. A medium-green tree, such as the common hackberry (*Celtis occidentalis*) may not have the most exciting foliage, but its mature form has a satisfyingly broad canopy with arching limbs, which stands out above small perennials in both mass and pattern.

Large groupings of brightly colored perennials, such as the hot yellow flower heads of the fernleaf yarrow (*Achillea filipendulina*), will lure the eye away from the details of the hackberry. But, perhaps, after sunset, your glance will wander up to the hackberry's tall form silhouetted against the fading colors of dusk.

The foliage of trees and shrubs alone offers the gardener an amazing array of choices. Their leaves and needles provide a rainbow of colorful tones—from yellows that border on golden to lime green; pale to the darkest of greens; red, burgundy, smoky vermilion, and purple shades; silver and white tones; and a wide range of the blue-green spectrum.

Variegated leaves come in more combinations than just yellows mixed with greens, including pink, white, and pale green; burgundy and green; and white with various shades of green. The bark can offer intriguing texture along with a patina of mixed colors not found in the adjacent foliage. Some barks can be smooth and range from rich gray to silvery; others offer reddish shades; and others peel to reveal cream, orange, auburn, umber, pale green, or pink underneath or in the shedding bark.

The choice of colors for your garden is a personal one. Some people paint their houses bright yellow or shocking purple. They don't do this to offend others, they do it to please themselves. While others may take offense, the color is a personal preference or style. While many artists assume all eyes see color the same way, the process is more like the variety of body chemistries in people that affect how hot or cold they feel or how their taste buds prefer different flavors. This is true for your garden as well.

The Challenges of Living Color

Unlike paintings, a garden is alive. Every moment of every day there are soft, subtle changes in the color on each leaf, petal, stem, or trunk. Paintings are mostly one-

---

Color Guidelines

For those who want more general guidelines for choosing trees and shrubs based on their foliage or bark color, here's a short list of pointers.

- Cool colors—greens, purples, and blues—mixed with grays and browns make plants appear to recede, adding distance from the viewer.

- Hot or warm colors—red, orange, and yellow—fore-shorten the view, making plants or flowers seem closer to the viewer.

- Spots of shade and green foliage accentuate the more vivid colors (see the photo on the facing page).

- Colors with low intensity (more pastel than hot) appear brighter in the evening's light.

- Humid, foggy, and misty places enhance the cool colors and make pastels and silver-gray plants look more vibrant. (Bright, direct, hot sun will tend to wash out some of the color.)

- Use highlights of a few hot or warm colors, surrounded by masses of cool or cooler-toned colors, to lead the eye in a desired direction.

- Pastels are associated with spring by some; summer is personified by purer, strong colors; fall is the dominion of warmer, richer colors; and winter is rep-resented by muted tones. (These guidelines are derived from gardens in the Eastern, Midwestern, Rocky Mountain, and Pacific Northwestern areas of the country. A completely different set of seasonal changes and colors occurs in the dry regions of the West.)

- Colors are modified by their "neighbors." Any tone can be intensified when planted next to a more neutral color such as white, buff, cream, or beige.

---

dimensional—except for some of the visible piles of paint used by artists such as Vincent van Gogh—and gardens are three-dimensional. It's one of the reasons why gardening is so rewarding and why trying to provide year-round interest is far more complicated and demanding than painting a canvas.

For starters, the sun changes color from the soft pinks of sunrise to the harsher yellows of midday to the orange-red spectrum of some sunsets. Leaves reflect the sun's colors differently depending on the time of day.

For example, several fruitless weeping mulberry cultivars (*Morus alba* 'Chaparral', 'Urbana', and 'Pendula') have cascading dark green foliage when the sun rises east of the tree. The leaf's somewhat shiny surface causes a bit of a noontime glare, but the late-daytime sun shines through each leaf, changing the tint toward an attractive, slightly yellow-green color. This transforms the tree into a more glowing, noticeable element, so it deserves a place in the yard where the setting sun will reveal this special display to people in the house or on a nearby summer patio. Thus the daily and seasonal orientation of light should be considered when placing your trees and shrubs.

Breezes and winds are also an important factor. They flutter leaves and flowers to reveal different colors or slightly different shades (a pure color mixed with some black). Consider the silver or white poplar (*Populus alba*): It has pale green on the top of each leaf, but a breeze reveals the woolly white underside—two colors for the price of one!

Rich, Dark Green Foliage

Green is the predominant color for plant foliage. Yet, green foliage ranges in a spectrum from almost pale yellow to the dark, almost burgundy or black-green.

Regardless of the shade or tone (a pure color mixed with white, gray, or black) of green, this is perhaps the most restful and relaxing of all the colors in the garden. The darker greens are good backdrops for lighter green foliage and other colors, allowing them to show off against the dark background. Without patches of dark or muted green, the eye is kept busy with a plethora of color. This is what I refer to as the "carnival" effect—lots of gaudy or bright colors

and no rest for the eyes. If you have enough room in your yard, a sizable tall backdrop of trees or intermittent groves of various green shrubs or trees separating hotter and brighter colors will provide a welcome visual interlude. The use of a green background can also help make a yard that's not very deep seem roomier, more generously proportioned.

Light green, nearly chartreuse foliage appears more vibrant against a dark green background of foliage.

Green-colored foliage is cooler to the eye and seems to cause hotter, brighter colors to appear closer to the viewer.

Many shades of green are available to the gardener. These eastern redbuds provide a rich backdrop for the shrub border.

Green is a cool color; it appears to recede and it makes hot colors seem even closer. This is why green foliage is often a backdrop in so many gardens, especially the evergreen hedges found as "living walls" in English gardens. There are hundreds of trees that can provide medium and dark green foliage for backgrounds. See the facing page for a listing of some distinctive dark green shrubs and trees.

Gray, Silver, and "White" Foliage

White is another restful color, although not as relaxing to the eye as greens. White has its greatest impact where the edge of white meets another color, creating a contrast. The range of tints that includes white, gray, and silver, and even stretches into the bluish silver color spectrum, radiates when set in front of dark green foliage.

The midday sun can make whites and silver-grays harsh to the eye. But white highlights add a wonderful touch to a garden in the late afternoon, early evening, and under the glow of a full moon. Silver-gray foliage can be used to mark pathways for nighttime strolls during much of the moon's brightest cycle. Of course, you'll want to use mostly small woody shrubs for this purpose.

Dark Green Foliage

Alnus cordata
ITALIAN ALDER

USDA ZONES: 5 to 7 (8)

SIZE: 30 ft. to 50 ft. tall; 20 ft. to 40 ft. wide

COMMENTS: This deciduous tree has perhaps the darkest green leaves of all the alders. There's some sheen to the 2-in.- to 4-in.-long leaves. Spring brings a display of catkins. Tolerates wet and dry conditions, less fertile soil, and high-pH soils. Will not tolerate water from sprinklers on the trunk. Not usually grown in the Northeast. Resists deer and tolerates clay and sandy soils in some areas.

Camellia japonica
JAPANESE CAMELLIA

USDA ZONES: 7 to 10

SIZE: 30 ft. tall; 25 ft. wide

COMMENTS: There are many named cultivars of this evergreen, and most have lustrous dark green foliage. Each cultivar has a slightly different edge and shape to the leaf (and a different blossom color). Requires acidic, well-drained soil and mulch. More hardy types are being introduced. Watch for mites, aphids, and scale infestations on indoor plants. Drought-tolerant in some areas.

Ilex aquifolium
ENGLISH HOLLY

USDA ZONES: 7 to 10

SIZE: 40 ft. tall; 20 ft. wide

COMMENTS: The species form has wonderful dark green, glossy, stiff evergreen foliage. Cultivars come in many sizes, but most share the trait of dark green leaves; some have leaves with prickly spines, others with smooth edges. Only the female trees form red berries, and they need at least one male tree nearby for a chance at good berry formation. Oak root fungus is not a problem. Some cultivars make good hedges and barrier plants. Deer-resistant in some areas. In the South, plant *Ilex* × 'Nellie R. Stevens'.

Magnolia × soulangiana
SAUCER MAGNOLIA

USDA ZONES: 5 to 10

SIZE: 20 ft. to 30 ft. tall; 20 ft. to 30 ft. wide

COMMENTS: The 3-in.- to 6-in.-long green leaves look good all summer, but fall color is usually disappointing. The plant is famous for a glorious display of fragrant, saucer-shaped, white flowers with a pinkish purple tinge up to 10 in. in diameter. Late-spring rains or frost can destroy this spectacular bloom, but the good years are worth the wait. Tolerates sandy soils in some areas. Superior cultivars are 'Rustica Rubra' and 'Alexandrina'.

Myrica pensylvanica
NORTHERN BAYBERRY

USDA ZONES: (2) 3 to 6

SIZE: 5 ft. to 12 ft. tall; 5 ft. to 15 ft. wide

COMMENTS: Glossy green, fragrant leaves up to 4 in. long that are typically evergreen but sometimes semievergreen. Tolerates saline and infertile soils. Will turn yellowish with chlorosis in soils with a high pH. Use *M. cerifera* in the South. Deer-resistant and wind- and drought-tolerant in some areas.

Stewartia monadelpha
TALL STEWARTIA

USDA ZONES: 5 to 8

SIZE: 20 ft. to 30 ft. tall; 20 ft. to 30 ft. wide

COMMENTS: Dark green leaves are 1½ in. to 3 in. long. Fall color is sometimes a dark reddish tone. Its attractive trunk is mottled with cinnamon red, grays, browns, and umbers. Flowers are also attractive with a creamy white midsummer bloom. More heat- and drought-tolerant and easier to grow than other *Stewartia* species. Male plant is required for fruit. *S. pseudo-camellia* is more popular in the Northeast and hardier. Tolerates sandy soils in some areas.

Other trees and shrubs with dark green foliage include: *Arbutus unedo* (strawberry tree) (p. 23), *Franklinia alatamaha* (Franklinia, Franklin tree) (p. 86), and *Nyssa sylvatica* (black tupelo, black gum) (p. 71).

Gray, Silver, and "White" Foliage

Abies concolor
WHITE FIR

USDA Zones: 3 to 10

Size: 30 ft. to 50 ft. tall; 15 ft. to 25 ft. wide

Comments: This evergreen conifer grows in a tall, narrow, conical form with nearly silver-blue foliage. Adapts to many yards and tolerates hot, dry summers. Drought-resistant in its natural environment. Not grown in the South. The cultivar 'Violacea' has the most silver-blue, or glaucous, needles of this species. 'Candicans' is also considered to have one of the best blue-toned foliage.

Lavandula angustifolia
ENGLISH LAVENDER

USDA Zones: 5 to 11

Size: 2 ft. to 3 ft. tall; 2 ft. to 3 ft. wide

Comments: An attractive evergreen shrub with romantic flowers on 6-in.- to 12-in.-tall stems. Blossoms come in many shades of blue, violet, mauve-blue, pink, and pure white, and the foliage in a wide range of whitish to glaucous to bluish green to sharp green. Prone to fungal foliage diseases where humidity is high. The cultivars 'Munstead' (darker blue blossoms) and 'Hidcote' (almost aster-violet flower heads) are much smaller and can be used for borders along pathways.

Perovskia atriplicifolia
RUSSIAN SAGE

USDA Zones: All

Size: 3 ft. to 4 ft. tall; 3 ft. to 4 ft. wide

Comments: Technically, a woody sub-shrub—a woody base cut to the ground like a herbaceous perennial in cold climates and merely sheared for form in warmer climates. Worth growing because of its marvelous, finely cut, gray-green foliage. Square stems are woolly white. An aromatic plant that also bears lovely violet-blue flowers from midsummer to fall. Prefers some winter chill. Evergreen in milder climates.

Picea pungens forma *glauca*
COLORADO BLUE SPRUCE

USDA Zones: 2 to 6 (7)

Size: 30 ft. to 60 ft. tall; 10 ft. to 20 ft. wide

Comments: Popular evergreen conifer because of its attractive silver-blue or blue-green needles. Avoid planting in overly moist soils. Overwhelming if planted in groves or quantity. May look somewhat ragged when grown outside its natural zone. Not grown in the South in Zones 7 to 10. Tolerates clay and sandy soils in some areas. The cultivar 'Moerheimii' has a rich blue foliage but a more open canopy. 'Montgomery' is a compact 3-ft. dwarf with gray-blue needles.

Pyrus salicifolia 'Pendula'
PENDULA
WILLOW-LEAVED PEAR

USDA Zones: 4 to 7

Size: 15 ft. to 20 ft. tall; 15 ft. to 20 ft. wide

Comments: A handsome, slightly weeping form of ornamental pear. The 3½-in.-long leaves are gray-green with a sensuous tomentose (hairy) texture. Leaves are slightly wavy and narrow, and silvery white with new spring growth. Prefers good drainage. The drawback is its susceptibility to fire blight. Keep a watchful eye and prune far past any visibly infected tissue. (Be sure to cleanse your shears after *every* cut.) Not grown in the South. Tolerates clay and sandy soils in some areas.

Teucrium fruticans
BUSH GERMANDER

USDA Zones: 7 to 10

Size: 4 ft. to 8 ft. tall; 4 ft. to 8 ft. wide

Comments: If untrimmed, has silver stems and gray-green leaves that have a much whiter underside. Lavender-blue flowers during much of the year if not heavily pruned. Do not overwater because root rot is a problem.

Other trees and shrubs with gray, silver, or "white" foliage include: *Calluna vulgaris* (heather) (p. 86), *Juniperus virginiana* 'Grey Owl' (Grey Owl eastern red cedar, hybrid eastern red cedar) (p. 21), and *Picea pugens* 'Tomsen' (Colorado blue spruce) (p. 53).

This lavender (*Lavandula dentata* var. *candicans*) has a silver-gray color to its foliage—a nice highlight near dark green leaves.

Excellent examples are santolina (*Santolina chamaecyparissus*), many forms of artemisias (*Artemisia* spp.), and some of the more silver-gray forms of lavender (*Lavandula* spp.).

Some people associate white blossoms with the emergence of early summer as the large, wide umbels of tiny white flowers such as Queen Anne's lace open. Foliage is a different matter. Shrubs and trees with white foliage often appear white because the *surface* of their leaves is tomentose. This means they have small, dense, matted, fuzzy hairs on the underside, usually whitish, silver-gray, or some tint of bluish gray. This same tomentose feature can be found on the entire leaf of a few woody shrubs, such as the more white-leafed form of French lavender called *Lavandula dentata* var. *candicans*.

(White variegated foliage is one exception discussed later in this chapter.) Trees and shrubs often have white blossoms (see Chapter 5).

Some designers say white is a safe color for beginners to work with because it's hard to overuse if there is a green or gray backdrop. On the other hand, you may want to use white with restraint, as it can easily overwhelm the eye. Instead, fall back to the more muted grays or the bluish white or bluish gray range of foliage. Use various shades of green as backdrops to feature or display the white foliage or blossoms of other shrubs and trees. A single dramatic tomentose-leafed tree or shrub, or one with a proliferation of white flowers, can be used as a single specimen for a seasonal focal point in the yard.

A bluish, grayish, or whitish bloom, or such a color on a leaf with a waxy coating, is considered glaucous. Glaucous plants are often found in arid climates as the waxy coating seems linked to water conservation.

Yellow and Chartreuse Foliage

The eye notes the yellow range (clear, pale yellows through yellow-green chartreuse) of color before all others. These warm to hot colors are intriguing but often troublesome to

The yellow on this juniper (*Juniperus communis* 'Depressa Aurea') is more toward the green end of the spectrum.

integrate into a balanced landscape design because they can easily overwhelm nearby plants or blossoms. Prudent use of the right tint of yellow or chartreuse can create an exciting focal point or a highlight in the background of the yard. Keep in mind that these hot colors will appear to move forward. These colors are particularly hard to use in masses with trees or large shrubs.

Some yellows are cool and blend well with the cool blue and pink range of color. Other yellows are richer, with a golden tone, and work best with the warm spectrum of colors.

If you're searching for yellow-colored foliage, look at the names, including the Latin-based cultivar names. 'Aureum', 'Aurea', 'Aureola', 'Aureus', 'Aureovargiegata', 'Aureo-reticulata', and 'Aureomarginatus' all indicate tints or shades of yellow.

Red, Burgundy, and Bronze Foliage

The range of reds, burgundies, and red-bronze tones adds a unique and exciting drama to any yard. This range of color is greatly under-utilized in America. These plants

Black locust (*Robinia pseudoacacia* 'Frisia').

A very hot yellow can be found on the Japanese false cypress (*Chamaecyparis pisifera* 'Filifera Aurea'), making it a noticeable element in any design.

Yellow and Chartreuse Foliage

Acer japonicum 'Aureum'
AUREUM HYBRID FULL-MOON MAPLE

USDA ZONES: (5) 6 to 9

SIZE: 10 ft. to 20 ft. tall; 10 ft. to 20 ft. wide

COMMENTS: An attractive form of the popular Japanese maple. The foliage has a lovely, vibrant yellow color unless summers are too hot. The leaves and branches layer out like wisps of fog. The fall foliage turns a richer golden yellow before cascading to the ground. Slow-growing tree that should be treated as a shrub. Prefers morning sun and light shade in midday and afternoon.

Ligustrum tschonoskii 'Vicaryi'
GOLDEN VICARY PRIVET

USDA ZONES: 5 to 10

SIZE: 10 ft. to 12 ft. tall; 10 ft. to 12 ft. wide

COMMENTS: A glorious hybrid with gold-yellow leaves all summer; cooler summers mean better coloration. Like all privets, it's very adaptable: tolerates pollution, salty soil, and other difficult soils. Can be clipped to less than 8 ft., even as low as 6 ft. Semievergreen. Wind-tolerant in some areas.

Philadelphus coronarius 'Aureus'
AUREUS YELLOW SWEET MOCK ORANGE

USDA ZONES: 4 to 8

SIZE: 8 ft. to 10 ft. tall; 8 ft. to 10 ft. wide

COMMENTS: Fragrant white flowers resembling citrus bloom from May through June. The young leaves provide a pastel yellow highlight. If left to grow in the hot sun, leaves will turn green and even scorch. Best with partial shade all day or complete afternoon shade. Requires consistent moisture to thrive.

Robinia pseudoacaia 'Frisia'
FRISIA HYBRID BLACK LOCUST

USDA ZONES: 3 to 10

SIZE: 25 ft. to 30 ft. tall; 15 ft. to 20 ft. wide

COMMENTS: Perhaps one of the clearest, lightest yellow leaves in the spring. Never looks anemic. The summer foliage gets some overtones of pale green, but the yellow still predominates, looking richer. Turns clear, vibrant yellow in the fall as the leaves drop. A great specimen tree. Short-lived but well worth growing. Wood is brittle. Some thorns and poisonous seeds; the foliage and seeds can occasionally cause dermatitis. Deciduous.

Sambucus racemosa 'Plumosa Aureus'
PLUMOSA AUREA HYBRID EUROPEAN RED ELDER

USDA ZONES: 3 to 6 (7)

SIZE: 8 ft. to 12 ft. tall; 8 ft. to 12 ft. wide

COMMENTS: Provides a luminous yellow against dark green foliage or on an overcast day. White flowers in the spring and red berries in the fall. The leaf has a decorative, finely cut pattern. Needs cooler summers to look good. Tolerates quite a bit of moisture.

Thuja plicata 'Zebrina'
ZEBRINA HYBRID GIANT or WESTERN ARBORVITAE

USDA ZONES: 5 to 10

SIZE: 30 ft. tall; 10 ft. to 15 ft. wide

COMMENTS: This form of the majestic giant or western arborvitae is graced with a delicate golden hue on all new growth. Some cultivars of this evergreen, such as 'Stoneham Gold', are slow-growing dwarf forms with orange or yellow new growth. Deer-resistant in some areas.

offer moody and pleasing additions to any planting.

Red summer foliage is often more muted than the hotter reds of new growth on some plants—such as the shrub Indian hawthorn (*Rhapiolepis indica*)—and certainly more restrained than the brilliant reds of the fall foliage of certain plants—such as sugar maple (*Acer saccharum*) and ornamental pear (*Pyrus calleryana*). Pure purple is seldom found in foliage.

The trick to mixing the red-burgundy-bronze foliage palette in your yard is to use temperance and provide a dark green backdrop for the tone to float on. Too many plants with red foliage in one section of the yard can be overwhelming or gaudy. Instead, use them in the middle ground or in the further reaches of the yard. The softer colors look striking near a clear, light yellow or shown against a dark or neutral green. One tree with such a soft color is the Purpureus smoke tree (*Cotinus coggygria* 'Purpureus'), whose foliage has one of the most pleasant matte finishes to be found, displaying wafts of pale smoky burgundy plumes of flowerheads in midsummer.

The sugar maple (*Acer saccharum*) develops an unforgettable display of blazing yellows on the interior and hot, vibrant oranges on the outer edges of its canopy.

The 'Bradford' pear (*Pyrus calleryana* 'Bradford') is famous for its resplendent show of earthy, red fall color, especially in cold winter areas.

Various shades of red-colored foliage make striking accents in a landscape, whether placed in contrast with yellow foliage or dark green leaves.

Acer palmatum forma atropurpureum
JAPANESE MAPLE

USDA Zones: 5 to 9

Size: 15 ft. to 25 ft. tall; 15 ft. to 25 ft. wide

Comments: One of the best ornamental trees, especially in its distinctive red forms. All Japanese maples have layered, cloudlike branches. The many purple-red cultivars are uniquely attractive. Needs some irrigation. Plant on the east side of the house or in filtered shade in hot summer areas to prevent leaf burn. In saline soil, there is burn on leaf edges. Two cultivars that withstand heat are 'Bloodgood' and 'Moonfire'.

Berberis thunbergii forma atropurpurea 'Rose Glow'
ROSE GLOW HYBRID RED-LEAF JAPANESE BARBERRY

USDA Zones: 4 to 9

Size: 3 ft. to 6 ft. tall; 3 ft. to 6 ft. wide

Comments: Best of the reddish forms of this shrub. Leaves marbled pink and white. Red fall color. Its spiny branches make it a good barrier plant. Multi-trunked. Plant only in arid areas where it won't spread. Tolerates light shade. Invasive in the East and Midwest. Green forms are less invasive. Resists deer and tolerates clay soils in some areas.

Cercis canadensis 'Forest Pansy'
HYBRID EASTERN REDBUD

USDA Zones: 4 to 9

Size: 15 ft. to 20 ft. tall; 15 ft. to 20 ft. wide

Comments: This beautiful cultivar opens new foliage each spring with rich maroon, red, and light green traces along the veins of each leaf and a slight luster. In warm summer areas, the color shifts toward green as the temperature rises; a shady location helps retain some of the reddish foliage color. In the Midwest, needs afternoon shade for protection. Can suffer some dieback in severe winters. Drought-tolerant in some areas.

Cotinus coggygria 'Purpureus'
PURPUREUS PURPLE LEAF SMOKE TREE

USDA Zones: 4 to 10

Size: 10 ft. to 15 ft. tall; 10 ft. to 15 ft. wide

Comments: One of the most spectacular maroon- or red-leafed plants. The pinkish bloom color in May and June is produced by light, silky hairs—thus the smokelike appearance. The roundish leaves on the wide shrub turn various purple shades in the fall. Cultivars like 'Royal Purple', 'Nordine' (the hardiest form), and 'Velvet Cloak' have the deepest, ruddiest foliage. Needs excellent drainage to avoid root rot. Resists oak root fungus. Deer-resistant and tolerant of sandy soils in some areas.

Prunus cerasifera
MYROBALAN PLUM

USDA Zones: 5 to 10

Size: 15 ft. to 20 ft. tall; 15 ft. to 20 ft. wide

Comments: There are many cultivars of this normally green-leafed tree in a range of red to purple-black foliage, including 'Allred' (red), 'Atropurpurea' (early leaves are copper-red, then turn dark purple), 'Krauter Vesuvius' (purple-black), and 'Newport' (purplish red). Some have white or pinkish flowers each spring. May be short-lived. Watch for canker. Deciduous. Tolerates drought and clay soils in some areas.

Rosa glauca
REDLEAF ROSE

USDA Zones: 2 to 8

Size: 5 ft. to 7 ft. tall; 5 ft. to 7 ft. wide

Comments: This very special species rose has glaucous bluish-red leaves with a hint of purple. The newer leaves are more purple-red. The petals of the midsummer, diminutive flowers are pinkish. The rose hips are dark red. The stems offer a maroon highlight. Defoliates in the Northeast if left unsprayed for fungus. Tolerates sandy soils in some areas.

Other trees with red, burgundy, or bronze foliage include: *Fagus sylvatica* 'Atropunicea' ('Atropunicea' purple beech) (p. 105).

One of the rarest, richest colors of any tree or shrub foliage is the deep burgundy found on the smoke tree (*Cotinus coggygria*). This cultivar, 'Velvet Cloak', looks particularly attractive next to the variegated tartarian dogwood (*Cornus alba* 'Saltouch').

Natural vs. "Unnatural" Foliage Color

MANY GARDENERS ARE FASCINATED by or drawn to shrubbery and trees with distinctive or different-colored foliage. The strange, odd, or unusual color is often first found as a rare, naturally occurring genetic mutation. In some cases, thousands of seeds are planted to look for individual plants with new characteristics—this is called selection. The grower who uses the selection process does not intentionally pollinate (cross) two parent plants—which is true breeding—but relies on nature's tendency to produce genetic variability. Sometimes a chance seedling in someone's yard will sprout with a variegated or reddish foliage not normally found with that species of plant.

Once a distinctively new plant is identified, it must be propagated vegetatively (via cuttings, layering, or grafting—not via seeds) to maintain the desired trait(s). Then it is eventually given a cultivar name—as in *Lavandula angustifolia* 'Alba' for a white-flowering form of the woody shrub English lavender.

Variegated Foliage

Some plants have more than a single shade of green in their foliage. Variegated leaves are streaked, striped, spotted, splashed, or edged with a second color, even with a third color. The range of colors includes pure white veins against a dark green background, egg-shell white colors, creamy white, buttery yellow, clear translucent yellow, the palest of greens mixed with several other shades of green on the same leaf, and even pink and rose colorations.

The variegation also comes in many patterns: just along the veins of the leaf, as a margin to the leaf, green margins with splotches of various colors on the interior of the leaf, odd rambling blotches of several colors throughout the leaf, and a pattern that's very close to stripes.

In the world of plants, gardeners seem to either love or hate variegated foliage. To some, the plant seems "ill." To others, the variegation represents the potential to lighten a dark corner of the garden. Variegated plants offer the same benefits of silver-gray foliage without the extreme of too much white or gray tones.

Use variegated plants to lighten a dark corner, to add drama to a shady nook, or as a specimen tree or shrub for a focal point or accent in the landscape. Most variegated foliage was originally found as a natural genetic mutation, so is not common

Variegated Foliage Options

To add interest to your landscape, consider the following variegated trees and shrubs.

Latin Name	Common Name	Foliage Colors
Acer negundo 'Variegatum'	Variegatum variegated box elder	Cream variegation, often concentrated on the leaf's margin; occasional reversion of some limbs to all green leaves
Caryopteris × clandonensis 'Worcester Gold'	Blue-mist shrub, Worcester Gold blue spirea	Lime-gold foliage
Citrus spp.	Sungold lemon, variegated lemon	Vertical green and yellow stripes on the fruit and leaves with splotches of creamy white
Cornus alba 'Argenteo-marginata'	Argenteo-marginata variegated tartarian dogwood	Creamy-white leaf margin to a subtle-gray leaf
Cornus florida 'First Lady'	First Lady flowering dogwood	Yellow-green leaves
Daphne odora 'Marginata'	Variegated winter daphne	Creamy-yellow edging to medium-green leaves
Euonymus fortunei 'Emerald and Gold'	Emerald and Gold winter creeper	Brilliant, dazzling yellow center with a bright green edge to the leaves; some leaves pinkish in winter
Hydrangea macrophylla 'Variegata'	Variegated hydrangea	Dark-green leaves have a creamy white edge
Lavandula dentata 'Linda Ligon'	Variegated French lavender	Mottled light yellow against a tomentose gray-green leaf
Lonicera nitida 'Baggesen's Gold'	Variegated box honeysuckle	Small, brilliant yellow leaves
Pieris japonica 'Variegata' or 'Aureo-variegata'	Variegated lily-of-the-valley shrub	Attractive pink-tinged growth in spring followed by creamy white on a solid green background

Lemon (*Citrus limon* 'Variegata').

Lily-of-the-valley bush (*Pieris japonica* 'Variegata').

or "normal." Keep that trait in mind and use such foliage modestly.

There are countless variegated herbaceous perennial and ground covers to use with trees and shrubs. The creeping ones, such as the variegated form of periwinkle (*Vinca minor*), make a lovely "skirt" crawling out from under darker-colored shrubs and trees—but be careful this particular ground cover doesn't spread too far afield.

Fall Leaf Color

I live where nearly pure stands of 500-year-old redwood trees (*Sequoia sempervirens*) are interlaced with a mixed woodland forest of Douglas fir (*Pseudotsuga menziesii*) and coastal live oak (*Quercus agrifolia*). This is an extraordinary environment to live in, but is does not bring forth much fall color.

The brightest red and orange fall color in my coniferous and evergreen woodlands comes from the vining or shrubby poison oak (the one I spend countless hours trying to banish). I have seen this plant streaking bright red some 125 ft. up the trunk of a redwood tree, a glorious sight—if it's not on your property! I do get some golden color, though.

The native bigleaf maple (*Acer macrophyllum*) turns a dull, unimpressive yellow if the fall stays warm, but a translucent yellow when crispy frosts slip into the canyons and valleys early in the fall. The impression of a single shimmering yellow leaf against the dark green shade of a coastal live oak is much like a vibrant van Gogh painting floating alone in the middle of a large, darkened gallery.

Small shrubs belonging to the currant genus (*Ribes* spp.) produce

Fall Leaf Color

Amelanchier arborea
JUNEBERRY or DOWNY SERVICEBERRY

USDA Zones: 4 to 9

Size: 15 ft. to 25 ft. tall; 15 ft. to 40 ft. wide

Comments: Fall color ranges from a musty, dull red to a yellow or orange. One of the best trees for feeding both people and birds. Berries, which have a flavor similar to highbush blueberries, make great pies, jams, and preserves. Very adaptable in acidic soil as well as wet and dry areas. Unaggressive roots.

Ginkgo biloba
GINKGO or MAIDENHAIR TREE

USDA Zones: (4) 5 to 9 (10)

Size: 35 ft. to 70 ft. tall; 50 ft. to 60 ft. wide

Comments: Blazing yellow fall color. Plant only male trees (such as the 'Magyar') to avoid the smell of the fruit. Visit the nursery in fall so you can see the color when you select a tree. Disease- and pest-resistant. Tolerates pollution, so a good city tree. Good lawn and street tree. Tolerates wind, drought, clay, and sandy soils in some areas.

Other trees with good fall color include: *Acer japonicum* 'Aureum' (Aureum hybrid fullmoon maple) (p. 65), *Diospyrus virginiana* (common persimmon) (p. 92), *Robinia pseudoacaia* 'Frisia' (Frisia hybrid black locust) (p. 65), and *Sassafras albidum* (sassafras) (p. 42).

Liquidambar styraciflua
SWEET GUM or LIQUIDAMBAR

USDA Zones: 5 to 9

Size: 60 ft. to 80 ft. tall; 40 ft. to 55 ft. wide

Comments: Outstanding fall color in many parts of the country. Can thrive in moist soils, especially along creeks. May be chlorotic in alkaline soils. Tops can break in wind. The cultivar 'Moraine' provides brighter red fall color and darker green summer foliage, and is more cold hardy in cold-winter areas. Good cultivars for fall color in California are 'Burgundy' and 'Festival'. Resists deer, attracts birds, and tolerates drought, clay, and sandy soils in some areas.

Nyssa sylvatica
SOUR GUM or BLACK TUPELO

USDA Zones: 4 to 9

Size: 30 ft. to 50 ft. tall; 20 ft. to 30 ft. wide

Comments: A harbinger of fall in many areas because the leaves begin turning red in September. The tree's 3-in. to 6-in. leaves are ablaze in the scarlet-maroon range with some yellow and orange, so the foliage appears to glow in the dark. Often rated as one of the top three most spectacular fall-color trees, even in mild winter areas. Almost pest-free. Tolerates a range of soil, but prefers acidic soil.

Pistachia chinensis
CHINESE PISTACHE

USDA Zones: 7 to 10

Size: 35 ft. to 50 ft. tall; 35 ft. to 50 ft. wide

Comments: Stunning rich fall color, from clear orange to warm red to scarlet. Always select trees during fall color period so you see what you're getting. Tiny red berries in early winter on female trees. Young, irregular-shaped crown matures to a dense, well-shaped round crown. Makes a good shade tree near pavement and in a lawn. Tolerates some lawn irrigation, but watch for verticillium wilt. Needs well-drained soil. Resists deer, attracts birds, and tolerates wind and clay soils in some areas.

Vaccinium corymbosum
HIGHBUSH BLUEBERRY

USDA Zones: 3 to 7

Size: 6 ft. to 12 ft. tall; 8 ft. to 12 ft. wide

Comments: The berries are tasty and the small shrub makes an astounding, flaming red, bronze, yellow, or orange color each fall. Leaves are long and a deep green on a multistemmed shrub. Fruit ripens in July or August, sometimes September. Must have sun, cool summers, plenty of moisture, acid soils, fertility, and drainage.

other shades of yellow, as do thimble berries (*Rubus parviflorus*).

In western and northwestern yards, many gardeners import their fall color with exotic specimen trees not native to their locale but reasonably adapted to the climate. A classic tree for this purpose in the San Francisco Bay area is the ornamental pistache (*Pistachia chinensis*), with its blaze of hot reds, clear yellows, and vibrant oranges. It also makes good fall color in desert climates. (The pistache is increasingly being planted because it is tolerant of some drought,

The exotic, ornamental pistache (*Pistacia chinensis*) is adaptable to many conditions and flaunts a remarkable array of clear yellows, soft oranges, and fiery reds each fall.

Early frosts and cold winters bring out the most vibrant sun-yellow fall color on the native bigleaf maple (*Acer macrophyllum*). Warm falls produce a softer, duller yellow.

of lawn irrigation, and of alkaline soils; it doesn't heave pavement; and it's resistant to oak root fungus.)

In much of the country where hardwoods and some softwoods abound, nature provides a blaze of color. Depending on each year's weather conditions, fall color may include fiery reds, dazzling crimsons, royal and luminous yellows, pale lemons, soft saffrons, burnt umbers, earthy oranges, clear and translucent oranges, and ruddy browns. The only task of the gardener (or builder) is to not remove too many trees, and to carefully select the trees and shrubs to keep on the basis of health, position, and color.

Bark Color for Winter Interest

In those same climates blessed with a glory of fall color, the dilemma is the lack of attractive foliage to give the landscape color throughout the winter. A dynamic approach to this problem is to plant shrubs and trees with colorful bark.

Consider where you'll be viewing the bark from when you place these trees. In cold winter areas, you're more likely to look at the landscape from within your warm home than while walking through the yard. In such cases, trees with attractive, large trunks that are visible from quite a distance can be a real asset. A perfect example is an older American beech tree (*Fagus grandiflora*) with its smooth, silver-gray bark.

Some trees have bark that exhibits fascinating exfoliation: The bark peels off in irregular patches to reveal different colors beneath. A prominent example is the paperbark maple (*Acer*

Colorful barks and those that peel back to reveal dramatic patterns along the trunk are an excellent way to provide colorful highlights during cold winters. The drama pictured here is from the birch bark cherry (*Prunus serrula*).

During the calm deciduous depths of winter, the gardener can fall back on colorful stems for accents of color. This is a close-up of the bright purple-red stems of tartarian dogwood 'Kesselringii' (*Cornus alba* 'Kesselringii').

Winter Colors

The following list provides some examples of colorful winter bark and stems.

Latin Name	Common Name	Bark or Stem Characteristics
Acer griseum	Paperbark maple	Peeling bark in various shades of red-orange, reddish brown, and cinnamonlike colors; stained-glass window effect of sun shining through peeling bark
Betula papyrifera	Paper or canoe birch	Peeling bark quite shiny; has occasional horizontal black markings
Cornus alba 'Sibirica'	Sibirica tartarian dogwood	Stems a strong red color throughout the winter if cut back each spring
Cornus sericea (*C. stolonifera*)	Redosier dogwood	Twigs of species form are a striking, warm red, almost reddish purple; 'Flaviramea' produces 2-ft.- to 3-ft.-long yellow-green stems.
Fagus grandiflora	American beech	Appealing silver-gray, smooth trunk and limbs in the winter
Salix alba var. *vitellina* (*S. alba* 'Tristis')	Golden willow	Must be cut back dramatically every winter to force vibrant yellow-orange shoots in the spring; stems have winter color that's hard to beat—a stronger orange-yellow.

griseum). The multitude of various reddish to brown tones is intricate and captivating. Also, the morning or evening sunlight passing through the shedding bark can make it look like a stained glass window. Since this tree is rather small, all these wonderful effects are lost if the tree is too far from a window or the pathway to the front door.

The paperbark maple (*Acer griseum*) displays a patina of reds, bronzes, and earthy browns on its defoliating bark year-round. The sun even illuminates the shedding bark like stained glass windows.

CHAPTER FIVE

Beautiful Flowers

FLOWER COLOR AND DRAMA are often foremost in the mind of the gardener. The color of a bloom can be so transitory, but its impact seems greater than the long-lasting color of foliage. Perhaps that's because the flowers themselves are so beautiful. While the entire rainbow of colors are available for herbaceous perennials and annual flowers, the palette of colors is more limited for shrubs and trees. For example, choices abound for green-flowering bulbs, annual bedding plants, and perennials, but very few trees have green blossoms. The tulip tree (*Liriodendron tulipifera*) is one of those few.

For other colors, such as a wide range of yellows, many shrubs and trees provide as remarkable a blossom as any perennial or annual. An example is the lively, pale green-yellow of the many species of the

Green blossoms are rather rare on trees and shrubs. One excellent example is the delicate, cupped blossom of the tulip tree *(Liriodendron tulipifera)*.

The bright yellow blossoms of the many species of Palo Verde (*Cercidium* spp.) are striking against its green limbs and as colorful as any annual flower.

deciduous Palo Verde tree (*Cercidium* spp.). This attractive large shrub or small tree is an option in desert environments, where it is much tougher than perennial and annual plants of a similar color.

Many gardeners desire a pattern of bloom that runs continuously from early spring through the summer and even, in rare occasions, into winter—mostly in the southwestern climates.

There are some select shrubs that, during a forgiving winter, bloom very early—almost on the heels of winter's retreat. Others provide a consistent floral display from year to year because their flowers open more

toward midspring after the danger of late frosts and snow. Early spring brings lots of new color, especially in the East and Midwest. Although the palette thins out, summer and early fall still provide a flurry of color.

A good way to plan for an uninterrupted blossom sequence is to look for a phenological calendar, a fancy name for a simple chart that plots the sequence of bloom and colorful fruiting throughout the year. Ask your local cooperative extension office for one. Occasionally, an avid gardener self-publishes a regional guide to the sequence to bloom, so check with your local bookstore or library. Or, begin to keep a calendar for just your neighborhood—the most local and accurate way to plot nature's unfolding beauty.

Spring Color

Many gardeners, especially those in cold, snowy winter areas, want shrubs and trees that bloom early in the yard—harbingers of the full-blown spring yet to come. The common risk is that late frost, heavy snow, wind, and heavy rains can demolish the delicate blossoms of such plants in occasional years. Nonetheless, hope springs eternal and these early signals of spring are commonly planted. Shrubs often fill this role as an accent color.

As the sun moves higher in the sky, arcing with more loftiness, the days become longer and the quality of light usually unfolds with a more luminous radiance. Such light begins, at first, to cause the hotter tones of color to radiate with more brilliance and vibrancy. By midspring, nature is rolling along with all kinds of trees and shrubs popping out in resplendent color.

During all portions of the spring, trees play a predominant role in color display because of the sheer amount of blossom. The larger canopy of a tree virtually guarantees more flowers and greater drama than shrubs. While flowering shrubs placed near the home add much appreciated color each spring, to get the same impact for plants placed further from the windows or main pathways, you'll need to use trees. An early-blooming plum tree or, in the West, an almond tree with the palest of pink blossoms, makes an impressive display easily appreciated from afar.

Edible Flowers

 TREES AND SHRUBS CAN PROVIDE brilliant and colorful edible flowers to sprinkle on top of a salad. Even though such flowers do not offer much in the way of real nutrition, the color is a delight to the eye. Examples include the following trees and shrubs:

- Redbuds (*Cercis* spp.)

- Apples and crabapples (*Malus* spp.)

- Elderberry (*Sambucus canadensis*)

- Hawthorns (*Crataegus* spp., a relative of apple trees)

- Lavenders (*Lavandula* spp., mostly the common English lavender *L. angustifolia* and its cultivars)

- Lilac (*Syringa vulgaris*)

- Orange (*Citrus sinensis*)

- Plums (*Prunus* spp.)

- Roses (*Rosa* spp.)

- Rosemaries (*Rosmarinus* spp.)

- Yuccas (*Yucca* spp.)

Always sample a *small* portion of any new edible flower to determine if you might have a rare allergic reaction to the blossom.

Shrubs for Spring Flower Color

Aesculus pavia
RED BUCKEYE

USDA ZONES: 4 to 8

SIZE: 15 ft. to 20 ft. tall; 15 ft. to 20 ft. wide

COMMENTS: Deciduous native buckeye blooms in April and May with dramatic intense red flower clusters 3 in. to 6 in. long, and rich green foliage. Prefers some light shade such as a woodland edge. Tolerates moisture, and actually needs some to prevent leaf scorching in late summer. Prefers good drainage. Wind-tolerant in some areas.

Abeliophyllum distichum
WHITE FORSYTHIA

USDA ZONES: (5) 6 to 8

SIZE: 3 ft. to 5 ft. tall; 3 ft. to 4 ft. wide

COMMENTS: A distinctive deciduous plant with white flowers (sometimes tinged with pink) on deciduous stems. This floral display happens as early as the middle of March in some climates, before the traditional (or true) yellow-flowering forsythia. The early bloom is susceptible to late frosts. Not a well-shaped shrub, so best set in the middle or background of the yard. Tolerates full sun. Lots of dieback occurs in upper Midwest and buds freeze in subzero temperatures in the middle Midwest. Not grown in the South. Attracts birds in some areas.

Corylus americana
AMERICAN FILBERT or AMERICAN HAZELNUT

USDA ZONES: 4 to 9

SIZE: 8 ft. to 10 ft. tall; 15 ft. to 18 ft. wide

COMMENTS: Drops long, attractive, pale yellow catkins in March that are soon followed by smaller yellow-green flowers. Great fall color in upper Midwest. Very adaptable, tolerating sun or shade, acidic or alkaline soil, moist or dry soil. The shrub expands by shallow roots. Can be pruned to a single trunk. Deer- and drought-resistant in some areas.

Daphne odora
WINTER DAPHNE

USDA ZONES: 7 to 9

SIZE: 4 ft. to 6 ft. tall; 4 ft. to 6 ft. wide

COMMENTS: The small flowers clustered together at the ends of this evergreen's branches are pink to reddish with pale pink throats. The flowers are best seen up close—plant near a path or door—but you can smell the fragrance from many yards away on a calm day. One of the earliest fragrances of the calendar year, blooming as early as January in warmer zones. Glossy, medium green leaves. Tolerates shade. Requires good drainage in a neutral soil. Easily gets root rot diseases.

Dirca palustris
LEATHERWOOD

USDA ZONES: 4 to 9

SIZE: 3 ft. to 6 ft. tall; 3 ft. to 6 ft. wide

COMMENTS: From early March through early April, small pale or bright yellow flowers open on deciduous stems. Good, bright yellow fall color. A special native plant for deep shade in a woodland garden; doesn't like direct sunlight in the summer. Tolerates very moist, high-humus, and acidic soils. May be difficult to find, but worth the search. Transplant in spring. Slow growing. Twigs are so supple they can be tied into knots without breaking. Resists deer, attracts birds, and tolerates sandy soils in some areas.

Erica carnea
SPRING HEATH

USDA ZONES: 5 to 7

SIZE: 6 in. to 12 in. tall; 6 in. to 18 in. wide

COMMENTS: This evergreen woody shrub is usually treated as a ground cover. It can't be beat for a wide range of early spring colors, from white to the hottest pink or fuchsia. Sometimes starts blooming in January, but certainly by March. Can be hurt by high heat and humidity. Deer-resistant in some areas. Many good cultivars to choose from: 'Ruby Glow' has one of the deepest red colors.

Garrya elliptica 'James Roof'
JAMES ROOF SILK-TASSEL

USDA ZONES: 8 to 10

SIZE: 10 ft. to 12 ft. tall; 10 ft. to 15 ft. wide

COMMENTS: It is the remarkable 6-in.- to 8-in.-long pale yellow to greenish yellow catkins' flower tassels that provide a resplendent display from December through February. The ever-green male shrub produces thousands of dangling catkins, almost like a cascade of tinsel. The catkins are offset against the dark green leaves, which have a gray, tomentose underside.

Hamamelis × *intermedia*
WITCH HAZEL

USDA ZONES: 5 to 8

SIZE: 10 ft. to 20 ft. tall; 10 ft. to 20 ft. wide

COMMENTS: This cross has more attributes than the native species of the plant. Bright yellow flowers can appear as early as January and are often the first shrub color in late winter or early spring. Many selections have a delightful fragrance. Fall leaf color is usually an attractive yellow to deep red tone. Tolerates moist and acidic soils. The cultivar 'Jelena' has a rich orange blossom. 'Arnold Promise' is one of the best yellow selections, blooming in February or March. 'Diane' has an rich red flower but little fragrance.

Lindera benzoin
SPICEBUSH

USDA ZONES: 4 to 9

SIZE: 6 ft. to 12 ft. tall; 6 ft. to 12 ft. wide

COMMENTS: Even in the North, this multitrunked deciduous shrub bursts forth with small, yellow flowers tinted with pale green. Also produces a lovely yellow fall color. This underutilized shrub prefers moisture, acidic soil, and some shade or full sun, but will take much more shade than many shrubs. Will naturalize.

Lonicera fragrantissima
WINTER HONEYSUCKLE

USDA ZONES: 4 to 8 (9)

SIZE: 10 ft. to 15 ft. tall; 10 ft. to 15 ft. wide

COMMENTS: Small, creamy white blossoms open along the long, arching deciduous shoots of this woody shrub. Provides a glorious perfume in March before the arching stems leaf out. Not a neat shrub, so give it plenty of room in the back section of the yard. Tough and somewhat aggressive. Tolerates alkaline soil, sun, and shade.

Other shrubs for spring flower color include: *Camellia japonica* (common camellia) (p. 61), *Chaenomeles speciosa* (common flowering quince) (p. 37), *Kerria japonica* 'Pleniflora' (Pleniflora Japanese kerria) (p. 37), and *Rhododendron* spp. (rhododendrons, azaleas) (p. 114).

Spiraea × *vanhouttei*
VANHOUTTE SPIREA

USDA ZONES: 3 to 7

SIZE: 6 ft. to 12 ft. tall; 6 ft. to 12 ft. wide

COMMENTS: Most popular spirea in America, with its profusion of pure white flowers floating above dark green leaves. The shrub is quite durable with a fountain of slender, arching branches. This large-diameter, multitrunk shrub can be used as a barrier plant or hedge. It does not spread. Resists deer and tolerates clay and sandy soils in some areas.

Syringa vulgaris
COMMON LILAC

USDA ZONES: 3 to 6 (7)

SIZE: 12 ft. to 20 ft. tall; 20 ft. to 35 ft. wide

COMMENTS: Famous sweetly scented flowers cover this shrub. More than 2,000 cultivars are available in a spectrum from white to mauve-pink to blue to violet-blue. Check with your local authorities for the cultivars best suited to your climate. Not suited to warm winter areas, although some cultivars have been selected for California. Prone to mildew in summer, leaf miner, lilac stem borer, and oyster shell scale. Attracts birds and tolerates sandy soil in some areas. *Syringa patula* 'Miss Kim' and *Syringa meyeri* are more compact and resistant to mildew.

Ornamental peach (*Prunus* spp.).

Chinese witch hazel (*Hamamelis mollis*).

Star magnolia (*Magnolia stellata* 'Royal Star').

Winter daphne (*Daphne odora*).

Enjoying Earlier Spring Color

ALTHOUGH SOME TREES AND SHRUBS BLOOM OUTDOORS as early as the spring bulbs, you can have their flowers even while the snow is still on the ground by forcing the blooms indoors. Yellow, pink, rose, and red flowers are most desirable for early spring color in a vase. The hot and clear yellow of the border forsythia shrub (*Forsythia* × *intermedia*) is a classic example. A simple spray of a handful of its gracefully arching stems will open in the warmth of the home—weeks ahead of the plant outdoors.

All members of the stone fruit family (*Prunus* spp.) are candidates for forcing. That includes white-flowering stone fruits, like some cherry trees, all edible plums and prunes, most apricots, and many "wild cherries" (whose small amounts of flesh are usually left for the birds). Peach, nectarine, almond, and some apricot and cherry trees offer a wide range of soft to warm pinks.

The *Malus* genus includes culinary apples with mostly pure white blooms. A notable exception is the apple cultivar 'Pink Pearl', with its delightful pale rose flowers (see p. 84). Ornamental crabapples supply more choices of pale pink to hot rose and nearly red bloom. All edible members of the pear family (*Pyrus* spp.) have white blossoms, although some of the Asian pear trees tend to open their buds a bit earlier than many of the European varieties.

The following short list offers a few examples of woody plants for forcing. Try cutting the end of the stems at a slight angle, and add several 2-in.-long slits along the bottom portion of the stem to help absorb moisture. Add 1 tablespoon of flower preservative to each gallon of water. Then be sure to change the water two to three times a week. Forcing seems to be becoming a lost art, so seek out some of the older gardeners in your town for details about plant choices and the best times to force blooms in your neighborhood.

Genus	Common Name	Weeks to Force
Chaenomeles	Quince, ornamental	4
Cornus	Dogwood	2
Forsythia	Forsythia	1-3
Magnolia	Magnolia	3-5
Malus	Crabapple, apple	2-5
Prunus	Plum, cherry, apricot, peach	2-5
Salix caprea	Pussy willow	1-3

Trees for Spring Flower Color

Amelanchier laevis
ALLEGHENY SERVICEBERRY

USDA Zones: 4 to 8

Size: 15 ft. to 30 ft. tall; 15 ft. to 30 ft. wide

Comments: In spring, white blossoms open on deciduous stems, followed by slightly bronze-red young leaves. The foliage turns dark green in summer. Edible red fruits and orange to red leaf color in the fall. A reliable performer in the colder Northern zones. Tolerates sandy soils in some areas. The selections A. × grandiflora 'Autumn Brilliance' and 'Princess Diana' both have a rich red fall color.

Cercis canadensis
EASTERN REDBUD

USDA Zones: 5 to 10

Size: 35 ft. to 50 ft. tall; 35 ft. to 50 ft. wide

Comments: Appealing hot pink spring bloom and excellent yellow to orange-red fall color. Flowers edible. Good choice for streets, patios, and lawns. Cankers and verticillium can shorten life in the Southwest and Southeast. May naturalize. Deciduous. Tolerates clay and sandy soils in some areas.

Cladrastis kentukea (C. lutea)
AMERICAN YELLOWWOOD

USDA Zones: 4 to 8

Size: 30 ft. to 50 ft. tall; 40 ft. to 55 ft. wide

Comments: A spectacular fountain of cascading white, fragrant flowers. The white flowers resemble short, fat clusters of a wisteria blossom cluster, but they're white against the pale, pea green young spring foliage of the tree. Prefers alkaline soils but can grow in acidic soils. Deciduous. Resists deer and tolerates sandy soils in some areas.

Crataegus viridis 'Winter King'
WINTER KING GREEN HAWTHORN

USDA Zones: 4 to 7

Size: 20 ft. to 30 ft. tall; 20 ft. to 30 ft. wide

Comments: The species produces a bounty of pure white flowers. This cultivar has dark green foliage in the summer and prolific red fruits set against a backdrop of gray stems in the winter. Be aware that a spray program may be needed to prevent defoliation from leaf spot. Fire blight and rust diseases may be severe in some years. Hardy, reliable tree for northern areas. Very popular in the East and Midwest.

Other trees for spring flower color include: *Aesculus parviflora* (bottlebrush buckeye) (p. 96), *Crataegus crusgalli* (cockspur hawthorn) (p. 92), *Magnolia × soulangiana* (saucer magnolia) (p. 61), and *Malus × moerlandsii* 'Profusion' (Profusion hybrid crabapple) (p. 32).

Davidia involucrata
DOVE TREE

USDA Zones: 6 to 7

Size: 20 ft. to 40 ft. tall; 20 ft. to 35 ft. wide

Comments: Gives the appearance of doves or white handkerchiefs floating above the stems. These are the large (2-in.- to 6-in.-long) bracts of the flower head. The true flowers have small red anthers and bloom in May (along with the dramatic bracts); the foliage is bright green. Golf-ball-sized fruits hang well into the winter on deciduous limbs. Hard to find and slow to come into flowering, but worth the effort. Leaves smell peculiar, so plant away from the house. The D. involucrata var. vilmoriniana is hardier and more common in nurseries in some areas.

Jacaranda mimosifolia
JACARANDA

USDA Zones: 10 to 11

Size: 35 ft. to 50 ft. tall; 35 ft. to 50 ft. wide

Comments: Spectacular lavender-blue blossoms from April through September. In warmest winter areas can be semievergreen. Needs protection from late Indian summer heat. Tender below 25°F. Has brittle wood. Best in urban areas where fire danger is low. Drought-tolerant in some areas. A white cultivar is 'Alba'.

Laburnum × *watereri* 'Vossii'
HYBRID GOLDENCHAIN

USDA ZONES: 6 to 7 (8)

SIZE: 30 ft. tall; 30 ft. wide

COMMENTS: Dramatic, spectacular yellow flower clusters hang like wisteria blossoms 18 in. to 24 in. long. Not long-lived, particularly in the Midwest. Best in cooler climates like that of England. May need staking. Member of the legume family. Alkaline soils lead to chlorosis. 'Vossii' is denser than the species form and makes just a few seedpods, which are poisonous.

Malus spp.
FLOWERING or ORNAMENTAL CRABAPPLE

USDA ZONES: 4 to 9

SIZE: Varies considerably

COMMENTS: Flower color stretches from snowy white through many shades of pink, to wild tones of rose and red. Small fruits make a nice winter display in deep red, yellow, or golden colors. There are over 800 named varieties of different species of the flowering crabapple. This is a versatile and common ornamental tree for the northern states and the Midwest. Watch for fire blight and mildews. Ask your nursery for resistant varieties for your local climate. Deciduous. Tolerates drought and sandy soils in some areas.

Prunus persica
ORNAMENTAL FLOWERING PEACH

USDA ZONES: 6 to 10

SIZE: 8 ft. to 15 ft. tall; 8 ft. to 15 ft. wide

COMMENTS: The flowering peach is a lovely show in the spring, but it can be troubled by many diseases and pests. The tree may not live longer than 5 to 10 years. Watch for gummosis, peach leaf curl, and borers. Tolerates drought and sandy soils in some areas. Many cultivars have hot-pink flowers, both single and double petaled. Look for 'Klara Meyer', 'Prince Charming', 'Pink Star', and, for Southern California, 'Daily News Four Star' and 'Saturn' (which also makes delicious fruit).

Prunus serrulata (hybrids)
JAPANESE FLOWERING CHERRY

USDA ZONES: 5 to 8

SIZE: 15 ft. to 25 ft. tall; 15 ft. to 25 ft. wide

COMMENTS: White to rich pink blossoms in early to midspring. Summer foliage is glossy dark green, but fall color can be a muted reddish. Some cultivars are seedless. Cultivars are much healthier than the species type. Watch for canker and fire blight. Tolerates sandy soils in some areas. Some hybrids are 'Beni Hoshi' (or 'Pink Star'), 'Shirotae' (or 'Mt. Fuji'), and 'Shogetsu'.

Pyrus calleryana 'Aristocrat'
ARISTOCRAT CALLERY PEAR

USDA ZONES: 5 to 10

SIZE: 40 ft. tall; 20 ft. to 25 ft. wide

COMMENTS: Covered with pure white blossoms in early spring (as early as February in warm winter climates). Late frosts can destroy the flowers. Glossy, dark green foliage; fall color is usually a vibrant, warm orange. Watch out for fire blight, especially in South. Tolerates clay and sandy soils in some areas. In the upper Midwest, also look for 'Autumn Blaze' and 'Chanticleer'.

Robinia ambigua 'Idahoensis'
IDAHOENSIS HYBRID BLACK LOCUST

USDA ZONES: 3 to 10

SIZE: 40 ft. to 50 ft. tall; 20 ft. to 25 ft. wide

COMMENTS: A delightful mauve, pinkish purple blossom similar to that of a typical black locust, but most like the fat blossom on a wisteria. Blooms a little after the true black locust, in April or May. New growth will be tinted bronze red and turn to a clear, warm green. Not as well known as typical black locust, but well worth seeking out. Sterile seed and no spines. Suckers severely from roots. Not grown in the South. Deciduous.

Common lilac (*Syringa vulgaris*).

Jacaranda (*Jacaranda* spp.).

The unique apple blossom of the heirloom cultivar 'Pink Pearl' is pale pink, unlike the pure white of the typical apple flower.

Callery pear (*Pyrus calleryana*).

Summer Bloom

As the sun moves ever so gradually toward its midsummer equinox, when it reaches its highest arc in the sky, its light becomes more dazzling and harsh—especially in the West and Southwest. The hotter-toned flowers tend to look more washed out in midsummer sunshine, whereas the pastels look better. The softer tones mediate the harsher light of summer and cool the entire garden visually, almost physically, making it more pleasant. Adding more white blossoms to your garden has a similar effect. This neutral color rests the eye and cools adjacent hotter or warmer colors. Don't rely on a solely white flower scheme, though, because you'll lose the excitement of accents, focal points, and splashes of captivating color.

Many of the popular shade trees have finished flowering with the passage of spring and now provide a cooler atmosphere with their protective foliage. This is the time gardeners look to the lower levels of the garden—the annuals, perennials, and flowering shrubs—for color. Trees and shrubs are far less likely to blossom in late summer and early fall. This season is the most difficult for finding woody plants to fulfill the need for garden color. However, see Shrubs for Summer and Fall Flower Color (pp. 86-87) for some good selections.

Strawberry tree (*Arbutus unedo*).

Franklinia (*Franklinia alatamaha*).

Calluna vulgaris
HEATHER

USDA ZONES: 4 to 6

SIZE: 4 in. to 3 ft. tall; 2 ft. to 4 ft. wide

COMMENTS: An amazing range of flower choices, from white to delicate pink to mauve-pink to rosy colors to even purple. The evergreen foliage ranges from silver-gray to dark green, even reddish and chartreuse. Blooms mid to late summer. Prune flower heads immediately after blooming. Must have well-drained soil with a high content of organic matter and consistent irrigation. Summer hardiness is questionable in hot, humid summer areas. Dislikes alkaline soil.

Disanthus cercidifolius
DISANTHUS

USDA ZONES: 4 to 7

SIZE: 6 ft. to 15 ft. tall; 6 ft. to 15 ft. wide

COMMENTS: Not well known yet, but worth looking for. Excellent wine-red fall color and interesting dark purple flowers that bloom in October. Plant near the house or a frequently used path, as the small flowers are best observed up close. The deciduous leaves are shaped much like the heart-shaped redbud foliage. Prefers sun and well-drained, acidic soils with a high content of organic matter. Attracts birds in most areas.

Franklinia alatamaha
FRANKLINIA

USDA ZONES: 5 to 8

SIZE: 10 ft. to 20 ft. tall; 6 ft. to 15 ft. wide

COMMENTS: Beautiful 3-in.-wide white flowers with a fuzzy orange center. Single petals are arranged in a circular pattern of five, not double sets of five petals as seen in some "double" blossoms. They are fragrant and open in July and last into August. Must have good drainage even though it requires moist acidic soil. Provide afternoon shade for sun protection. Can get cold damage in the Midwest.

Genista tinctoria
DYER'S GREENWOOD

USDA ZONES: (4) 5 to 7

SIZE: 2 ft. to 3 ft. tall; 2 ft. to 3 ft. wide

COMMENTS: Ablaze in clear yellow in June. Each flower is only ½ in. to ¾ in. wide, but together they fill a vertical flower stem up to 3 in. tall. This evergreen is loaded with blooms early and continues to sporadically bloom, if left unpruned, throughout the summer. Won't spread by seed as the taller bright yellow-flowering scotch broom (*Cytisus soparius*) does. Will spread some in urban settings in the Pacific Northwest. Drought-resistant in some areas.

Hydrangea macrophylla
BIGLEAF HYDRANGEA

USDA ZONES: 6 to 10

SIZE: 3 ft. to 10 ft. tall; 6 ft. to 10 ft. wide

COMMENTS: Classic favorite plant for foundation plantings. Blooms last for weeks and transform through myriad color shifts. Flowers on old wood, so prune just after blooming. An acidic soil makes the flowers blue; alkalinity creates pink blooms. Tolerates salt and partial shade, but needs rich, well-drained soil. Hundreds of cultivars. 'All Summer' is a good cultivar that blooms blue in acid soils and pink in a nearly neutral pH.

Hydrangea paniculata 'Tardiva'
TARDIVA HYBRID
PEEGEE HYDRANGEA

USDA ZONES: 3 to 8

SIZE: 15 ft. to 25 ft. tall; 10 ft. to 20 ft. wide

COMMENTS: While the structure of the canopy is rather coarse, this tall deciduous shrub produces an abundance of pure white pyramidal blooms in September when little else is in flower. More common in northern states, but still underutilized. Look for cultivars 'Unique', 'Pink Diamond', and 'Kyushu'.

Other shrubs for summer and fall flower color include: *Buddleia davidii* (butterfly bush) (p. 96), *Lavandula* spp. (lavenders) (p. 96), *Perovskia atriplicifolia* (Russian sage) (p. 62), *Rosa* spp. (countless rose varieties) (pp. 67), and *Teucrium fruticans* (bush germander) (p. 62).

Hypericum prolificum
SHRUBBY ST.-JOHN'S-WORT

USDA ZONES: 3 to 9

SIZE: 1 ft. to 4 ft. tall; 1 ft. to 4 ft. wide

COMMENTS: Intense yellow blossoms from June through August. In the center of each flower is a noticeable stamen ball-like cluster up to 1 in. wide. Requires good drainage and full sun. Other species to consider are *H. × moserianum* (1 ft. to 2 ft. high and wide, Zones 7 to 9) and *H. × 'Rowallane'* (5 ft. tall and wide, Zones 7 to 9). (Note: *None* of these species are the herbs claimed to be useful for treatment of depression.) Resists deer and tolerates drought and clay soils in some areas.

Magnolia grandiflora 'St. Mary'
ST. MARY SOUTHERN MAGNOLIA

USDA ZONES: 7 to 10

SIZE: 15 ft. to 20 ft. tall; 15 ft. to 20 ft. wide

COMMENTS: Heavy bloom of pure white flowers up to 8 in. to 10 in. across with a wonderful fragrance. Blooms randomly over the canopy from midsummer to early fall. The evergreen leaves are ornamental—dark green and very glossy. Deer-resistant and drought-tolerant in some areas. 'Little Gem' and 'Victoria' are both narrower than 'St. Mary'.

Osmanthus fragrans
SWEET OSMANTHUS or SWEET OLIVE

USDA ZONES: (8) 9 to 10

SIZE: 10 ft. to 20 ft. tall; 10 ft. to 20 ft. wide

COMMENTS: Has powerful apricotlike fragrance. Blooms from early to late summer, although it may bloom sporadically all year in mild winter climates. Traditional glossy, medium green, evergreen foliage. Young plants prefer shade. In the West, highly susceptible to oak root fungus if irrigated near the trunk. Deer-resistant and drought-tolerant in some areas.

Potentilla fruticosa
SHRUBBY CINQUEFOIL

USDA ZONES: 2 to 7

SIZE: 1 ft. to 4 ft. tall; 1 ft. to 4 ft. wide

COMMENTS: These woody, deciduous shrubs are covered with bloom from June until they're killed by frost. Available in many sizes and colors, from golden or bright yellow to white to pastel pink, and occasionally reddish. Foliage ranges from darkish green to gray. Likes most soils except overly wet ones. Two worthy cultivars for the upper Midwest are 'Primrose Beauty' and 'Pink Beauty'. Deer-resistant and wind-tolerant in some areas.

Rosa rugosa
RUGOSA or SALTSPRAY ROSE

USDA ZONES: 2 to 9

SIZE: 4 ft. to 6 ft. tall; 4 ft. to 6 ft. wide

COMMENTS: An attractive deciduous plant with a long summer blooming period from June through October in some climates. Fragrant blossoms come in many shades depending on the cultivar—from pure white to various pinks—and with single and double petals. Hardy, disease-resistant, and reliable, but give it room to roam. Hybrids of the species, such as 'Sarah von Fleet', are tall, vase-shaped, and do not spread. Drought-tolerant in some areas.

Vitex agnus-castus
CHASTETREE

USDA ZONES: (6) 7 to 10

SIZE: 6 ft. to 20 ft. tall; 6 ft. to 25 ft. wide

COMMENTS: In midsummer this deciduous tree usually has dramatic lilac-blue, purple, white, or pink flower heads from 6 in. to 18 in. long. The foliage is gray underneath and reasonably dark green on top. Thrives in full sun with regular watering and fertilization. In colder climates, prune all growth to the ground each fall. In warmer climates it can develop a treelike form, where new growth will flower each summer. At its best in Arizona. Tolerates drought and sandy soils in some areas.

Late-Summer and Fall Blossoms

Much of nature slows down before the respite of fall and winter, except in the West, Southwest, and Deep South, and it's only natural that flowering be minimal in late summer and early fall for woody ornamentals. Fortunately, there are some interesting exceptions, mostly in the warmer zones of the West and Southwest.

There are many cultivars of *Camellia sasanqua* that bloom in some climates from fall through midwinter.

		Late Bloomers	
Here are a few examples of trees with showy late-summer and fall bloom.			
Latin Name	Common Name	Bloom Time	Zones
Arbutus unedo	Strawberry tree	Small flowers from September through October; decorative and marginally edible fruits through the winter	7-10
Camellia japonica	Japanese camellia	Flowers from midwinter through early spring	7-9
C. sasanqua	Sun camellia	Colorful, large blossoms from September through December	7-9
Lagerstroemia indica	Crape myrtle	Flowers in August and September	7-10
Myrtus communis	True myrtle (shrub)	Flowers in August or later	9-10
Schinus molle	California pepper tree	Tiny yellow flowers from late winter until summer	9-10

CHAPTER SIX

Birds & Butterflies

For THOUSANDS OF YEARS, people were inspired to pursue the idea of flight—stimulated by the inspiration of soaring birds and the graceful fluttering of butterflies. We have learned much about aviation, but birds and butterflies continue to fascinate and enthrall us. Some gardens are designed to do nothing but attract these airborne friends. All types and sizes of plants can attract and provide shelter for these winged beauties. Trees and shrubs provide food, nesting places, and habitat for birds. Butterflies and moths gather nectar for sustenance, their caterpillars forage on leaves, and their chrysalises or cocoons are often hidden among the stems of trees and shrubs.

89

Attracting Birds

The first step in attracting birds to your yard is to restrain your cat. Either keep the cat indoors, fenced in, or on a short leash outdoors—and certainly have all female cats spayed. (Bells on their collars actually do little to protect birds, unless the bell weighs more than the cat!)

Now you can move on to selecting trees and shrubs to attract birds. Many people focus on feeding birds, but nature provides nuts, seeds, fruits, insects, worms, grubs, and all manner of edibles for bird life. As a very general rule, those birds with short, stubby, and triangular beaks, such as finches, grosbeaks, towhees, and sparrows, feed on fruits, nuts, and seeds. The shape of the

---

Those Sweet Hummingbirds

MANY WOODY PLANTS HAVE FLOWERS that attract hummingbirds, although they play a lesser role than perennials and annuals. Hummers are lured to long, trumpet-shaped flowers, whose nectar and pollen are too deep for bees. Here are some trees and shrubs, both with and without tubular flowers, that the hummers love:

- Arizona honeysuckle (*Lonicera arizonica*)

- Bottlebrush shrubs (*Callistemon* spp.)

- Chastetree (*Vitex agnus-castus*)

- Currants (*Ribes* spp.)

- Desert willow (*Chilopsis linearis*)

- Grevilleas (*Grevillea* spp.)

- Lilacs (*Syringa* spp.)

- Ocotillo (*Fouquieria splendens*)

- Rhododendrons and azaleas (*Rhododendron* spp.)

- Twinberry (*Lonicera involucrata*)

Members of the sage family, with their tubular flowers, are especially attractive to hummers. Some shrubby forms include blue sage (*Salvia clevandii*), gray or autumn sage (*S. greggii*), Mexican bush sage (*S. leucantha*), and purple or gray sage (*S. leucophylla*).

Hummers also visit all members of the apple family (apple, pear, hawthorns, roses, and other pome fruiting plans from the genera *Rosaceae*) even though they don't have the deep tubular flowers so commonly associated with the birds' long beaks.

The throat of legume blossoms is well suited to being pollinated by hummingbirds. Examples of shrub and tree members of the legume family are black locust (*Robinia pseudoacacia*); wisteria (*Wisteria* spp.), which can be trained as a free-standing tree; the scarlet wisteria tree (*Sesbania tripetii*); the goldenchain tree (*Laburnum* spp.); and honeylocust trees (*Gleditsia* spp.).

Besides nectar, hummingbirds also relish eating insects such as mosquitoes, flies, leaf hoppers, small weevils, aphids, beneficial wasps (yes, the good guys), spiders, gnats, and white flies. While the bugs aren't a large portion of the hummers' diet, these foods may represent up to 10 percent of their daily protein uptake. That means any form of spraying, whether chemical or organic, will decrease the food supply for the speeding, hovering beauties we call hummers.

Even as winter covers this hawthorn shrub (*Crataegus* spp.) with snow, the vivid red berries are available to help sustain birds.

beak gives them the power to crush nutmeats and small seeds. Birds with long beaks, such as a wide range of woodpeckers and nuthatches, often pursue insects and grubs in the cracks and crevices of trees. Birds with both short and long beaks eat ripe flesh from any number of fruits.

In addition, many birds sip nectar from flowers, but, except for hummingbirds, this is not a primary source of nourishment—it's more like a treat. There are exceptions to these guidelines, but a diversified garden planting can provide a plethora of food sources and habitat for birds.

In addition to eating parts of trees and shrubs, all birds eat insects, both those we consider beneficial and those we consider harmful. Many insects inhabit the living and dead portions of trees and shrubs. To maintain a healthy ecosystem for our winged friends, you should attempt to avoid using insecticidal sprays— whether organic or chemical. Restraint and very carefully targeted spraying helps protect the insect populations so important to many birds. In the greatest of ironies, not spraying certain caterpillars feeding on a favorite tree helps maintain both

birds that search out this food source *and* colorful and fluttering adult butterflies.

Some bird lovers question the ethics of feeding birds through the winter with purchased seed concoctions, suet blends, and countless inventive feeding stations. This interrupts the birds' natural migratory instinct and makes them dependent on you—seed or suet junkies getting their daily fix. If you offer supplementary food, do it year-round. You also need to provide a water source; a small heater can be purchased to keep a bird bath unfrozen in winter.

Trees and shrubs provide many tasty treats throughout much of the year, and, in the warmer winter areas of the West, fruit and seed are available virtually year-round. And most birds are highly adaptable to a variety of food sources. For instance, besides capturing unsuspecting worms as they wiggle upward after a spring rain, American robins eat from the following menu:

- *Wild cherries and plums all summer* (Prunus *spp.*)
- *Summer juniper berries* (Juniperus *spp.*)
- *The fall fruit of honeysuckle shrubs* (Lonicera *spp.*)
- *Midsummer crabapples* (Malus *spp.*)
- *Summer mulberries* (Morus *spp.*)

Alnus rugosa (A. serrulata)
SPECKLED ALDER

USDA ZONES: 2 to 5

SIZE: 20 ft. to 35 ft. tall; 20 ft. to 35 ft. wide

COMMENTS: A native tree that feeds many birds, including the American goldfinch, black-capped chickadee, mourning dove, and purple finch. It provides only habitat for the song sparrow and the yellow warbler. Needs moist soil, but will grow in loamy as well as gravely soil. Spreads fast, so give it plenty of room. *Alnus glutinus* (common alder) is a better performer in the South.

Crataegus crusgalli
COCKSPUR HAWTHORN

USDA ZONES: 4 to 7

SIZE: 20 ft. to 35 ft. tall; 20 ft. to 35 ft. wide

COMMENTS: A native understory tree with fruit through the winter. It feeds cedar waxwing, evening grosbeak, hermit thrush, northern bobwhite, northern flicker, and purple finch. Also provides cover to American robin, blue jay, brown thrasher, northern cardinal, and mockingbird. Grows in flood plains, near open meadows, and in open woodlands. Tolerates a range of acidic and alkaline soils, and a small range of moist to dry soil. Drought-resistant in some areas.

Diospyrus virginiana
COMMON PERSIMMON

USDA ZONES: 4 to 9

SIZE: 35 ft. to 60 ft. tall; 20 ft. to 35 ft. wide

COMMENTS: A common deciduous native tree in some areas. The small orange fruits in the fall and winter feed American robin, cedar waxwing, Steller's jay, and gray catbird. Great rich orange or red fall color. Tolerates drought and sandy soils in some areas.

Fraxinus pennsylvanica
GREEN ASH

USDA ZONES: 3 to 9

SIZE: 30 ft. to 40 ft. tall; 30 ft. to 40 ft. wide

COMMENTS: The wood duck, bobwhite, cardinal, evening grosbeak, pine grosbeak, and purple finch feed on the winged seeds. Offers many advantages: tolerates alkaline soils, hot and dry winds, a wide range of dry or moist soils, and clay soil in some areas. Patmore' is a 50-ft., upright form that may be hardier for northern gardens. 'Urbanite' is a good cultivar for the upper Midwest.

Other trees and shrubs to attract birds include: *Amelanchier arborea* (Juneberry, downy serviceberry) (p. 71), *Amelanchier laevis* (allegheny serviceberry) (p. 82), *Celtis occidentalis* (common hackberry) (p. 32), and *Prunus* spp. (wild cherries, wild plums) (p. 96).

Sorbus americana
AMERICAN MOUNTAIN ASH

USDA ZONES: 3 to 7 (8)

SIZE: 10 ft. to 30 ft. tall; 20 ft. to 25 ft. wide

COMMENTS: Cedar waxwings, gray catbirds, northern bobwhites, and orchard orioles feed on the bright orange or red berries well into winter. Not a particularly good habitat plant. Grows in moist, well-drained soils in full sun. Tolerates both alkaline and acidic soils. Tolerates clay soils in some areas. Not shapely, so use in the background. Not common in the nursery trade but available at local plant sales or from a specialty mail-order company.

Tsuga caroliniana
CAROLINA HEMLOCK

USDA ZONES: 5 to 7

SIZE: 40 ft. to 60 ft. tall; 15 ft. to 25 ft. wide

COMMENTS: This pyramidal evergreen conifer is best at providing cover and nesting sites for American robin, blue jay, mourning dove, and wood thrush. The nuts provide food for American goldfinch, black-capped chickadee, dark-eyed junco, and pine siskin. Prefers well-drained and acid sites. Tolerates sandy soils in some areas. *T. canadensis* serves a similar function in the landscape and is easier to find in nurseries in the Northeast.

There are many species of the shrubby honeysuckle that produce berries birds love to devour. This is the tatarian honeysuckle (*Lonicera tatarica*) that thrives in Zones 3 through 9.

- *Late-summer serviceberries (Amelanchier spp.)*
- *Late-summer bayberries (Myrica spp.)*
- *Late-summer hawthorn fruits (Crataegus spp.)*
- *Late-summer, early-fall dogwood fruits (Cornus spp.)*
- *Fall hackberries (Celtis spp.)*
- *The late-fall fruits of the sumac (Rhus spp.)*

When winter is too cold or snowy to provide a good supply of food, the birds head south, returning as a harbinger of spring.

To keep birds around your yard during the seasons when they are

The formal garden and lawn in the foreground soon give way to a wilder mixture in the background of this Pacific Northwest garden. The mixture of layered shrubs and trees provides needed habitat for birds as they flit in and out of the garden.

naturally in your neighborhood, you'll want to provide an attractive habitat. Many small birds need a thicket of foliage with many different levels, from low shrubs to taller trees. The foliage provides a place for birds to hide (from cats and other predators), find shade, roost, and nest.

A mixed woodland planting that gradually descends from trees to lower shrubbery to create several layers, together with an edge next to a meadow or lawn area, provides an excellent habitat for a variety of birds and other wildlife. This planting, which need not be ornamental, should be at least 8 ft. wide in all directions. A jungle of

vines, shrubs, and small trees may do the trick, but keep it dense, unpruned, and undisturbed. In larger yards, piles of uncomposted brush are helpful if they aren't visually intrusive. In the West, brush piles are great habitat for the threatened California bobwhite.

If you can allow a portion of your yard to remain (or become) wild, it will provide natural nesting sites. In dead trees, dead limbs, and stumps, woodpeckers hunt for grubs and insects and drill holes for nesting. (But make sure nothing will be harmed when a dead tree falls over.)

Don't delay pruning until late spring, as this is when some birds are

Trees That Provide Protection

Fortunately, many living trees provide protective cover for birds. The following are just a few of these trees and shrubs, and the birds they help shelter.

Latin Name	Common Name	Birds Protected
Acer rubrum	Red maple	American robin, prairie warbler, American goldfinch
Betula spp.	Birches	American woodcock, hairy and downy woodpeckers, black-capped chickadee, northern oriole
Cornus spp.	Dogwoods	Grouse, bobwhite, American woodcock, eastern kingbird, mockingbird, brown thrasher, American robin, wood thrush, cedar waxwing, cardinal
Ilex opaca	American holly	Bobwhite, mockingbird, brown thrasher, American robin, eastern bluebird, cardinal
Juniperus communis	Common juniper	Ruffed grouse, bobwhite, chipping sparrow
Malus spp.	Crabapple	Ruby-throated hummingbird, blue jay, mockingbird, gray catbird, eastern bluebird, orchard oriole, northern oriole
Tsuga canadensis	Eastern hemlock	Ruffed grouse, mourning dove, blue jay, brown thrasher, American robin, wood thrush, various warblers, northern junco, song sparrow

Leaving a few dead limbs or tree tops in the wildest portion of the yard encourages birds such as these pileated woodpeckers to grace your landscape.

looking for a place to nest. And when you prune, keep in mind that many birds prefer to make their nests where there is a 70-degree angle between a branch and limb (or between the limb and trunk), so leave branches of that description uncut.

Attracting Butterflies

I once visited a butterfly house where many beautiful, tropical butterflies fluttered about and rested on nearby plants. I noticed a staff person gently rubbing leaves throughout the greenhouse, so I asked what was going on. The answer was, "We have to rub off any eggs laid by the butterflies so the caterpillars don't hatch to eat holes in the plants' foliage. We buy 'fresh' adult butterflies from butterfly farms on a regular basis to keep the greenhouse stocked."

This illustrates the dilemma faced by a butterfly "gardener." The beauty of the butterflies comes with some destruction of the foliage in the garden. Still, although caterpillars can eat massive quantities of foliage, even they can be magical in their beauty and form. Many of the swallowtails and large moths such as the cecropia come from spectacularly beautiful and oddly shaped caterpillars.

The fragrant blossoms of the woody shrub English lavender (*Lavandula angustifolia*) help draw butterflies into any garden. Pictured here is the cultivar 'Munstead'.

Adult butterflies flit from flower to flower in search of nectar—the "fuel" they require to seek a mate and, in the case of females, to lay eggs. Some butterflies feed on only one family of plants, or even only one genus. For example, as its name indicates, the anise swallowtail feeds primarily on members of the anise, or fennel, genus, including blooming carrots. Other butterflies are adapted to the host plant of their caterpillar stage.

The western tiger swallowtail consumes the leaves of cottonwoods (*Populus* spp.), quaking aspen (*Populus tremuloides*), willows (*Salix* spp.), white alder (*Alnus rhombifolia*), red alder (*A. rubra*), western sycamore (*Platanus racemosa*), other native trees, and even many members of the fruiting *Malus* genus such as apple trees.

All butterflies prefer a sheltered place away from the wind where temperatures hover between 75°F and 90°F during the day. The margin where the shrubs and trees meet the open lawn or meadow is ideal. The trees and shrubbery also provide welcome coolness during heat waves.

Unlike birds, butterflies don't drink water directly from birdbaths or ponds. They gather in a muddy area around a source of water and drink a bit of moisture. From the

Shrubs and trees attract many colorful butterflies. Here, an eastern swallowtail is drawing nectar from the blossoms of this apple tree (*Malus* spp.).

The leaves of the quaking aspen (*Populus tremuloides*) can provide needed sustenance for the caterpillars of the western tiger swallowtail.

Attracting Butterflies

Aesculus parviflora
BOTTLEBRUSH BUCKEYE

USDA ZONES: 4 to 8

SIZE: 8 ft. to 12 ft. tall; 8 ft. to 15 ft. wide

COMMENTS: With its dramatic 12-in.-long white flowers, this is one of best plants for attracting butterflies in late spring. 'Roger's' has flowers 18 in. to 30 in. long. All flowers bloom in shade or sun. Bronze leaves in spring and dark green summer foliage. Nuts are poisonous. Needs well-drained soil.

Buddleia davidii
BUTTERFLY BUSH

USDA ZONES: 5 to 10

SIZE: 10 ft. to 15 ft. tall; 10 ft. to 15 ft. wide

COMMENTS: The species form has long, slender, arching branches tipped with 4-in.- to 10-in.-long, conical, fragrant flower heads in an array of colors, from pale pink to mauve to almost red. The introduction of many new cultivars offers a considerable choice of flower color, including dark purple, lavender, white, and yellow-orange. Compact forms—up to 5 ft. to 6 ft. tall—are more formal and easier to manage. Grows in all kinds of rocky soil. Deer-resistant in some areas.

Nectar sources: *Amelanchier laevisi* (allegheny serviceberry) (p. 82) and *Syringa vulgaris* (common lilac) (p. 79).

Caterpillar hosts: *Fraxinus americana* (white ash) (p. 34), *Lindera benzoin* (spicebush) (p. 79), and *Sassafras albidum* (sassafras) (p. 42).

Lavandula spp.
LAVENDERS

USDA ZONES: 5 to 11

SIZE: Varies from 6 in. to 4 ft. tall; 6 in. to 6 ft. wide

COMMENTS: All forms of lavender attract various butterflies, especially the small ones called skippers, which can reach the sweet nectar in the throat of this romantic blossom. Blossoms come in shades of blue, violet, mauve-blue, pink, and pure white, and foliage comes in a wide range of grayish to green. Prone to fungal foliage diseases where humidity is high. The cultivars 'Munstead' (dark blue) and 'Hidcote' (almost aster-violet) are much smaller.

Prunus spp.
WILD CHERRIES, WILD PLUMS

USDA ZONES: 2 to 9

SIZE: Varies by species

COMMENTS: Many caterpillars graze on the foliage, forming chrysalises from which they metamorphose into two-tailed and western tiger swallowtails, among others. Easy to grow, provided they have good drainage and aren't planted in heavy clay soils, although they can thrive in a clayey loam. Seeds sprout easily and can become a maintenance problem. Wind- and drought-tolerant in some areas.

Rhamnus californica
CALIFORNIA COFFEEBERRY

USDA ZONES: (7) 8 to 10

SIZE: 3 ft. to 15 ft. tall; 3 ft. to 15 ft. wide

COMMENTS: The caterpillars of the gorgeous pale swallowtail (which resembles the showy, bright yellow tiger swallowtail) love to munch on the foliage of this shrub. This very attractive shrub has dark green leaves with a hint of blue and berries that turn from red to black. It can be pruned to just about any shape. Wind-tolerant in some areas—even wind-resistant along the coast.

Salix discolor
PUSSY WILLOW

USDA ZONES: 3 to 10

SIZE: 10 ft. to 20 ft. tall; 10 ft. to 20 ft. wide

COMMENTS: Provides fodder for the viceroy caterpillar, whose wings mimic those of the monarch in color and pattern. The leaves are oval and bright green. This species is popular for forcing indoors in late winter because of its attractive, soft, and pearl gray catkins. All willows evolved on flood plains or along riparian habitats (near flowing water) and tolerate periodic flooding. Roots will find cracked water pipes and septic leaching fields. Tolerates clay soils in some areas.

mud, the males absorb nutrients that increase their concentration of pheromones, the chemicals they release to attract females. So a constant puddle of mud is essential to a thriving butterfly garden.

Most butterfly gardens focus on annual bedding plants, herbs, and herbaceous perennials. But there are many woody shrubs and trees that can also be used in the wilder areas of the garden where both birds and butterflies love to hang out. (Don't

One of the favorite foods of the caterpillars of the eastern swallow tail butterfly is red ash (*Fraxinus pennsylvanica*).

Woody Plants That Attract Butterflies

Here's a list of some of the woody plants that attract these gossamer delights to our gardens—either as adults or as caterpillars. See also Attracting Butterflies on the facing page.

Latin Name	Common Name	Zones
Alnus spp.	Alders	4-9
Amelanchier spp.	Serviceberries	4-9
Asimina spp.	Pawpaws	6-8
Betula spp.	Birches	4-8
Carpinus caroliniana	American hornbeam	3-9
Carya spp.	Hickories	5-8
Ceanothus spp.	Wild lilacs, tick brush	8-9
Cornus spp.	Dogwoods	2-9
Fraxinus spp.	Ashes	4-9
Lantana camara	Lantana	9-10
Liriodendron tulipifera	Tulip tree	4-9
Rosa spp.	Roses	4-9
Rosmarinus spp.	Rosemaries	7-10
Salvia officinalis	Culinary sage (woody herb)	6-9
Sassafras albidum	Sassafras	5-8
Vaccinium spp.	Blueberries	2-9

forget about the duality of nature— some birds love to eat butterflies!) Native plants are preferred by local butterflies as a leaf or nectar source.

In the West, try the family of plants often referred to as wild lilac, tick brush, buck brush, or deer brush (*Ceanothus* spp.). These plants support the California tortoise shell butterfly without massive destruction to the plant's foliage. In the East, the spicebush swallowtail feeds on sassafras (*Sassafras albidum*), camphor tree (*Cinnamomum camphora*), and spicebush (*Lindera benzoin*), while the eastern tiger swallowtail feeds on sassafras (*Sassafras albidum*), tulip tree (*Liriodendron tulipifera*), choke cherry (*Prunus virginiana*), white ash (*Fraxinus americana*), and red ash (*F. pennsylvanica*).

CHAPTER SEVEN

Special-Purpose Trees

THE URGE TO CLIMB TREES and build forts, houses, and lookouts seems to be personal. For some, the treehouse is a lofty refuge for privacy. Others like being closer to the clouds and enveloped within the cool, protective canopy of a tree on a hot summer day. Bird watchers find they can use a treehouse like an arboreal duck blind, to observe without being noticed. Maybe it's a primordial urge reaching back to a distant time and culture where treehouses were safe havens from hostile people below.

Treehouses have a long and enchanting history. Consider the

Some treehouses have more than one level, requiring safe steps for entry and sturdy, weather-proof construction.

behind by the carpenters to redeem for two pennies each to buy the paint for the walls and the composite shingles for the roof.

I had the "neatest" treehouse in the neighborhood. Other families had a carpenter come in and build a fort on four posts 8 ft. off the ground, but all those kids came over to play in my tree fort, with its mandatory trap door entry. A tornadolike wind blew out the top 60 ft. of the oak tree just above the treehouse, but the treehouse itself remained intact. It was used by neighborhood kids for more than a decade after I left home.

Treehouses are going through a revival. Baby-boomers who had kids

Jacobean Tree House in England, built in 1772. Restored and reinforced with additional support, it remains open to visitors by appointment to this day. You may look for a tree like the one holding the Jacobean Tree House to make your own memorable legacy, with or without a treehouse.

Treehouses

When I was young, my treehouse was a frequently used refuge and overnight campground for the guys—no girls allowed. It was about 20 ft. up an old oak, whose trunk was 3 ft. in diameter near the ground. My dad helped me build a sturdy floor with 2x4s and the old tongue-and-groove paneling pulled out when my Grandma Tevis's porch was remodeled. The walls were of conventional 2x4 stud construction and covered with plywood. All the wood other than the flooring was scavenged from the proliferation of houses being built in the ever-expanding suburbs. My friends and I collected daily the soda bottles left

The new generation of treehouses are built with solid construction techniques; they resemble real homes or arboreal retreats set within the trees.

This charming treehouse and play area provides many activities for children. At the same time, a nearby ornamental planting adds color and unites the treehouse with the rest of the landscape.

later in life are building these fun forts for their own children (girls are now allowed). But baby boomers who had their kids early and now have an empty nest also want treehouses. It serves as a private retreat in a tree, like the good ol' days.

New standards for treehouses

In the old days, any old decrepit tree that wasn't lying flat on the ground was a candidate for a ramshackle tree fort. Not now. Safety standards are much stricter. More thought is given to selecting one or more trees with firm, solid trunks and well-attached main limbs. Now, the structure itself is more likely to resemble conventional house construction in how it is built, sheathed, and roofed.

The new-generation treehouses are really just small houses in trees. As an example, walls may be fashioned with studs and may even have protective insulation. (Sometimes the studs are reduced from the standard 2x4s to 2x2s to reduce the weight of the treehouse.) The new-generation treehouses tend to be located 6 ft. to 30 ft. high in the trees. Many of the treehouses constructed by people like Peter Nelson, founder of the World Treehouse Association, have electricity, modem access, and kitchens. Some of these retreats cost up to $30,000. This is a far cry from my sturdy, but modest, retreat in St. Louis in 1965.

Locating the right tree

It takes too long to plant a tree and wait for it to be sturdy enough to support a treehouse, so begin by surveying the trees and the place in the yard where you or your child would like to have a treehouse. Involve your children from the beginning. Usually, locating the proper tree or cluster of trees is the first step. The shape of the fort or house will evolve from the specifics of the trunks and main limbs. You can build a treehouse around one, two, three, or even four trees. Have the kids tie colored ribbon to likely candidates as the selection process begins.

Once you've identified the possibilities according to location, you must consider safety. Not all trees are sturdy enough to support the weight of a treehouse. In general, hardwood trees usually have more strength than softwoods. An exception is the blue

Treehouse Inspiration

THE WORLD TREEHOUSE ASSOCIATION has had two national annual meetings at one of the country's best treehouse sites—the Out 'n' About Treesort near Takilma, Oregon. (You can actually rent one of four treehouses for an aerial vacation at this site.) The World Treehouse Association was formed in part by one of the current gurus of treehouse construction, Peter Nelson. You can get some inspiration from this group, or you can use a resource not available in my childhood—the Internet. (See Resources on pp. 180-181.)

Sturdy Trees

Here's a list of the most frequently recommended trees for a sturdy foundation for a treehouse.

Latin Name	Common Name
Acer spp.	Maple
Carya spp.	Hickory
Fagus grandiflora	American beech
Lithocarpus densiflorous	Tanbark oak
Malus spp.	Apple and pear
Picea spp.	Spruce
Pinus spp.	Pine
Pseudotsuga menziesii	Douglas fir
Quercus spp.	Oak (many species)
Ulmus spp.	Elm

Another tree that makes a worthy candidate for a treehouse is an older, sturdy Douglas fir (*Pseudotsuga menziesii*).

gum eucalyptus (*Eucalyptus globulus*), which is technically a hardwood but easily shatters. While the lower portion of a large blue gum eucalyptus may not fail, limbs are likely to split off during high winds, becoming potentially dangerous projectiles for the treehouse's roof or its occupants. Be sure to check with local arborists. Nowadays, the experts recommend that a treehouse for children be built

The American beech (*Fagus grandifolia*) is a sturdy tree for supporting a treehouse and often produces lower limbs attached to the trunk at an angle approaching 90 degrees.

within 6 ft. of the ground, to help prevent injury should someone fall. While the genus of a tree is important, it's also crucial to favor major limbs attached to the trunk near the ground. A full inspection of potential trees includes trying to deduce the anchorage afforded by the roots, the strength and health of the trunk, and how the limbs join the trunk. There are several parts of the tree to consider, and—since the tree can't be cut apart for inspection—it must be scrutinized from the outside.

Roots Locate shallow roots or buried parts of the trunk and unearth some for inspection. Look for disease where the trunk meets the ground. Peel back a small portion of the upper roots with a sharp knife; the tree should have pink, red, and bright green tissue just under the bark. Do not use trees that have had the soil over their roots compacted by frequent foot or car traffic, because their roots may have already been damaged.

Trunk Check the tree for a hollow core or rotten heartwood. Look for rotten tissue or discolored wood. Trees rotten to the core are often visibly hollow. If no hollow spots are visible, take a length of 2x4 and tap along the trunk. A distinctive change in the tone of the thud as you strike the tree is a bad sign. (Don't whale away so hard

that you do damage to bark and the active layers of transport underneath.)

Branch collar Zen Buddhists say attachments are not important, but they probably don't live in treehouses! A sturdy treehouse requires limbs and branches that are well attached. You can judge sturdiness by inspecting both the branch collar and the branch bark ridge.

The branch collar is the bulging, shoulderlike lump at the base of the limb, just where it connects to the trunk. Within the base of the branch is an area with special cells and chemicals that prevent the spread of any decay or pathogens into the interior of the woody plant. The phenomenon is called compartmentalization. When a branch begins to die naturally, the branch collar swells, becoming more conspicuous as it seals off the wound, and looking like a callus after pruning. Use the branch collar to locate the branch bark ridge—the key element in determining the sturdiness of a limb's attachment.

Branch bark ridge The branch bark ridge is the diagonal, dark or raised portion of bark opposite the branch collar on a tree that denotes where the branch's wood meets the trunk's wood. A healthy branch bark ridge usually puckers outward. Sometimes,

Tree Anatomy

The branch collar is indicated by the bulging or shoulderlike lump at the base of a limb. The branch bark ridge is the dark area, or raised portion of bark, which denotes where the branch's wood meets the trunk's wood. The best angle of attachment to support a treehouse is a 45- to 90-degree angle.

though, it is nearly as flat as the surrounding bark but has a darker discoloration and more texture.

But what you're looking for on the branch bark ridge is included, or invaginated, bark. Included bark indicates a narrow angle of attachment, which causes an inherent weakness of the internal tissue of the tree. To identify included bark, see if the branch bark ridge folds in on itself. Included bark often has a raised, folded pattern to both sides of the branch bark ridge, giving rise to the alternate term invaginated. This tissue growing back onto itself makes an internal fissure, or separation, where well-knitted tissue should be. The presence of included bark indicates a weak union for the branch or limb. Often a limb with included bark will eventually split off at the tree's trunk, or from another limb.

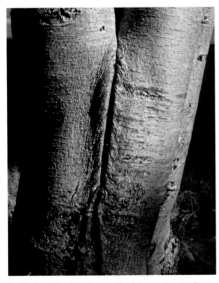

Included bark, also called invaginated bark, indicates an interior weakness of the wood. These two main trunks have included bark; one or both may split off from the tree—not a good choice for a treehouse.

The white oak (*Quercus alba*) is a splendid example of a tree to plant as a legacy. An older specimen has a wide, rounded canopy and immense, rugged limbs. It would make a sturdy tree for a treehouse.

Trees with 90-Degree Angles

Latin Name	Common Name
Abies balsamea	Balsam fir
Abies concolor	White fir
Carpinus caroliniana	American hornbeam
Cercis canadensis	Eastern redbud
Cornus florida	Flowering dogwood
Crataegus spp.	Hawthorns
Fagus grandiflora	American beech
Gleditsia triacanthos	Common honeylocust
Larix laricina	Tamarack or eastern larch
Nyssa sylvatica	Black tupelo
Pinus ponderosa	Ponderosa pine
Pinus resinosa	Red pine
Platanus occidentalis	American plane tree, sycamore
Prunus americana	American plum
Quercus alba	White oak
Q. macrocarpa	Bur oak
Q. stellata	Post oak
Taxodium distichum	Canada hemlock

Included bark also occurs when there are two competing vertical leaders (the most upright shoots in the middle of the tree). These leaders are called codominant shoots or branches. Many shade trees have codominant leaders. Technically, a codominant tree has, somewhere above the ground, two or more trunks of equal diameter and equal height.

Such trees can still make good places to build a treehouse if the main floor supports are attached or mounted to the sturdier of the two trunks, or lower on the tree where there is just a single strong trunk. If you remove one of the two competing leaders, the remaining shoot will grow into a single strong leader (vertical shoot) without included bark.

These points of attachment cannot be controlled by pruning because genetics is a far more powerful influence. If a tree or shrub typically grows with a narrow angle of attachment, then there's not much you can do to cause a wider angle. If the angle of a shoot or branch is so narrow that the branch bark ridge looks as though it has a fissure or is folded in on itself, then it's best to prune it off. You'll be left with only the stronger limbs for the support of the treehouse.

Natural branching patterns The natural branching pattern of a tree varies from genus to genus. Certain trees have limbs that customarily grow with wide, strong angles of attachment—these are the trees to seek out in your yard.

Branches attached at a 90-degree angle to the main trunk have the most potential for treehouses. The genetic angle of attachment is wide and "structurally" sturdy. Also, the wide angle of attachment makes it much easier to construct the platform for an arboreal abode or fort.

Trees with a 45-degree angle of attachment aren't ideal, but they're still useful for treehouses. These trees require extra inspection time to look for internal flaws. When in doubt, brace the fort from the ground with posts, or use wire bracing (cabling by

Trees as a Living Legacy

Carpinus caroliniana
AMERICAN HORNBEAM

USDA Zones: 3 to 9

Size: 20 ft. to 30 ft. tall; 20 ft. to 30 ft. wide

Comments: This tree has an upright round canopy with foliage that turns mottled yellow, reddish, or slightly red-purple in the fall. Well adapted as a lawn or small street tree. Prefers deep acidic soil with moisture but can tolerate some more hostile soils in the Midwest. The largest known specimen in the wild is 69 ft. tall and 56 ft. wide.

Fagus sylvatica 'Atropunicea'
ATROPUNICEA PURPLE BEECH, COPPER BEECH

USDA Zones: (4) 5 to 7

Size: 50 ft. to 60 ft. tall; 35 ft. to 65 ft. wide

Comments: Very rich bronze-red foliage. The cultivar 'Riversii' has large, shiny copper beech leaves. Does not like saline soil. Tolerates drought and sandy soils in some areas. Sometimes gets canker-causing fungi and beech coccus. A record-holding purple-leaved beech in Everett, Washington, is 97 ft. tall, with a 106-ft.-wide canopy.

Picea englemannii
ENGLEMAN SPRUCE

USDA Zones: 3 to 5

Size: 30 ft. to 40 ft. tall; 15 ft. to 20 ft. wide

Comments: Tolerates a wide range of soils. Drought-tolerant in some areas. May get aphids in the late winter, causing needles to drop. If it gets pine needle scale, a sooty mold may form on some of the needles. Also susceptible to spruce gall aphid. In the Rocky Mountains, can get tussock moth or spider mite infestations. The largest known specimen is 179 ft. tall, with 43-ft.-wide foliage.

Pinus sylvestris
SCOTCH PINE

USDA Zones: 2 to 6 (7)

Size: 30 ft. to 60 ft. tall; 30 ft. to 40 ft. wide

Comments: A young tree left to mature naturally develops a striking, wide-open, spreading branch structure with a mushroom-shaped, domed canopy. Wind- and drought-tolerant in some areas. The largest is 60 ft. tall by 62 ft. wide.

Other legacy trees include: *Carpinus betulus* (European hornbeam) (p. 114), *Carya illinoensis* (pecan) (p. 42), and *Ginkgo biloba* (ginkgo tree) (p. 71).

Quercus alba
WHITE OAK

USDA Zones: 3 to 8

Size: 50 ft. to 80 ft. tall; 50 ft. to 80 ft. wide

Comments: A mature tree is majestic, rounded, and mushroom-shaped. Hard to transplant but easy to grow from a seed planted in the fall. Prefers well-drained, deep soils that are acidic and moist. Tolerates drought, clay and sandy soils in some areas. Diseases include anthracnose, oak leaf blister, oak wilt, and root rots. Pests include caterpillars, scale, and skeletonizers specific to oaks. In spite of this, some trees are reputed to be 350 to 500 years old. A record tree reached 182 ft. tall.

Quercus suber
CORK OAK

USDA Zones: 7 to 10

Size: 50 ft. to 60 ft. tall; 30 ft. to 40 ft. wide

Comments: An oak with fascinating bark: Its deep fissures have hints of orange. The evergreen foliage is also attractive. Tolerates most soils except alkaline types or poorly drained clay. Deer-, wind-, and drought-resistant in some areas. The largest recorded is 85 ft. tall; its spread is 67 ft.

Trees with 45-Degree Angles

Trees with 45-degree angles of attachment still make good places for treehouses, but they require extra inspection for internal flaws.

Latin Name	Common Name
Acer rubrum	Red maple
A. saccharinum	Silver maple
A. saccharum	Sugar maple
Betula lenta	Sweet birch
B. lutea	Yellow birch
B. nigra	River birch
Carya cordiformis	Bitternut hickory
C. glabra	Pignut hickory
C. illinoensis	Pecan
C. ovata	Shagbark hickory
Juglans cinerea	Butternut (walnut)
J. nigra	Eastern black walnut
Liquidambar styraciflua	Sweet gum, liquidambar
Liriodendron tulipifera	Tulip tree
Quercus coccinea	Scarlet oak
Q. velutina	Black oak
Robinia pseudoacacia	Black locust

a certified arborist) above the treehouse for extra strength. If you're uncomfortable with depending on reinforcements, abandon such trees.

For safety, avoid narrow-angled, upright trees altogether. Their branches range from almost vertical to less than 45-degrees from vertical.

Trees for Future Generations

One of the most poetic legacies is a tree. It will grow into a glorious, wide, statuesque reminder for current and future loved ones. For centuries, trees have been figurative and literal examples of longevity, continuity, and a testament to nature's will to procreate and thrive. Your legacy can come in any size. The maximum size of some long-lived trees is often much smaller than you'd imagine.

One of the best places to learn about the most suitable trees for your area is a very old cemetery. (Modern cemeteries cut costs by not allowing anything but turf.) An examination of the trees there will teach you at least two important points. First, you'll see how they have been used as living monuments for people. Wide, spreading canopies; large, sturdy limbs; and massive trunks provide a welcome feeling of durability, reverence, and peacefulness. Second, you'll immediately know what trees are long-term survivors, those that thrive for decades, even hundreds of years. If you can't identify the tree, take a sample leaf to a local nursery.

Older public parks also serve as a good scouting place. Many parks from the late nineteenth and early twentieth centuries have wonderful specimen trees. Ask the grounds-keeping staff for the names of the most appealing trees. Or visit older arboretums and botanic gardens, which usually provide signs for the large, mature specimens, or a map of what's growing in their collection.

CHAPTER EIGHT

Problem Trees & Shrubs

GOOD PLANT SELECTION involves knowing what *not* to plant. This chapter covers trees and shrubs to avoid or to use with discretion. For example, a young woman I know bought a house with a large, 40-year-old redwood tree (*Sequoia sempervirens*), originally planted 4 ft. from the foundation. After living there a while, she noticed the tree's root system near the trunk was lifting and cracking the house's foundation. It cost many thousands of dollars to have a tree service remove the tree.

This is a danger that many trees pose if planted too close to pavement. Fortunately, it can be avoided by planting the tree or shrub in the back portion of the property, more than 40 ft. from the house. (This also helps to avoid the fire danger of the dry summers in the West.)

In a similar vein, some trees make a real mess when they drop ripened fruit on your flagstone walkway or terracotta tiled patio. By planting them in their own woodland setting, where the mess won't even make mowing difficult, you can avoid a myriad of maintenance problems. Knowing which trees are less messy lets you plan your landscape for streamlined efficiency and low maintenance.

With young kids in the family, poisonous trees and shrubs can pose a threat. Knowing which plants have poisonous parts is a priority. Use the list on p. 116 as a starting point when you plan your landscape.

Prickly, thorny trees and shrubs can also be a nuisance. The key is to use them to your advantage by locating them on the perimeter as barrier hedges. Or you may want to avoid them altogether.

Trees That Heave Pavement

The genetics of any tree or shrub influences how the roots will grow (see pp. 50-51). Some trees and shrubs have roots that grow near the surface and will likely heave pavement, while others have deeper roots that will be less likely to do so. However, genetics is not the only factor. It is often the predominance of an anaerobic condition in the upper layers of the soil that forces roots to the surface. For example, in sandy soil, roots will travel further and may not surface as readily.

Fortunately, you can choose trees that are less likely to cause problems. Trees genetically programmed to have deep roots are good candidates closer to pavement. Trees and shrubs that are recommended for lawns because they are less likely to surface also work well near pavement (refer to p. 53 for more suggestions).

Keeping trees and shrubs far away from paved areas, including favorite

---

Trees and Shrubs Not to Plant Near Paved Surfaces

These temperate climate trees are traditionally planted in front yards along the sidewalk or the road. However, to avoid heaving nearby pavement, don't choose them.

Latin Name	Common Name
Acer platanoides	Norway maple
A. saccharinum	Silver maple
Cinnamomum camphora	Camphor
Hippophae rhamnoides	Sallow thorn
Liquidambar styraciflua	Sweet gum
Morus spp.	Mulberry
Pinus pinea	Italian stone pine
Platanus spp.	Sycamore, plane tree
Populus spp.	Poplars (columnar)
Quercus palustris	Pin oak
Rhus spp.	Sumac
Salix alba	White willow
Ulmus pumila	Siberian elm
Zelkova serrata	Japanese zelkova

patios and paths, is important. Although little research has been done, a good general rule is to keep the root crown (where the main roots meet the trunk just below the soil's surface) as far from the masonry or stonework as possible. It is the main roots as they form the root crown that develop the largest diameter and do the most damage. The canopies of many trees are quite wide, so you can maintain trunk distance and still get effective shade. If you don't have enough room and you have to choose between shade and the possibility of cracked pavement, err on the side of caution and don't plant the tree.

It's easier to use attractive patio umbrellas for cool shade than to repair a cracked patio.

You should also pay attention to the type of soil you're planting in. A layer of clayey soil under the pavement forces even those roots naturally prone to grow deeper to turn upward toward the soil's surface to buckle or break a driveway, patio, or path. Loose soil, on the other hand, allows more naturally deep root systems, such as those found with the Aristocrat pear (*Pyrus calleryana* 'Aristocrat'), to grow and stay below the surface.

However, loose soil is not a firm surface for pavement, brick

walkways, and flagstone patios. So you're faced with a predicament. For walkways and garden paths, make the construction as permeable as possible so water and air can percolate into the soil beneath. This more aerobic environment is healthier for the roots, which won't have to go searching for a healthy environment on the surface where they might do damage. Setting bricks in sand, placing large flagstones as individual stepping stones, using precast permeable lawn pavers (which have vertical cavities to be filled with soil and planted), and even resorting to heavily mulched paths when needed far from the home's doors (so no litter is tracked inside) will help sustain aerobic soils.

For driveways and other surfaces that must carry a heavy load, compacting the soil before pouring cement is a must. In this situation, keeping the trunk of the tree or shrub as far from the paved surface as possible is the only remedy.

Root barriers, which come in many shapes (mostly circular) and materials (primarily plastics), are another option (see the drawing on p. 110). The theory is that the young roots grow sideways, hit the wall of the barrier, grow down some 12 in. to 48 in. deep (depending on the barrier), and then continue to grow sideways out from under the barrier at the deeper level. The barriers are

Trees and Shrubs Less Likely to Heave Pavement

Here's a list of trees and shrubs generally considered less risky for planting near pavement. Keep in mind, though, that the farther from the pavement you can plant, the better.

Latin Name	Common Name
Aesculus spp.	Horse chestnut
Betula spp.	Birch
Crataegus spp.	Hawthorn
Fagus spp.	Beech
Fraxinus spp.	Ash
Malus spp.	Apple/crabapple
Pyrus spp.	Pear
Quercus spp.	Oak (but not *Q. palustris*)
Tilia spp.	Linden

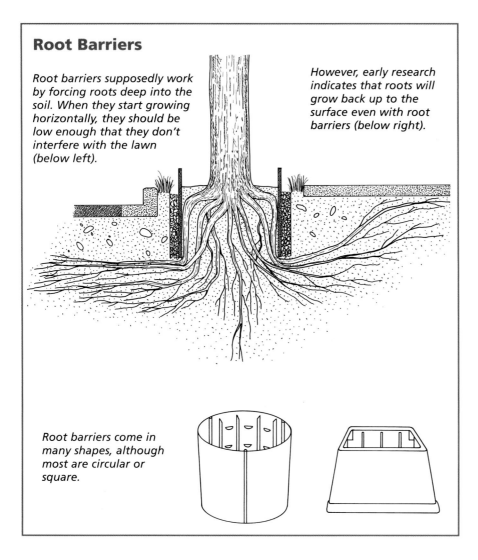

Root Barriers

Root barriers supposedly work by forcing roots deep into the soil. When they start growing horizontally, they should be low enough that they don't interfere with the lawn (below left).

However, early research indicates that roots will grow back up to the surface even with root barriers (below right).

Root barriers come in many shapes, although most are circular or square.

often used when planting trees near pavement in the hopes of keeping roots from growing upward to heave the pavement.

Some landscape architects and consulting arborists have apparently been successful with deep, vertical root barriers in the tree-planting areas between the street and the sidewalk. If one or more trees are being planted in the strip between the curb and your front sidewalk, and the soil runs continuously along the length of the front yard, you may be able to add a 48-in.-deep root barrier around the entire perimeter of the strip (maintaining 2 in. to 6 in. of the barrier above the soil). This allows enough room for the roots to roam sideways within the root barrier to explore for water and nutrients. The assumption is that the larger, longer volume of soil is enough to keep the roots satisfied without having to roam out from under the root barrier and up under the street or sidewalk.

While these larger root barriers may work, individual barriers for single trees are often a waste of time, money, and effort. Studies have shown that although individual circular barriers placed around each new tree resulted in fewer roots, the roots still surfaced (sometimes abruptly, other times more gradually) 1 ft. to 2 ft. beyond the barrier. In these studies, the average root depth of the barrier-encircled trees equaled that of the trees without barriers. There were no roots circling within the root barrier, or sinker roots. The roots all developed laterally. In heavy soils, the roots were in the top 6 in. of the soil, and if the barrier was at soil level or covered with mulch, some roots would search out the duff, growing up and over the barrier and back into the soil beyond the barrier.

The researchers found that the root barrier type does not substantially affect root distribution or size. But

Choosing and Planting Street Trees

PERHAPS THE TOUGHEST PLACE TO CHOOSE a tree for is the narrow space between the sidewalk and the road. The more urban the setting, the more difficult it is for a tree to survive. Street-side plantings have to deal with wayward cars and trucks, undisciplined dogs, sometimes air and water pollution, poor or compacted soil, perhaps a limited soil volume, and, in some places, high salt levels from winter deicing.

Yet many cities and suburban neighborhoods require street-side plantings. As the trees mature, the arching, widening crown makes the neighborhood look more settled, and the environmental benefits of trees—cooling shade, filtering out of dust and pollution—transform the streets and homes into more comfortable places to live.

Most urban and suburban municipalities or neighborhood homeowners' associations have a short list of

Too often, trees are planted in a very narrow strip between the street and the sidewalk. Cracking or lifting of the sidewalk is inevitable, as these ornamental cherry trees reveal.

what is legal to plant in the narrow space between the sidewalk and the street. This limits the homeowner's options, but it also reduces the burden of decision making and legal liability due to injury from uneven sidewalks caused by heaving roots.

Call your local department of public works, homeowners' association, or the county office of planning, and ask for the guidelines for your neighborhood. Then visit a nursery to see what the trees look like. While the choices are restricted, you can still choose between different bark colors and textures, foliage colors, fall leaf colors, and overall shapes, at least to some degree.

Within your property, the impact a tree or shrub makes on sidewalks, driveway, patio, or any other pavement is under your own control.

Chinese chestnut *(Castanea mollissima)* is an excellent example of a picturesque canopy, but the spiny burrs create a mess if they fall on a lawn. This tree is best reserved for wilder sections of the yard or in mulched areas.

Some trees, like the paulownia *(Paulownia tomentosa)*, have very attractive blossoms. But the flowers fade to produce these seed capsules, each with as many as 2,000 winged seeds—thus spreading like a weed.

Liquidambar fruit littering the ground *(Liquidambar styraciflua)*.

they added two caveats: If the soil outside the barrier is heavy or compacted, the roots will grow closer to the surface regardless of the tree's genetic tendency, whereas if the soil is loose and well aerated, the root growth is more likely to be determined by genetics. And, the thinner the layer of soil, the more the roots will be near the surface, lurking beneath your patio, driveway, or walkways.

Messy Trees and Shrubs

With busy lives, many gardeners want to focus on the joy of tending the annual bedding plants, pruning and nurturing herbaceous perennials, growing a few vegetables and perhaps some fruit, and shaping and maintaining small shrubs. They don't want the hassle of cleaning up messy trees and shrubs. Trees add a fantastic sense of place and a feeling of longevity to the home and yard, but if they are too messy, they are more a burden than a pleasure.

Of course, there's no such thing as a completely clean tree. All trees make some mess during the year. Deciduous trees provide plenty of leaves to rake, blow, or bag. Wet fallen leaves are slippery and can permanently stain pavement. So can tree flowers and fruits. Even conifers drop needles—a year-round nuisance. The needles must be swept or collected with a garden vacuum. (Needles in uncleaned gutters in the arid West are high fire hazards.)

So you have to decide how much mess is tolerable (there's a big difference between falling leaves and falling rotten fruit), and the decision depends on both the variety and the location of the tree. Some fruit trees don't require much attention: The birds eat most of the fruits before they drop. On the other hand, persimmons make fruits that can get very soft and mushy in the late fall or midwinter. Those that jettison from

In midwinter, these Hachiya persimmons (*Diospyros kaki* 'Hachiya') become soft, so unharvested fruits will make a considerable mess if they fall on decking or paving.

Messy Trees and Shrubs

The following list contains some messy trees and shrubs to avoid if you want the canopy to extend over paved or wooden surfaces.

Latin Name	Common Name	Messy Parts
Araucaria araucana	Monkey puzzle tree	10-15 lb. of sharp-spiny seed cones
Castanea mollissima	Chinese chestnut	Prickly burrs surrounding nuts
Catalpa speciosa	Northern catalpa	Long seed pods
Gledistia triacanthos	Common honeylocust	Pods
Juglans spp.	Eastern and black walnut	Husks surrounding nuts
Ligustrum lucidum	Glossy privet	Small purple berries stain
Maclura pomifera	Osage orange	Heavy fruits on female trees
Malus spp.	Crabapple trees	Tiny fruits
Morus spp.	Fruiting mulberry trees	Berries
Paulownia tomentosa	Royal paulownia	Fruits release thousands of small, winged seeds per fruit
Pinus coulteri	Coulter pine	Huge, heavy cones
Platanus spp.	American and London plane tree	Ball-like fruits, prolific deciduous leaf fall, and lots of twiggy litter
Prunus serotina	Wild black cherry	Fruit

the tree leave a slimy splat on pavement or wooden surface. But alongside a "meadow" in the yard, a persimmon would be just fine.

On the smooth surface of a patio, acorns are like marbles with their potential for causing you to lose your footing. On the driveway, your car will crush acorns into a mess that can stain the pavement. But the oak tree is a handsome addition to the back of a yard.

Furthermore, don't forget that a messy lawn can be just as unpleasant

"Cleaner" Trees and Shrubs

Carpinus betulus
EUROPEAN HORNBEAM

USDA ZONES: 4 to 7 (8)

SIZE: 40 ft. to 60 ft. tall; 30 ft. to 40 ft. wide

COMMENTS: This tree's premier virtue is its evenly shaped, round or oval canopy. The leaves last into the late fall and early winter, spreading the cleanup further into the fall season. Prone to scale problems. Produces winged seeds each fall, but they blow away or are easily swept off dry surfaces. Wind-tolerant in some areas. A popular cultivar for hedging is 'Fastigiata', with an oval-pyramidal form.

Cryptomeria japonica
JAPANESE CRYPTOMERIA

USDA ZONES: (5) 6 to 10

SIZE: 50 ft. to 60 ft. tall; 20 ft. to 30 ft. wide

COMMENTS: Evergreen conifer with a well-defined conical or pyramidal shape. The cultivars are hardier than the species. Bark peels off in strips to reveal a beautiful red. Resistant to oak root fungus in the West. Deer-resistant in some areas.

Other "clean" trees and shrubs include: *Abies concolor* (white fir) (p. 62), *Camellia japonica* (common camellia) (p. 61), *Jacaranda mimosifolia* (jacaranda) (p. 82), *Pinus strobus* (white pine) (p. 34), and *Syringa vulgaris* (common lilac) (p. 79).

Ilex × meserveae
MESERVE HOLLY HYBRIDS

USDA ZONES: (4) 5 to 6 (7)

SIZE: 6 ft. to 10 ft. tall; 6 ft. to 10 ft. wide

COMMENTS: Typical spiny-leafed holly. The female cultivars make copious amounts of beautiful red berries. To prevent berries and reduce maintenance, plant only male cultivars. The dense foliage makes a good low screen or barrier plant. Don't plant near coastal areas because leaves burn in strong winds. Needs well-drained soil. Watch for holly leaf miner and holly aphids. Prone to root rot in the heat of Zone 7. Resists deer and attracts birds in some areas.

Metasequoia glyptostroboides
DAWN REDWOOD

USDA ZONES: 5 to 9

SIZE: 70 ft. to 90 ft. tall; 20 ft. to 30 ft. wide

COMMENTS: Not a true redwood. Develops a magnificent pyramidal form without pruning. Turns a stunning bronze-orange in the fall; drops needles (requiring annual cleanup). Tolerates dry soils when it is older, but prefers moisture (even thrives in lawns). Can grow 4 ft. to 5 ft. per year. Few pests. Resistant to oak root fungus in the West. Wind-tolerant in some areas.

Rhododendron spp.
RHODODENDRON or AZALEAS

USDA ZONES: 3 to 9

SIZE: Height and width vary

COMMENTS: Rhododendrons or azaleas can be evergreen or deciduous and are available in a tremendous array of sizes. The evergreen forms are particularly low maintenance; few leaves fall, and flowers naturally fall off and quickly decompose. In dry and hot areas, provide shade from late morning on. Watch for yellowing foliage, a sign of iron deficiency (if the veins remain green) or of root rot (if the entire leaf yellows, then quickly browns). Watch for root weevils. Not suited for arid areas due to leaf margin burn.

Thuja plicata
WESTERN or GIANT ARBORVITAE, or WESTERN RED CEDAR

USDA ZONES: 5 to 7

SIZE: 50 ft. to 75 ft. tall; 15 ft. to 25 ft. wide

COMMENTS: Perhaps the most beautiful of the arborvitaes, this evergreen grows in a uniform broad or narrow pyramidal shape. Prefers a moist, acidic soil with good drainage. Needs shade in areas with hot, dry summer; prefers the cooler coastal belts when grown in the West. Resists deer and tolerates sandy soil in some areas.

These European hornbeam trees (*Carpinus betulus* 'Fastigiata') are examples of well-shaped trees that are "cleaner" than other deciduous trees.

This Mediterranean-style landscape features a sizable olive tree (*Olea europaea*). To prevent a mess on any pavement, use the fruitless cultivars 'Swan Hill' or 'Wilsonii'.

as a messy deck or driveway. The mature form of the popular shade tree sweet gum (*Liquidambar styraciflua*) makes hundreds of pounds of prickly, round fruits, which clutter the lawn or paved areas and make walking awkward. (My dad picks up over 250 gallons of sweet gum balls every year from one 30-ft.-tall tree!)

There are some relatively "clean" trees that merit consideration. Although conifers drop needles, they usually require only small amounts of maintenance spread throughout the year, compared to the massive strategic maneuver required each fall by deciduous trees. Some deciduous trees, such as the California buckeye (*Aesculus californica*), actually drop their leaves in late summer as a water-conserving, drought-resistant adaptation. This early defoliation spreads leaf-raking over a couple of months, reducing the amount you have to do in the fall.

Trees with large fruits that can turn soft and mushy—persimmons, apples, pears, and plums—can be surrounded by mulch. Then the fruits fall harmlessly.

You also have the option of using nonfruiting cultivars of some trees. For example, to avoid the messy seed balls of the sweet gum (*Liquidambar. styraciflua*), plant only the fruitless cultivar 'Rotundiloba'. The messy fruits of olive trees readily stain paved and wooden surfaces, so select only nonfruiting cultivars such as 'Swan Hill' or 'Wilsonii'.

Poisonous Trees and Shrubs

All plant poisons injure by chemical means and can cause irritation, illness, or death. Leaves, berries, stems, and sometimes even whole plants can cause the symptoms. Sometimes the effects are subtle, and sometimes only some people are affected.

For instance, the white, viscous sap from a fig tree (*Ficus carica*) has a chemical that can cause a lingering dermatitis, but only in those who are sensitive to the chemical. The white sap of poinsettias—members of the euphorbia family—can produce a similar response. There is usually a delay between getting the sap on your skin and the onset of itching and redness, but prevention

When pruning a fig tree (*Ficus carica*), be careful not to get the white sap on your skin because it may cause an irritating dermatitis.

Both the leaves and the fruit of the European burning bush (*Euonymus europaea*) are poisonous, so don't plant this shrub where young children play.

is the best medicine. The prudent pruner of a fig tree wears long pants, a long-sleeved shirt, and gloves, and showers immediately after pruning.

A more frightening example is the castor bean plant (*Ricinus communis*). The glossy, colorfully speckled seeds are attractive and lure children to pick them up, but they are poisonous

Caution! Poisonous Plants

The following plants should be avoided if you're concerned about young children eating plants in your garden.

Latin Name	Common Name	Poisonous Parts
Aesculus × carnea	Horse chestnut	All parts
Buxus sempervirens	Boxwood	Leaves (cause rash)
Daphne spp.	Daphne	All parts
Euonymus europaeus	European burning bush	Leaves and fruit
Heteromeles arbutifolia	Toyon or Christmas berry	Leaves
Hydrangae spp.	Hydrangea	Leaves
Ilex aquifolium	English holly	Berries
Juniperus communis	Juniper	All parts
Kalmia latifolia	Mountain laurel	All parts
Ligustrum vulgare	Privet	Leaves, bark, and fruit
Nerium oleander	Oleander	Leaves
Rhododendron spp.	Rhododendrons and azaleas	Leaves
Robinia pseudoacaia	Black locust	All parts, including young shoots (cause cramping or colic)
Sambucus canadensis	American elderberry	Shoots, leaves, and bark
Taxus baccata	English yew	Bark, needles, and seeds
Thuja occidentalis	American arborvitae	Foliage (causes rash)

Some cultivars of oleander (*Nerium oleander*), such as 'Calypso', have dramatic and colorful flowers, but the leaves are poisonous.

scientific name of the plant. Bring a piece of the plant to the phone with you to describe it if you aren't sure about its name.

Prickly Plants

There are varying degrees of prickly: true thorns (such as found on roses and pyracanthas); slightly hard, pointed, serrated leaves (holly shrubs); and irritating plants such as the scratchy foliage of junipers. Thorny plants are effective whether clipped or unsheared. Prickly leaves like hollies and scratchy juniper foliage are soft enough that heavy

All species of barberry (*Berberis* spp.) have stickery thorns, which can be useful in a barrier hedge along the edge of the yard.

when chewed and swallowed. Even the leaf can cause skin allergies.

To make your yard safer for children, choose your trees carefully. Research the poison content of all parts of your trees or shrubs, not just the berries. For instance, the hollow, pithy stems of American elderberry (*Sambucus canadensis*) are poisonous. Children who use them for blow darts can be poisoned. The best way to

prevent an accident is through knowledge.

Fortunately, many poisonous plants have such a foul taste or are so caustic that going as far as swallowing them is unlikely. If someone does swallow a plant that you know or suspect to be poisonous, call your poison control service (an 800 telephone number in the front of your telephone directory) immediately. Try to remember the common or

A thorny hawthorn (*Crataegus* spp.) hedge.

Prickly Trees and Shrubs

Avoid these plants in places where you plan to play or next to a walk-way. Or plant them as a barrier hedge.

Latin Name	Common Name
Berberis × *mentorensis*	Mentor barberry
Carissa grandifloria	Natal plum
Chaenomeles speciosa	Common flowering quince
Crataegus spp.	Hawthorn trees
Ilex spp.	Holly trees
Mahonia aquifolium	Oregon grape
Pyracantha spp.	Firethorn, pyracantha
Rosa spp.	Countless rose varieties

shearing reduces the effect somewhat, and new leaves are not as stiff as mature foliage.

Although you'll want to avoid prickly plants in places where you're likely to rub against them, you can use them to good effect. As shrubby borders or clipped hedges, prickly trees and shrubs keep out unwanted people. Place them close to the perimeter of your yard where unwanted foot traffic occurs. Allowing these plants to grow above 6 ft. means outsiders won't be able to see into your property—an added benefit in some situations.

The best use of these plants is as a sheared hedge. Shearing is usually required so that foliage is maintained from the top down to ground level, to prevent kids or adults from slipping *under* the barrier. Regular pruning also keeps the foliage dense, preventing the development of "caverns" or hollow spots beneath the canopy.

Barrier plants should be placed close together. To exclude dogs, plant shrubs as close as 6 in.; to restrain people, plantings should be spaced 12 in. apart. When the planting is young, consider putting up chicken wire or other wire fencing to begin to give a "hint" as to where you don't want uninvited guests. If you have the time, bend some of the young branches horizontal to the

The spiny-toothed Oregon grape (*Mahonia aquifolium*) leaves.

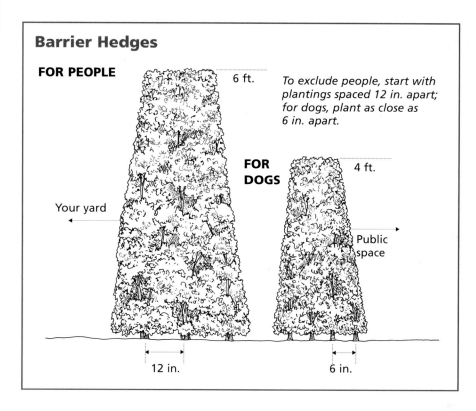

Barrier Hedges

FOR PEOPLE

6 ft.

To exclude people, start with plantings spaced 12 in. apart; for dogs, plant as close as 6 in. apart.

FOR DOGS

4 ft.

Your yard

Public space

12 in.

6 in.

ground and weave them through the limbs of neighboring plants (wear gloves and a long-sleeved shirt). This informal weaving and yearly shearing will form a fairly formidable living fence.

If deer are a problem, barrier plants and thickets of thorny plants alone will never keep them out of your yard (they may even eat them!). You'll need an 8-ft.-tall fence to do that.

Monrovia firethorn (*Pyracantha coccinea* 'Lalandei Monrovia') has thorns.

Planting & Maintenance

CHAPTER NINE

Buying Trees & Shrubs

YOUR BUYING DECISIONS are not over when you have chosen the tree or shrub you want to plant. Trees and shrubs are sold in many forms, including balled-and-burlapped (B-and-B) and bare-root. Each option has its own pros and cons, and you should understand them before you make your purchase. Plants also come in all sizes, which have different impacts on the landscape. You'll have to decide what size is right for you.

Buying Options

Most nurseries offer many varieties and sizes of plants to the avid gardener. B-and-B stock is best sold only while fully dormant, but container-grown plants can be sold throughout the spring and summer. Large plants sold in containers or as B-and-B make an immediate impact because of their size, but the root system on such trees isn't wide and sturdy. For decades, bare-root stock has been the best value for the money because, unlike B-and-B and container plants, there are no soil, wrap, or container costs. Some innovative nurseries are now offering smaller plants grown and sold in long, narrow tubes (and tall square containers called deep cells) for a better root system for transplanting *and* a lower cost.

Balled-and-burlapped stock

Balled-and-burlapped trees and shrubs are grown in the nursery field. In much of the country, B-and-B stock is dug up in the early spring near the end of the dormant season. When they are dug, their roots and a surrounding lump of soil are wrapped in a burlap binding. Digging up a B-and-B removes up to 98 percent of the roots on larger trees. The tree is often grown in fairly heavy soil to

Balled-and-Burlapped Stock

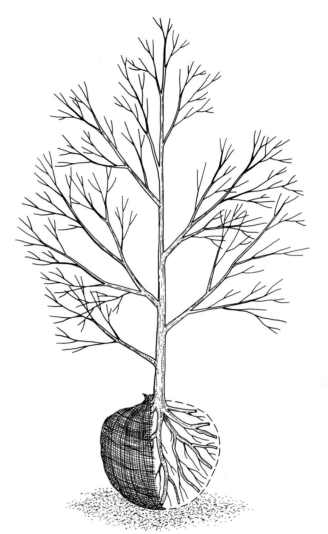

Here you can see a B-and-B plant wrapped in burlap (left) and after it's unwrapped and the roots are exposed (right). Landscapers often leave the burlap in place. If the soil in the B-and-B ball is very different from your native soil, remove most of the soil from around the roots of the B-and-B and cover with native soil.

Transporting B-and-B Stock

BALLED-AND-BURLAPPED STOCK up to about 2 ft. (maybe 3 ft.) in diameter can often be lifted by two people with strong, healthy backs and transported in a station wagon, car trunk, or truck. Be sure to wrap the trunk with cloth padding where it might hit metal, and secure it with well-padded rope. Once you get the stock home, you can cart it around in a wheelbarrow. The safest way to tote B-and-B stock is to use a special tree/shrub carrier. This device has aluminum-tube pipes that fit beneath the ball like a cradle, with two handles to divide up the weight (see Resources on pp. 180-181). In a pinch, you can slide the ball onto planking or plywood for a makeshift carrier. Larger specimens need to be transported and set in place by the nursery or a landscape contractor.

A tree/shrub carrier is an easy way for two people to transport heavy B-and-B stock.

ensure that the soil clings to the root mass for an intact root ball. This means that B-and-B stock is considerably heavier than container stock of a similar size, an important factor when it comes to handling the plant and avoiding lower-back pain.

The health of a B-and-B tree or shrub is dependent in large part on the amount of soil around its roots while it's held in the nursery. Look for a plant with the smallest top relative to the size of its root ball. Figure the ball you purchase should average at least 10 to 12 times the trunk's diameter 6 in. above the soil—bigger

is even better. (See also What Size to Buy on p. 130.)

Always look at the condition of the ball itself, and avoid plants that have a sloppy wrapping job. It's best to get a freshly dug and balled plant. Plants that sit into the summer may have soil and roots spilling out; roots growing through the wrapping into the mulch used to "heel in" the stock; or a ball that looks intact until you lift it and find the soil loose or fractured, exposing roots to air damage. Any roots growing through the burlap may have to be trimmed off as you plant. Watch out for plenty of

blooming foliage above a small container, as well.

Most landscapers and gardeners leave the burlap intact. If the soil from the field where the tree was grown is much different from your garden's soil, it's better to remove the burlap and most of the soil in the ball. When you plant, pack native soil around the root mass so the roots will quickly adjust to the soil they must live in for the rest of their lives. B-and-B roots are easily frayed when the burlap is removed, so check them carefully after you remove most of the soil. Look for cracked, broken, snapped

Judging B-and-B Size

This tree has several problems:
- *Lower limbs too high*
- *Small-caliper trunk*
- *Trunk too tall for the size of its root ball*

This tree has the correct proportions and is healthier. For example, it has the following:
- *Sturdy lower limbs*
- *Large-caliper trunk*
- *Shorter trunk that corresponds to the size of its root ball*

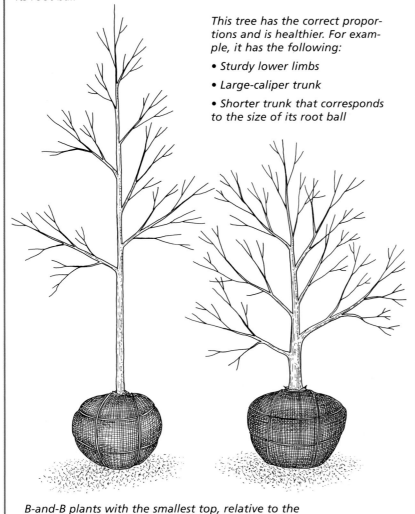

B-and-B plants with the smallest top, relative to the size of the root ball, are generally healthier.

roots with uneven edges. Trim to a clean cut with pruning shears. Cut back to an existing side shoot on the roots, if it's not too close to the trunk. There should be few, if any, circling roots because the plant was field-grown—but check for them anyway.

When buying a B-and-B deciduous tree, make sure none of its flower or leaf buds have swollen or opened. Ideally, you want the buds to open only *after* the tree has been planted so that the new root hairs stimulated by the new leaf buds come into immediate contact with moist, native soil.

Evergreen conifer and broadleaf plants and shrubs are often sold as B-and-B stock. This option also is also appropriate for deciduous trees over 6 ft. tall.

Container-grown plants

Any plant can be grown in a container, which is usually plastic. The most common sizes are 1, 2, 5, or 15 gallons. More and more nurseries are switching to container plants, as they allow less-frequent watering in the nursery—a benefit to the seller but not necessarily to the buyer. Also, the plants can be held through the summer before they are planted. The special artificial soil mix in a container planting is often considerably lighter than the soil of a B-and-B tree, making transport and transplanting less troublesome.

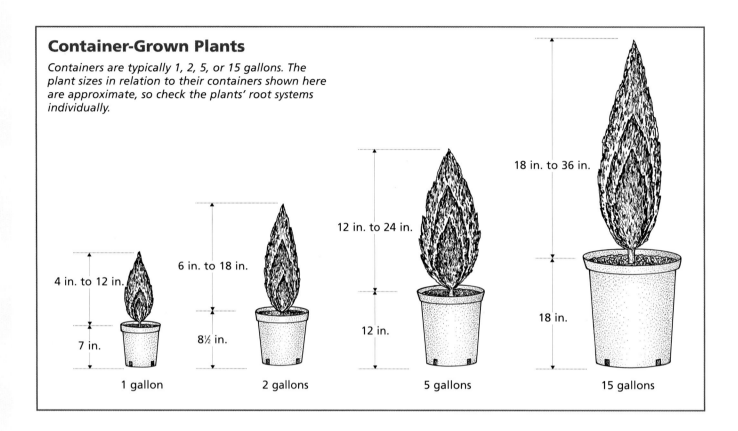

Container-Grown Plants

Containers are typically 1, 2, 5, or 15 gallons. The plant sizes in relation to their containers shown here are approximate, so check the plants' root systems individually.

4 in. to 12 in.

7 in.

1 gallon

6 in. to 18 in.

8½ in.

2 gallons

12 in. to 24 in.

12 in.

5 gallons

18 in. to 36 in.

18 in.

15 gallons

Because the industry has promoted large plants as a good value, many container plants are left to grow too large in the pot. They have root masses that fill the container and may circle the bottom of the pot. Containers with smooth sides may have more circling roots. Some containers have vertical ridges to force the roots down the sides of the pot and prevent circling near the top of the soil mass.

When buying container stock, make sure the plant has been transplanted into its container fairly recently. Inspect the roots, some of which should be visible near the top at the outer edge of the root mass. It's best if you can also check the roots inside the container. Ask permission from the nursery staff; if they don't want you to check the roots without buying the plant, they are probably selling overgrown stock. Gently pull the plant from its container. This is very easy to do with 1-gallon container plants. A gentle tap of the potting mix should cause some soil to crumble from the bottom of the root ball.

For bigger plants or trees, you'll need help. Rock the container onto its side; one person jiggles the bottom of the container while another pulls slowly and carefully on the trunk where it meets the potting soil. Slide the root-and-soil mass slowly sideways until you can see the roots. If the plant comes out with the soil firmly attached to an extensive root system, the plant is overgrown. You'll need to inspect only one or two plants (one with a small canopy and one with a large canopy) to get the picture.

One sign of a recently potted plant is new root growth, which is a healthy white, pink, or light tan color (dark brown or black root-tips are usually dead). Also, look for a root mass that hasn't completely filled the volume of soil-mix, and avoid any container plant that shows signs of circling roots, which indicate a rootbound plant. Finally, check to make sure that foliage or deciduous limbs appear healthy and vigorous, that the plant can stand without the support of a stake, and that, if the plant is grafted, it has no cracks, fissures, or incomplete fusing (callusing) of the graft.

Bare-root trees and shrubs

Because bare-root trees are sold without soil around their roots, the freight costs and hassle of shipping are reduced—making them less expensive than container or B-and-B plants. Primarily, only fully dormant deciduous trees are sold bare-root. Evergreen trees can become dehydrated via their foliage if they aren't getting any moisture through the roots. Some evergreen plants are shipped mostly bare rooted via mail, but with some moist moss or packing material to keep the roots fresher. (Soak the roots of such plants immediately upon receipt for an hour or so, and plant in the ground or a pot directly.)

Just about any size deciduous plant can be purchased bare-root. It is very common for nurseries to offer a wide selection of bare-root fruit trees and shade trees in the early spring. As soon as these trees begin to leaf out, they are planted in containers and the price increases dramatically.

Removing Big Plants from Containers

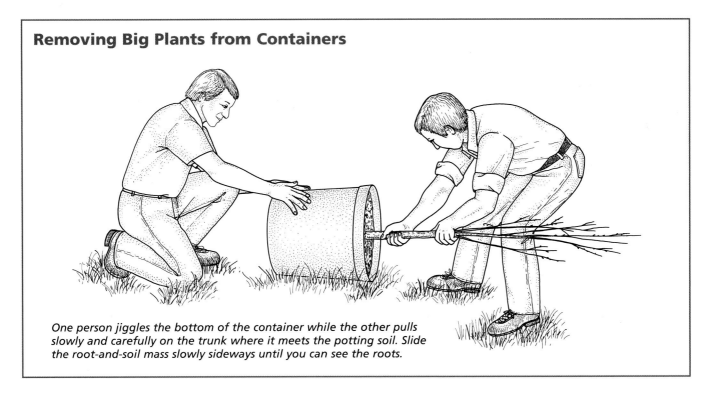

One person jiggles the bottom of the container while the other pulls slowly and carefully on the trunk where it meets the potting soil. Slide the root-and-soil mass slowly sideways until you can see the roots.

Identifying Potential Problems

If the plant is grafted, make sure it has no cracks, fissures, or wounds.

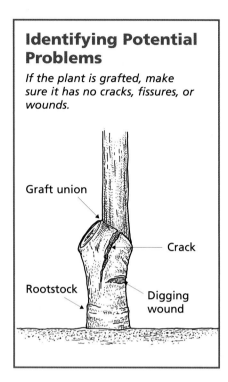

Graft union

Crack

Rootstock

Digging wound

The process of digging bare-root stock may leave even more of the root system in the ground than a B-in-B tree. Look at the roots to make sure most have been cleanly cut and are not too shattered by the digging process. (You can trim the ends of slightly damaged roots with pruning shears, but you don't want to remove too much of the already limited roots.)

Tube-grown stock

Some nurseries now use these tall, narrow containers to force the roots downward to prevent circling and to

Bare-Root Plants

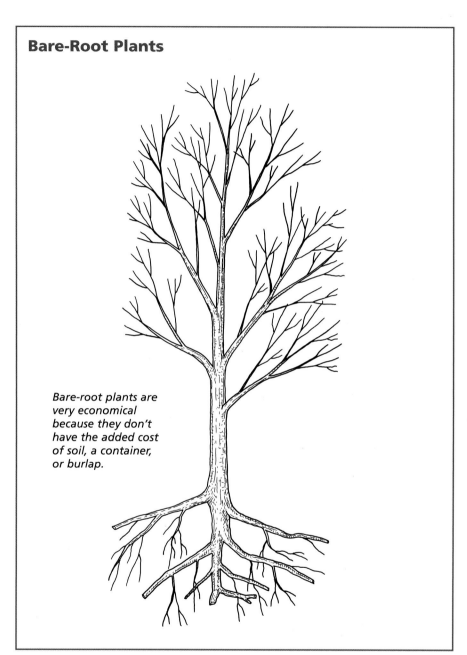

Bare-root plants are very economical because they don't have the added cost of soil, a container, or burlap.

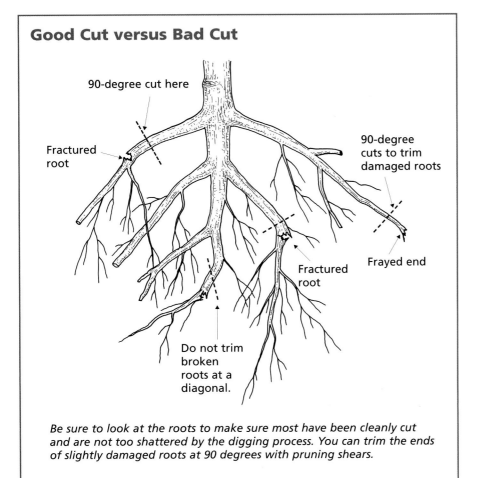

Good Cut versus Bad Cut

90-degree cut here

Fractured root

90-degree cuts to trim damaged roots

Frayed end

Fractured root

Do not trim broken roots at a diagonal.

Be sure to look at the roots to make sure most have been cleanly cut and are not too shattered by the digging process. You can trim the ends of slightly damaged roots at 90 degrees with pruning shears.

stimulated. The proliferation of lateral root hairs reduces transplant shock because there are more root hair tips to absorb moisture and nutrients. Trees with taproots must have very little shoot growth above the soil if the entire taproot is to remain intact without getting air pruned. (Still, air-pruned taprooted trees are also easy to transplant.)

Unfortunately, this innovative and inexpensive type of plant stock is still difficult to find at retail nurseries. To find tube-grown stock, look for nurseries specializing in plants for hedgerow (windbreak) plantings, reforestation, revegetation, and wildlife-habitat plantings. Or, you can pester your favorite nursery to carry tube-grown plants. Fortunately, a few mail-order sources are becoming available (see Resources on pp. 180-181). Look in the back of horticultural magazines for some options.

To inspect tube-grown plants, pull a sample seedling out of its tube and examine the roots. (Ask the permission of the nursery staff first.) After a few such examinations, you'll get a sense of the look and feel of a healthy plant without having to remove it. There should be a number of healthy white, pink, or pale tan root tips. Once removed, the roots should hold most or all of the tube's soil mix together. Ideally, the top

stimulate more tiny root hairs for a better root system when transplanting. On top of these advantages, they cost less than 1-gallon container-grown stock.

The drainage holes at the bottom of each tube or deep container probably won't prevent circling, but they will air-prune the roots. With most trees and shrubs, the roots that try to grow out of the small holes at the bottom of the tube are killed because of the lack of protective, moist soil—called air pruning. Air pruning acts much like pruning a shrub or tree above ground: Each cut causes two or more side shoots to develop. In this case, root hairs are

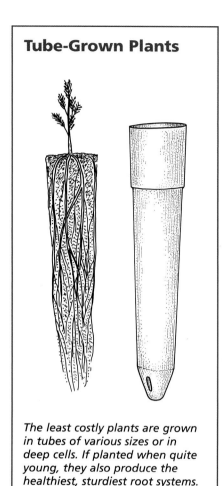

Tube-Grown Plants

The least costly plants are grown in tubes of various sizes or in deep cells. If planted when quite young, they also produce the healthiest, sturdiest root systems.

of the seedling should be about one-quarter the length of the tube. The smaller the plant, the more quickly it will become established, the healthier its root system will be, and the more vigorously it will grow.

Other criteria to look for include easy removal of the seedling; solid walls so roots don't grow from one container to another; ribbed sides (which direct roots downward and help prevent circling); sufficient soil volume to support healthy root growth; and an opening at the bottom to air-prune roots. It's best to look for tube-grown plants in containers 6 in. to 18 in. deep and 1½ in. in diameter to 8 in. square.

All trees and shrubs benefit from being grown in tubes, as long as the root mass has not outgrown the tube. The low cost makes this type of nursery stock ideal for hedges and screen plantings where many plants are required. Tube-grown plants are especially useful when planting windbreaks to withstand the strongest winds. The roots grow naturally to form the widest and sturdiest development of lateral roots to bolster the canopy against any onslaught by fierce winds. Such plants are also the best way to start a tree to leave as a living legacy for future generations to appreciate.

What Size to Buy

Very large trees give a well-established look to the garden. They come in 48-in. to 72-in. (or larger) boxed containers or B-and-B stock. Large stock (but smaller than 48 in.) is usually desired when a screen or hedge needs a quick fill-in. These plants can be purchased as either large B-and-B or 5- to 15-gallon container plants. Smaller stock, whether as smaller-diameter B-and-B or in 1- or 2-gallon containers, is often chosen to save money and fill the same needs—but this takes longer to create solid foliage. The smallest and most economical stock is grown in various-sized tubes or deep cells.

Contrary to popular opinion, bigger is not necessarily better when it comes to buying plants. Smaller container-grown plants can outgrow large-sized plants within a few years, because the roots have been less damaged by confinement in their container. And smaller plants adapt to their environment faster. This is particularly important for tall shrubs and trees because of the stress they take from wind and ice. Often, a larger plant will not be able to establish as healthy a natural root system, and it will be the first to blow over in severe winds. If your screen is doing double-duty as a hedgerow, the sturdiest long-lived plants are often the smaller transplants with unencumbered roots.

The practice of some growers is to fit as many plants to the acre as possible, forcing their trees to grow in a very shady and wind-protected environment (especially the lower limbs and trunk). This usually results in overly tall trees without sturdy trunks capable of resisting strong winds or ice. A top-heavy canopy flexing against a puny stem is a formula for disaster. For B-and-B and container-grown trees, check the American Nursery & Landscape Association guidelines, *American Standard of Nursery Stock* (see Resources on pp. 180-181). These guidelines will help you find a tree with a good diameter-to-height ratio for the trunk. Ask your local nursery-men if they use these guidelines.

While small plants develop the sturdiest root systems, the largest-diameter trunks, and the most resistance to wind and ice, you may still want to block your view quickly or have shade as soon as possible. You can do this by planting both large and small windbreak or shade trees at the same time. The large plants will act as nurse plants, buffering the winds and allowing the seedlings to grow without staking. The seedlings will develop a larger-diameter caliper and more wind and ice resistance. The smaller plants will quickly attain the height of the larger plants. Within 5 to 10 years, the former seedlings will be as tall as the more costly and less sturdy trees. Then you can selectively remove the weaker trees and leave only those with the best anchorage and the most robust trunks.

Finally, it's necessary to determine how many plants to buy. Even though

you'll be selecting the best plants available, many hazards await each young seedling. Tiny trees can succumb to nibbling rabbits, dry soil, persistent gophers, browsing deer and their trampling feet, hungry caterpillars. In light of all these hazards, you will probably lose the plant lottery if you plant just one seedling of each tree. A good strategy is to purchase four to six inexpensive

tube seedlings or very small trees in 1-gallon containers for each permanent tree. Plant them in an irregular cluster at the approximate spot where you want one tree to flourish. After a year, remove one or more of the weaker seedlings. By the second or third year, you'll be left with the most vigorous, healthy, and well-rooted young sapling.

Considering Your Soil

ONCE YOU'VE NARROWED THE CHOICES to those trees and shrubs that appeal to you and that appear to be growing well in the nursery, analyze your yard's soil. Many people forget that their soil may be different from that of their neighbors down the street or across town. Dig some test trenches, get into the trenches, and look at and feel your soil—get dirty! Take samples to your local nursery if you're confused about how to classify it on the continuum from sandy to loamy to clay-loam to heavy-clay soils. Each root system thrives in one range of soils and many languish in other soil

types. Those trees and shrubs that prefer good drainage in sandier soils often don't like to be planted in heavy clay soils. On the other hand, trees and shrubs that can handle clayey soils often grow quite well in sandy soils—if they have or are given enough fertilization.

Soil preferences of some trees are listed in the Plant Finders (note the icons). Check with local nurseries, landscapers, and knowledgeable landscape architects about the specific roots best for your soils. Anchoring your tree with a rootstock well adapted to your soil will ensure a long and healthy life.

CHAPTER TEN

Planting

PLANTING A TREE OR SHRUB seems easy enough: Just dig an enormous hole, fill it up with lots of amendments and fertilizers, bind a stake to the trunk, water like there's no tomorrow, and sit back. According to many recent studies, though, all this is literally overkill. Thanks to research, we now know that proper planting begins with choosing the best rootstock or plant for your soil, adjusting the hole depending on the type of soil, leaving out amendments or fertilizers, and staking only when necessary. The process is still simple (perhaps simpler), but it's much better suited for growing success.

Preparing the Plants

You can buy bare-root trees or shrubs when they first arrive at the nursery so as to get the best selection, but you may need to store them until the soil is drained enough to plant. The simplest way to hold the plants until planting time is to lay the bare-root stock on the ground and cover the roots with moist, aged sawdust, or sand. (You can also stand them up and cover the roots.) Be sure the plants are in deep shade on the north side of a building to delay the opening of buds for as long as possible. (Foresighted gardeners in the West, where winter rains predominate, prepare the planting spot in the summer or fall so they need only open the soil enough for the plant in early spring.) The process is much the same for balled-and-burlapped (B-and-B) stock, except most people aren't inclined to lay the plants sideways.

If gophers are a threat, lay a piece of ½-in. mesh aviary wire over the area to be covered by the sawdust or sand to prevent root damage. Where mice chew on bark in the winter, wrap the trunks with trunk guards, available at the nursery.

When you're ready to plant, cut off any wire used to hold the B-and-B together before planting. With fully dormant B-and-B plants, remove all burlap, especially the newer synthetic substitutes, so the roots will more easily grow into the native soil. If the B-and-B stock has already leafed out, it is safer to leave true burlap in place—but the synthetic material must go. If the soil texture around the B-and-B root mass is dramatically different from your soil, remove some or most of the B-and-B's soil, and replace with firmly packed native soil.

Container plants are the most convenient because they can be held for long periods of time after purchase with only frequent watering and an occasional application of liquid fertilizer to keep them healthy. Keep them in slightly filtered sunlight to prevent dehydration on hot days. Containerized plants can be planted during the spring, summer, or fall. Early fall planting can be done anywhere, and the roots may even grow a bit below the level at which the soil will freeze during the winter. Where there are mild, rainy winters and arid summer; fall plantings are superior. Roots established during the winter will be ready for the dry season and will require little or no supplemental irrigation.

With container plants, you should remove as much of the potting soil as possible before planting—especially if the native soil is heavier than the potting soil. Be careful not to injure roots, and cover them with native soil immediately.

Planting Patterns

The usual guideline for spacing is based on the mature width of the trees or shrubs. For example, cinnamon viburnum (*Viburnum cinnamomifolium*) grows to be 15 ft. wide, so you would space viburnum plants about 15 ft. apart. With this method, the two plants will, theoretically, grow to have their canopies just about touch.

In a traditional English flower, shrub, and tree border, the waist-high shrubs begin mostly 10 ft. from the viewer. The larger shrubs at eye level have their foliage beginning 20 ft. away. Trees and large shrubs that tower above the gardener's head are set back 24 ft. to 30 ft. or more from the front of the border.

However, the forest doesn't read gardening books. For a more natural look in a portion of your yard, try planting like the forest—in a more random pattern. The first approach is to plant trees in odd-numbered clusters on irregular centers for a more natural and dynamic look. If you're brave, simply take 3, 5, or 7 golf balls and toss them up into the air. Where they fall is where you plant. The hard part is to not move any of the balls once they land! It's a tough exercise in "letting go."

In urban and suburban settings, there are concerns not found in the

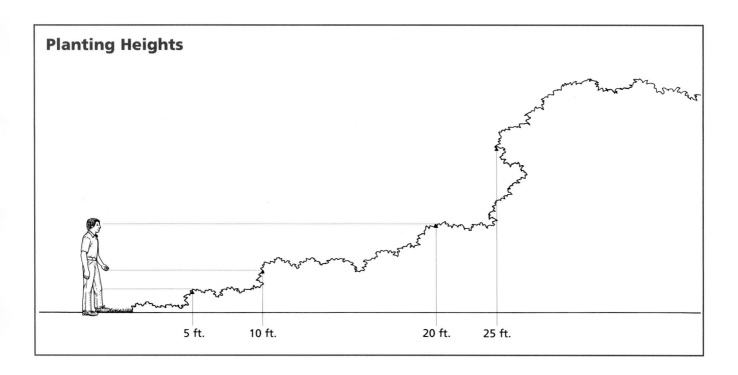

Planting Heights

5 ft.   10 ft.   20 ft.   25 ft.

forest. Don't plant beneath telephone or power lines, to prevent mangled or unshapely trees over time. Or, be sure to choose a shrub or small tree that won't grow tall enough to interfere with the maintenance of the wires. Always remember that tree roots will get rather large over time, so young trees should be planted as far as possible from the foundation. (Use the guidelines in Chapter 8.) With large shade trees, 6 ft. is the *minimal* clearance from the foundation or any hardscape for long-term protection.

Planting Guidelines

Knowing the depth of your soil can help you gauge how well your new plant will grow. As a general rule, if the layer of good soil is 5 in. or less, tree and shrub growth will tend to be poor. Ten inches allows fair growth; 16 in., good growth; and 20 in. to 30 in., excellent growth. Oddly enough, soils deeper than 30 in. often decrease the vigor of plants because such soils tend to have been leached of valuable nutrients.

Next, it's important to have sense of the type of soil you'll be planting in, as this will greatly affect the method of

planting. Sandy soils can be identified by their gritty, granular feel, and a clod of sandy soil will easily fall apart. Heavy clay soils feel slicker, smoother, and sometimes denser, and any clod will not fall apart. An ideal loam soil has the best of both extremes—some sand or minerals for drainage, some clay for nutrients and moisture-holding capacity. A loamy soil also has well-decomposed organic matter (humus) that prevents the leaching of nutrients, retains moisture, and keeps the soil well aerated and drained. A clod of compressed loam crumbles much more easily than clay but doesn't fall apart as easily as sandy soil.

Sandy and loamy soils

If you have sandy or loamy soil, always select a tree or shrub whose roots are compatible with it. The plant lists throughout this book indicate which shrubs and trees, grown on their own roots, tolerate sandy soils. Before you plant, double-check that there is a sandy-soil icon for the tree or shrub you want. Trees and shrubs in all sizes fit this category, so the selection is bountiful.

In loamy and sandy soils, planting a tree or shrub requires only a planting hole. Digging a hole seems like a simple task, yet a hole poorly dug has a detrimental effect on the plant for decades and may even kill it. Perfectly good-looking small shrubs can be pulled out of the ground years after planting, and their roots will

Planting in Sandy or Loamy Soil

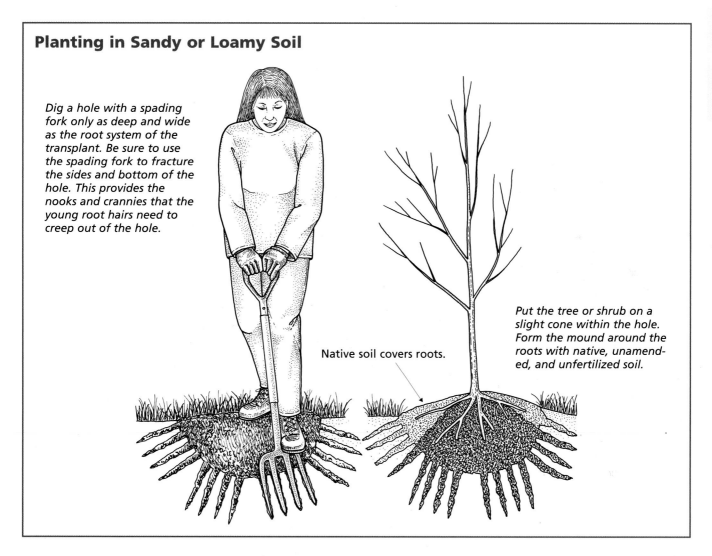

Dig a hole with a spading fork only as deep and wide as the root system of the transplant. Be sure to use the spading fork to fracture the sides and bottom of the hole. This provides the nooks and crannies that the young root hairs need to creep out of the hole.

Native soil covers roots.

Put the tree or shrub on a slight cone within the hole. Form the mound around the roots with native, unamended, and unfertilized soil.

still be conforming to the shape of the planting hole. That's alarming when you remember the roots of most trees and shrubs will, if unrestricted, grow to be up to three times wider than the canopy in sandy soil. For a wonderful shade tree like a pin oak (*Quercus palustris*), with a 40-ft. spread, this means roots 120 ft. wide in sandy soil!

Make a hole only as deep and as wide as needed to fit the well-spread root system of the tree or shrub. (If your rootstock is well chosen for the soil, a wider hole isn't worth the effort.) The depth is basically determined by the depth that the roots were grown at the nursery. You can determine where the depth was on the roots in the nursery by a distinctive change in color: Usually, the above-ground portion of the trunk is darker than the portion that grew in the soil. In the case of B-and-B plants, the hole must be wide enough to cut away the wrapping and pack your soil around the ball.

Reserve the soil, minus any living weeds or plant material, to add back over the roots after planting. Finish preparing the hole by using a spading fork to fracture the sides and bottom. This is important because it provides nooks and crannies for the young root hairs to creep out of the hole.

Next, in the bottom of your hole, make a cone of native topsoil 12 in.

to 18 in. high and about as wide. The cone is used to spread the roots out so they are less likely to be cramped and grow in a circular fashion. This cone is important no matter what type of plant you purchase. However, you needn't make a cone of soil for planting when a burlap ball is intact; simply place the B-and-B firmly on the bottom of the fractured planting hole.

When you place the tree or shrub on the cone, with the roots splayed over the sides of the cone, note the true soil line on the tree. Position the tree so that this line will occur at the same level as the surrounding uncultivated soil, or slightly higher. The soil that fills the hole should come up to this line. Be sure to settle the soil and eliminate air pockets by watering thoroughly, and by carefully treading on the surface of the planting area. Finally, add a protective layer of up to 4 in. of mulch starting 6 in. to 12 in. out from the trunk. During a heat wave, you may have to provide extra water and shelter the plant with a shade cloth.

Clay soils

Unfortunately, fewer trees and shrubs tolerate heavy clay soils than sandy soils. The icons in the plant lists will identify the best trees and shrubs for this difficult situation. Dig only when the soil is slightly moist but not wet.

(Sandier soils can be worked when they are wetter.) Turning over a shovelful of wet clay soil causes the platelike structure of the clay to compress, excluding air and further destroying what little loose structure the soil had. The result is a stickier, more anaerobic soil—conditions tough on young root hairs.

Before you dig the hole, do a test. Take a small shovelful of soil from the planting area, carefully turn it over on the surface, and gently tap the heap of soil with the back of the shovel blade. If it crumbles easily, the soil is in good condition for digging. If you must batter the soil to break it apart because it's too wet or too dry, working the soil will actually make the clay more dense and anaerobic. If your soil passes the test, switch to a long-handled spading fork with forged tines for the digging.

Clay soils promote root rot because of the dampness of the soil. Many ornamental and fruiting trees die of this disease (caused by the fungus *Phytophthora* spp.) of the upper portion of the roots, near the soil's surface, without anyone even suspecting the culprit. The fungus damages the sapwood of the tree, either killing limbs or the entire plant. Once the symptoms appear (pale yellow, wilted leaves), it's too late to do anything.

Planting in Clay Soil

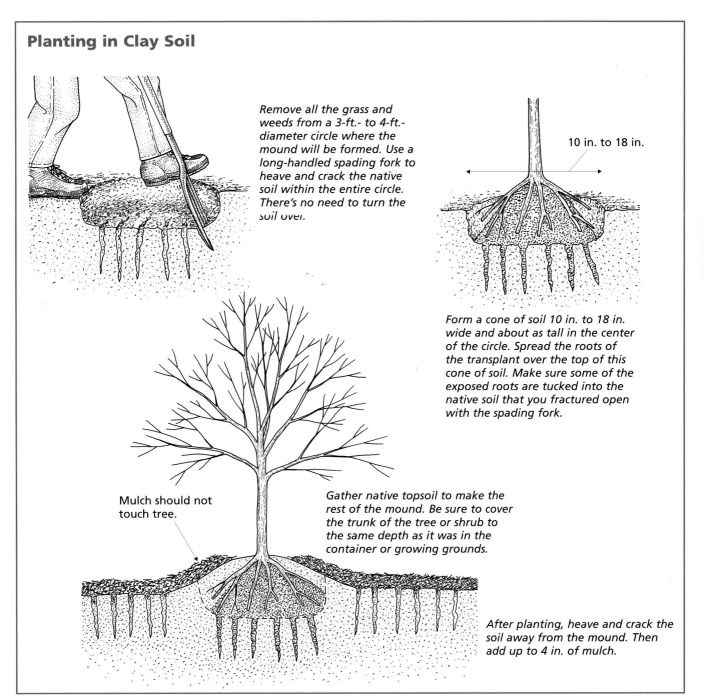

Remove all the grass and weeds from a 3-ft.- to 4-ft.- diameter circle where the mound will be formed. Use a long-handled spading fork to heave and crack the native soil within the entire circle. There's no need to turn the soil over.

10 in. to 18 in.

Form a cone of soil 10 in. to 18 in. wide and about as tall in the center of the circle. Spread the roots of the transplant over the top of this cone of soil. Make sure some of the exposed roots are tucked into the native soil that you fractured open with the spading fork.

Mulch should not touch tree.

Gather native topsoil to make the rest of the mound. Be sure to cover the trunk of the tree or shrub to the same depth as it was in the container or growing grounds.

After planting, heave and crack the soil away from the mound. Then add up to 4 in. of mulch.

Fortunately, you can work to ensure healthy plants in clay soil by planting on mounds well above the natural level of the surrounding soil. The mounds act as preventative medicine in climates where it rains during the summer, because the crown rot fungus thrives in damp and warm soil. (If you keep the mound well mulched, the bark of the trunk will also be protected from lawnmower scalping.)

When planting a tree on an 18-in.-high mound in clay soil, a true planting hole isn't even required. Instead, remove all the grass and weeds from the 3-ft. to 4-ft. diameter of the mound-to-be. Then, with a spading fork, heave and crack the native soil within the entire circle.

Planting from Tube Containers

TUBE-GROWN SEEDLINGS OF NONTAPROOTED TREES or shrubs should have a few air-pruned vertical roots and plenty of lateral roots. A mound may not be required if the soil is well drained or matched to that of the rootstock. Mounding won't hurt the plant, but it does take extra time.

With a spading fork, heave open a crack in the soil. Turn the tube upside-down and jostle or tug the seedling out. Shake off as much of the potting soil as possible. Spread or fan out the roots and place the seedling's trunk so that the soil level is the same as it was in the tube. To close the planting hole, lift the fork out, place it 4 in. to 6 in. away from the seedling and parallel to the previous insertion, and press the handle toward the seedling to compress the soil around the roots. Water thoroughly and add a ring of mulch that doesn't touch the trunk.

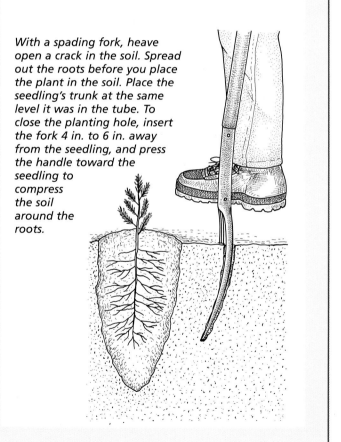

With a spading fork, heave open a crack in the soil. Spread out the roots before you place the plant in the soil. Place the seedling's trunk at the same level it was in the tube. To close the planting hole, insert the fork 4 in. to 6 in. away from the seedling, and press the handle toward the seedling to compress the soil around the roots.

Scrape up good soil from the surrounding area (after the weeds have been skimmed off) and make a small cone of soil in the center of the circle, 10 in. to 18 in. tall and wider at the bottom than the total height. (I soak bare-root trees in water while making the mound, to rehydrate the tissue and wash off anything clinging to the roots.) Then spread the roots of the tree over the top of the soil cone. (If you're planting a container-grown or tube-grown plant, make sure to tear apart any well-knit roots, knock off most of the planting mix, and spread out any circling roots on the soil cone.) Make sure some of the exposed roots are tucked into the native soil that was fractured open with the spading fork.

After the roots of the trees are spread out evenly on the cone of soil, gather plenty of topsoil to make the rest of the mound. Cover the tree's trunk to the same depth as it was in the nursery, as noted by the marked change in color on the trunk. Tamp the soil with your shoes to eliminate air pockets that can desiccate young roots. (The soil in the mound can be amended for better drainage as long as some of the tree's roots are placed in unamended soil.) Rake the finished mound to look like a gentle knoll.

After planting, soak the entire mound once or twice. Then mulch the mound and beyond about 4 in. deep,

making sure that the mulch stays at least 6 in. to 12 in. away from the trunk.

Amendments and Fertilizers

Amendments such as sand, peat moss, compost, and rice hulls have traditionally been added to planting holes to improve drainage and keep the soil loose and friable. Fertilizers, such as blood meal, cottonseed meal, greensand, and wood ashes, were added to provide nutrients. Some amendments, such as compost, also acted as mild fertilizers. The prevailing opinion was to add lots of amendments and fertilizers, especially to new plants. But now studies have shown that plantings with no amendments or fertilizers outperform those with added amendments or fertilizers. In fact, when I had a landscape business, I was amazed to observe that the trees with the most amendments were the most likely to blow over.

The loose soil of the amendments makes something like an underground swimming pool full of water when it rains hard, drowning important root hairs. Also, adding a lot of amendments at planting time leaves the roots unprepared for the shock of what lies beyond the amended area. Often, the roots fail to

make it out of the well-amended hole and merely circle around in the loose planting medium; the result is the same as a pot-bound plant in a nursery—weak plants that blow over in storms. The trees most tolerant of wind, ice, and snow are those with the widest root systems.

Sandy soil can tolerate more amendments because adding them doesn't significantly change the soil structure. However, because the fiber of the amendments absorbs plenty of water, adding a lot of amendments to drought-prone sandy soils will concentrate the roots in the moister, amended area, again leaving the tree or shrub vulnerable to weather damage.

For the most self-sufficient tree, avoid fertilizer as well—at planting time or anytime thereafter. The plant needs fertilizer only if a discoloration of leaves indicates a specific mineral or nutrient deficiency. Roots are relatively lazy, so they feed where it's easiest. Fertilizers further encourage the tree's roots to stay in the planting hole. Compost, especially in quantity, is one of the worst additions because it is both an amendment and a fertilizer. If you don't feel comfortable not fertilizing, add the material well beyond the planting hole to encourage the roots to spread into the native, unamended soils. After trying the no-amendments and

Brace Height

To tell where to place the ties, grab the trunk beneath the first branches with your left hand. Bend over the canopy of the tree with your right hand. Release the canopy, and the top will return to an upright position. Move your left hand down a few inches and bend over the canopy again. Repeat until the top of the tree stays flopped over. Place the ties 6 in. higher than the last position of your left hand, as shown by the woman's right hand in the figure on the right.

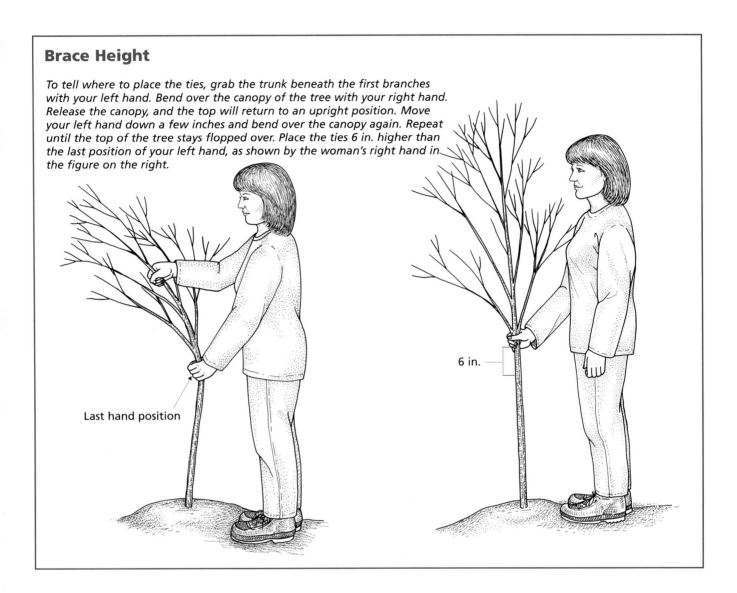

Last hand position

6 in.

no-fertilizer approach for over 10 years, with the best trees for the soil, I'm convinced it works, and gardeners should experiment to wean themselves from this extra effort and expense.

Proper Staking

You can avoid staking altogether by purchasing only trees with sturdy trunks that don't require staking. However, if a limited choice forces you to buy a spindly tree, remember that the more a tree flexes in the wind, the stronger it gets. That means you should allow the tree some flexing even when it's staked.

The stakes should be nowhere near the trunk. The best support comes from two pressure-treated pine, cedar, or redwood stakes, each 2 in. to 3 in. in diameter, placed 8 in. to 10 in. from the trunk, so that the tree doesn't hit the stake when the wind blows it, and so that the stakes don't hit too many roots when they're pounded in place. If you're planting a large B-and-B tree, you may have to drive the stakes through the root ball. In windy areas, place the stakes so that a line drawn between them is perpendicular to the direction of the strongest winds.

The lower you tie the tree, the more flexing you'll allow. Grab the trunk with your left hand near the top and bend the top over with your right hand. You'll notice that the tree is able to return to an upright position. Move your left hand down the trunk and try bending and releasing the top with your right hand. At a certain point, the top will stay flopped over and not regain its upright position. Tie the tree to the stakes at a point 6 in. higher than the last position of your left hand.

If you have poorly grown, spindly trees, whose top is disproportionately taller and wider than the root ball, you should thin them by about half to reduce the "sail effect" and allow a better proportion of roots to top.

Finally, use small-gauge (#22) 6- or 10-strand wire to run from each

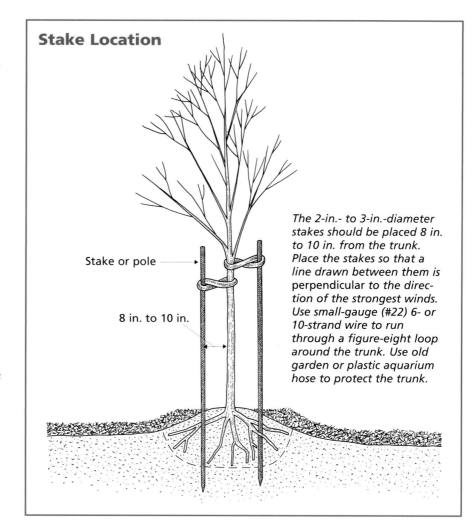

Stake Location

Stake or pole →

8 in. to 10 in.

The 2-in.- to 3-in.-diameter stakes should be placed 8 in. to 10 in. from the trunk. Place the stakes so that a line drawn between them is perpendicular to the direction of the strongest winds. Use small-gauge (#22) 6- or 10-strand wire to run through a figure-eight loop around the trunk. Use old garden or plastic aquarium hose to protect the trunk.

stake to a figure-eight loop around the trunk. The loop should pass through a piece of old garden hose to keep the wire from cutting into the trunk. The loops should be firm, but not so tight that they injure the bark. Make sure the combination of wires allows the trunk to sway 6 in. to 8 in.

Then let 'er blow! As the trunk builds diameter, take the loops off one at a time, over a period of time, so you'll know when the tree can ride the wind without support. This may take only a year or two with healthy stock, or much longer if you purchased a spindly trunked plant.

CHAPTER ELEVEN

Water & Food

❧ THE ULTIMATE GOAL OF A low-maintenance garden is to avoid the effort of watering or fertilizing altogether. In an ideal situation, this can be done, but it takes years to perfect your timing and planting techniques within the limits of your locale's seasons, microclimates, and soil variations. A more expedient approach involves some irrigation, mulch, and perhaps a little fertilization for a healthy start to the plant's roots. After a few years of gentle nurturing, natural rainfall, and your yard's inherent fertility, the tree or shrub's extensive root system can thrive without irrigation or fertilizer.

The Roots of Good Irrigation

Remember, for the sake of growth, bloom, or yields, the upper 1 ft. to

2 ft. of the soil supplies at least 50 percent (or even more) of all the nutrients *and* moisture a plant absorbs. Often, the upper 6 in. is more important than the top 12 in., which provides more fertility and moisture than the next foot down, and so on. There are places where glacially deposited topsoil extends for dozens of feet, but this is more the exception than the rule. If you have such a deep, loamy soil, then rejoice, but remember that the majority of moisture and nutrient absorption still happens in the top 2 ft. (or less) of the soil.

Consistent moisture in the upper layer of soil helps promote the best growth. Moisture in the upper few inches acts as a cap to prevent moisture losses from deeper in the soil, so the lower levels of soil never dry out. Supplement erratic rains with irrigation to keep the top few inches moist (not wet) and you'll actually keep the upper 2 ft. moist.

Good humus and moisture

In the upper layers of the soil live the highest populations of bacteria and other soil life. These valuable decomposers act as some of nature's fertilizing machines—liberating mineralized (unavailable) nutrients into a soluble form absorbed by tiny root hairs. At the same time, humus holds on to moisture containing nutrients in a soluble form.

Decomposed fallen leaves, leaf mold, mulch, compost, or any other form of organic matter gradually becomes humus. Humus itself is constantly decomposing. Excessive cultivation, bare soil, hot soils, and drought usually speed up this natural degradation of humus. To slow the process down, you can create dufflike mulch, which will constantly renew the humus.

Plants absorb their nutrients primarily in a thin soil-water solution coating the humus and/or the clay particles. The structure of humus is such that it both holds onto and releases many of the nutrients plants utilize.

The soil has minute channels collectively referred to as its pore structure. The pore structure within a crumbly soil allows water to percolate down, harmful gases to vent away, and refreshing air to permeate the soil. The humus also helps hold the pore structure open.

Cycles of dry and wet

Infrequent irrigation tends to reduce or prevent optimal growth by two mechanisms. First, when the soil is too dry, nutrient uptake is inhibited because the soil microorganisms, which solubilize the nutrients, don't thrive in a parched soil.

Second, when lots of water is supplied all at once to the dry soil, the pore structure is saturated to the point that the root hairs and air-loving soil life are stressed or killed from *too much* water. Nutrient assimilation is inhibited by the anaerobic conditions. Even after the soil has drained (via the pore structure), it takes some time for the aerobic soil bacteria to repopulate the soil. So there is a biological lag before the root hairs can "feed" again.

Watering Options

One of the oldest watering methods in the world is the watering moat. Then various forms of sprinklers appeared. The most recent development in the last 20 years is drip irrigation, which is becoming increasingly popular as a way to provide moisture between rainy periods. Regardless of the method, though, it's a good idea to increase the available water to get the tree or shrub off to a good start, then to wean the plant off the supplemental water so that it develops an extensive root system.

Moats and sprinklers

Many gardeners like to water their shrubs and trees for the first year or more. If they were transplanted from containers in the summer, some

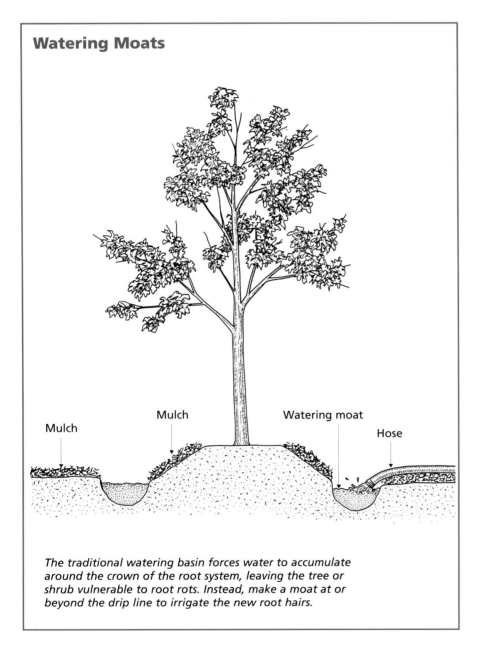

Watering Moats

Mulch

Mulch

Watering moat

Hose

The traditional watering basin forces water to accumulate around the crown of the root system, leaving the tree or shrub vulnerable to root rots. Instead, make a moat at or beyond the drip line to irrigate the new root hairs.

amount of irrigation is often required. A simple way to irrigate a newly planted shrub or tree is to dig a shallow basin around the trunk and fill it occasionally with water. You can use a garden hose or a bucket of water to fill the shallow trench. Often these basins lead to damage or death due to the *Phytophthora* fungus. Also, although the roots want to grow well beyond the drip line, a water basin near the trunk keeps the roots localized to that area, which is a good reason not to use this technique.

Instead, modify the basin by making a watering moat located at or beyond the drip line of the tree. Keeping the wet soil away from the trunk will encourage the roots to grow out into new soil. This method is appropriate for individual trees and shrubs scattered far apart in the yard, or when you plan to water for just 1 or 2 years to help a tree or shrub get established before it becomes self-reliant.

Sprinklers are another option. But both sprinklers and watering moats, with their high flow rates, are more likely to flood the soil's pore structure, overwhelming its ability to drain surplus water. This causes drowning of root hairs and the soil's flora. The heavy application of water by a sprinkler or moat also means that much of the water is pulled by gravity into the deeper, anaerobic soil depths—away from the root hairs that could benefit from moisture.

To solve this problem, allow your sprinklers to cycle off periodically instead of being on continuously. This allows the pore structure of the soil to drain and become aerobic. The intervals for the on-and-off cycles have to be determined by careful observation and much testing. Soil type and climate have a dramatic impact on the duration of each cycle. Poke around in the soil as you experiment with this healthy option to continuous irrigation. For moats, use less water with each application, perhaps some each day.

Drip irrigation

Instead of flooding the trees or shrubs with moats or sprinklers, try drip irrigation when it becomes necessary to water trees and shrubs. Drip irrigation is a gentler technique, and it avoids the hassle of turning the sprinkler on and off, lugging buckets of water, or dragging snarls of hose to each plant.

Drip irrigation uses small devices called emitters to dribble droplets of water into the soil. It is not unlike the old-fashioned, flat garden soaker hose with hundreds of tiny little holes that emitted a small arc of water if facing up. The difference is the tiny holes of

the soaker hose more easily clog, especially with well water. Also, the flow rate from the beginning to the end of the line is less regular than with most emitters.

Compared to sprinklers and moats, drip emitters minimize waterlogging. The secret is that drip emitters form a moist spot beneath the soil's surface without flooding much of the soil's pore space. As the drops of water fall onto the soil, capillary action helps wick some of the moisture sideways to keep the soil moist but not overly wet. Drip irrigation gives the gardener the most

Moisture Zones

Laterals

Irrigate with parallel lines of in-line tubing (called "laterals") with spacings between the lines equal to the distance of the emitters along the tubing. The moist spots blend together some 2 in. to 6 in. below the surface to irrigate the entire root zone.

Shaded areas indicate zone of continuous moisture.

control over how slowly and with what frequency the soil is irrigated.

A drip system results in a water savings of at least 15 percent compared to even the most perfectly tuned sprinkler system, because no water is lost to the wind, evaporation from puddling, or runoff. When compared to the more conventional, poorly adjusted sprinkler system, water savings may reach 50 percent. Because some emitters are designed to have pressure-compensating action, the water comes out of each emitter at the same rate over the entire area of a steep slope— something no sprinkler can do.

Drip systems can greatly reduce mildew and fungal diseases in many climates, as long as the natural climate is not too humid or damp.

Drip irrigation is much more than a last-ditch strategy for a drought-parched landscape. It's a way to help *all* gardens prosper, and that includes trees and shrubs, whether planted in borders, hedges, or as specimens in mulched islands in the lawn. Gardens with well-designed drip systems display plentiful foliage growth; a tangible increase in bloom; and a marked reduction in diseases such as mildew, crown rot, and rust.

Where rains fall intermittently during the summer, drip irrigation is used to maintain ideal moisture levels so small amounts of stress from short-

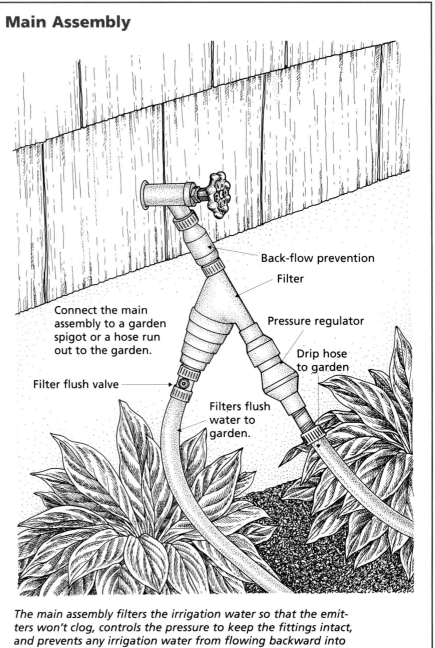

Main Assembly

Connect the main assembly to a garden spigot or a hose run out to the garden.

Back-flow prevention

Filter

Pressure regulator

Drip hose to garden

Filter flush valve

Filters flush water to garden.

The main assembly filters the irrigation water so that the emitters won't clog, controls the pressure to keep the fittings intact, and prevents any irrigation water from flowing backward into the drinking water supply.

term droughts are avoided. Drip irrigation hardware can foster better plant growth than any other irrigation technology, with increases in plant productivity—whether that be in yield or beauty.

Drip irrigation systems are best suited to those plantings of trees and shrubs requiring ongoing irrigation, such as a dense privacy hedge or screen or any plant you want to grow with a bit more vigor than what the rains will provide for. Yet drip systems are also very adaptable. Newer fittings allow you to actually take apart any length of drip hose and reconfigure it for a newer planting. Thus, a few circles or spirals of drip tubing with emitters can be "recycled" through the yard for a year or two on each new plant or planting.

Drip system basics All drip systems begin with a main assembly attached to a hose faucet or spigot. This assembly has an antisiphon device to keep any dirt that sneaks into the irrigation system from flowing backwards into the drinking water pipes in the home. A filter screens out any small amounts of rust, dirt, or debris that might clog the emitters (the actual watering devices) over time. (A Y-filter is a good device: It has a valve that allows you to flush dirt off the screen without having to take the filter apart.)

The simple fittings of a drip system for the yard don't require wrenches or glues, but they can't withstand pressure over 25 lb. per sq. in. (psi). The final element on the main assembly is a pressure regulator, which keeps the pressure at or below 25 psi. The pressure regulator must come after the filter so that the higher pressure of the home's water supply can be used to flush the filter's screen. Then the water leaves the main assembly and enters the tubing, which distributes the water to each emitter in the landscape. Emitters are usually rated at a flow of ½ to 1 gallon per hour (gph).

The out-dated approach to drip irrigation placed just one or two emitters near the base of each plant's stem or trunk, not at regular intervals. This may conserve water, but moistening such a small portion of the soil confines the natural shape of the root system. Often, emitters were punched into a solid ½-in.-diameter tubing that snaked through the landscape. Such emitters, and the small ¼-in. "spaghetti" tubing often used with them, regularly snapped off the ½-in. tubing, or the "spaghetti" got tangled up in a frightful mess.

A revolution in drip irrigation technology makes it easier to install a drip system and promotes superior plant growth. Emitters in the new ½-in. tubing occur at regular intervals (you can buy it with 12-in., 18-in., or

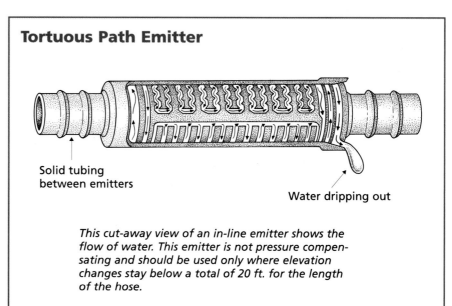

Tortuous Path Emitter

Solid tubing between emitters

Water dripping out

This cut-away view of an in-line emitter shows the flow of water. This emitter is not pressure compensating and should be used only where elevation changes stay below a total of 20 ft. for the length of the hose.

24-in. intervals). This change means there are no protruding punched-in emitters or "spaghetti" tubes to crack off. The emitters come in the same ½- or 1-gph flow rates.

New in-line emitters have a long tortuous path (also called a complex maze) that is more self-cleaning that many older emitters. A cut-away view (see p. 147) of the emitter reveals that the complex path makes the water turn many times. Each angular turn creates a small sideways tornado; the swirling keeps and dirt and sediment suspended and helps prevents clogging. To further prevent clogging, newer in-line emitters have much bigger openings for the water to drip through than some of the older emitters.

Putting it together To install a drip irrigation system, you first need to know which spacing between emitters best matches your soil. Start with a small test. Punch one old-fashioned, 1-gph emitter into the bottom corner of a plastic 1-gallon milk jug. Set the jug on some dry soil until the water runs out. Dig a trench along side the emitter to see how wide the moist spot is; the width determines the spacing of the emitters in the in-line tubing.

With very sandy soils, you'll most certainly want to only use emitters 12 in. apart. Some clayey soils spread

the moist spot so wide that the emitters can be 24 in. apart.

For the best root system, irrigate the entire planting area—and well beyond the drip line—with many properly spaced emitters. The in-line

tubing makes the installation easy. Here are the steps to follow:

1. *Run a solid ½-in. drip hose from the main assembly to the edge of the planting area. Run a section of in-line emitter tubing along the surface*

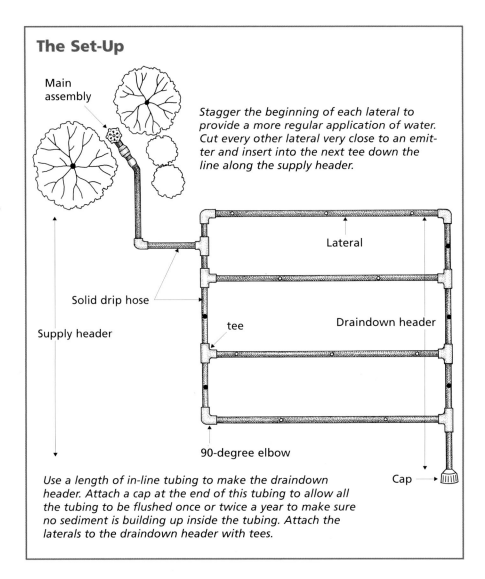

The Set-Up

Main assembly

Stagger the beginning of each lateral to provide a more regular application of water. Cut every other lateral very close to an emitter and insert into the next tee down the line along the supply header.

Solid drip hose

Lateral

Supply header

tee

Draindown header

90-degree elbow

Cap

Use a length of in-line tubing to make the draindown header. Attach a cap at the end of this tubing to allow all the tubing to be flushed once or twice a year to make sure no sediment is building up inside the tubing. Attach the laterals to the draindown header with tees.

Location around a Trunk

Make sure the emitters don't sit on top of a plant's root crown and cause rot. Snake the tubing around the base of existing plants—24 in. or more from the trunks of established shrubs and trees, 12 in. to 24 in. from new plantings, depending on your soil.

Supply header

Drip line

24 in.

Wet spot on surface

of the soil down one side of the area, because roots will soon grow into this area to utilize the moisture. This is called the supply header and it's attached to the drip hose.

2. Now place tubing on top of the soil over the entire area of the root zone you are going to plant (or have already planted). Lay the in-line tubing in parallel lines (called laterals) with spacing between the

lines equal to the distance of the emitters along the tubing. (You can use landscape pins to hold the tubing down before it's covered with mulch.)

3. Stagger the beginning of every other row of lateral tubing to provide a more regular application of water to the soil beneath the emitters. Attach each lateral to the supply header with a fitting called a tee. To attach the first lateral, cut halfway between two emitters on the supply header and insert the tubing into the first tee. Every other lateral should be cut very close to an emitter and inserted into the next tee down the line in the header.

4. On the opposite end of the root zone area from the supply header, attach a length of in-line tubing called the draindown header. Add a cap to the end of this tubing. Unscrew the cap once or twice a year to flush the tubing to make sure no sediment is building up inside. The laterals are attached to the draindown header with tees.

5. You don't want the emitters to sit on top of a plant's root crown and cause rot. So don't run the laterals rigidly parallel; instead, snake the tubing around the base of each plant. Place the emitters at least 12 in. to 24 in. from the trunks of shrubs and trees, depending on your soil type.

How much water

No matter what gizmos you choose for irrigating, you'll need to know how much water to apply. There are complicated ways to calculate the number of gallons. Yet the simple answer may be found by asking your neighbors, the cooperative extension office, or the Master Gardeners. When I asked local gardeners who had lived nearby for 50 or so years what a new fruit tree needed during dry California summers north of San Francisco, they replied "about 15 gallons per week." The cooperative extension office also recommended 10 to 15 gallons per week, depending on the month—not much of a discrepancy.

However, to get a tree or shrub off to a good start, you can apply much more water for the first few years and then wean the trees off irrigation. I've routinely watered three times more than the suggested weekly total (45 gallons for new fruit trees) for the first two or more years.

I prefer to water frequently (I think of it as topping off the tank of the soil). The goal is to replace each day approximately the amount of moisture lost due to evaporation from the soil and transpiration from the plant's leaves. In my previous example, I'd divide the 45 gallons by 7 to find out the daily rate (about 6 to 7 gallons per day). My trees establish a good root system because the source of the water is well beyond the drip line. As the irrigation is slowly

Spotting Nutrient Deficiencies

 TREES AND SHRUBS PROPERLY CHOSEN for the soil in which they are to be planted rarely experience a nutrient deficiency. But sometimes trees and shrubs have a little trouble getting started, or they hit a bad season. Instead of fertilizing automatically, wait until the plant gives you a signal that something is awry. Always look for unusual coloration in leaves—it's an excellent way to deduce nutrient problems.

Leaf symptoms are even more accurate than soil samples. The soil may have plenty of a particular nutrient, but numerous conditions—from cold soil to the wrong pH, compaction, or low amounts of humus—may prevent the uptake of the nutrient by roots. If a number of leaves have become yellow or purplish, or they exhibit some other discoloration, take samples to the local nursery, cooperative extension office, or a Master Gardener for diagnosis.

The visual symptoms of iron and nitrogen deficiency are similar: The leaves on the shrub or tree turn pale to bright yellow. On a plant with nitrogen deficiency, the entire leaf, including its veins, turns yellow and may turn brown and fall off the limb.

On a plant with iron deficiency (called chlorosis), the leaves are yellowish green except for the veins, which remain green. Trees and shrubs that exhibit iron chlorosis are forms of citrus (*Citrus* spp.), river birch (*Betula nigra*), liquidambar (*Liquidambar styraciflua*), pin oak (*Quercus palustris*), and rhododendrons and azaleas (*Rhododendron* spp.).

Abnormally yellow leaves are a good indicator that a carefully

withdrawn over several years, the extensive root system is in place to pick up the task of finding its own water supply.

Mulch for Health

Reduced weeding is often touted as an important benefit of drip irrigation, but the effect pertains only to arid climates. The dry surface between the emitter's wet spots discourages weeds because dormant seeds don't have enough moisture to germinate. But any periodic summer rain will negate that effect.

Mulch, which is routinely used to hide a drip irrigation system, can be used to suppress any weed seeds that might germinate, and to conserve water at the same time. But don't pile mulch up against the trunk of any shrub or tree, or it will promote root rots, and it may provide places for bark-eating mice to hide in the winter. Use no more than 4 in. of a purchased, loose mulch (such as hay, wood chips, or shredded bark); anything more gives diminishing returns when the water conserved is compared to the cost of the material.

Mulch far away from the trunk of the tree, especially if you have limited amounts of mulch. The mulch around existing trees needn't be very close at all to conserve moisture. A study of a 10-year-old apple tree done in England with radioactive phosphorous isotopes found that the

staged approach to treating visible leaf deficiencies is needed. The symptoms may show most during the colder times of the year. If the yellowing continues once the soil warms, it's time to take action. First, you can try a foliar spray, often called a feeding spray, which will provide quick but temporary results. Spray the foliage with iron chelate, iron sulfate, or soluble organic iron, carefully following the directions on the package. Spray after the soil is warm, at intervals of 2 to 4 weeks, until the foliage turns green.

Unfortunately, this "cure" lasts only as long as you go on spraying, so you need to attack the underlying problems. Begin by improving the soil with the addition of organic materials such as leaf mulch or well-aged compost, at and beyond the drip line. Make sure there is decent drainage.

The most frequent cause of iron deficiency is an alkaline soil. If the pH isn't acid enough, ideally between 5.0 and 6.5 (7.0 is neutral), the root hairs can't absorb iron. Blueberries, azaleas, and rhododendrons prefer a pH as low as 4.5. Test your soil's pH at a local nursery or cooperative extension office.

To increase the soil's acidity, add powdered, pure "garden" sulfur, aluminum sulfate, iron sulfate, or chelated iron materials. Spread on the soil surface—well beyond the drip line of the canopy—at the recommended rate based on your soil test, and soak it into the soil with irrigation if there isn't enough rainfall. You will see faster results if the chemicals are tilled into the soil—but don't cultivate so deep that you damage larger roots.

first 4½-ft. radius from the trunk accounted for less than 10 percent of the absorbed water and nutrients. In fact, the best use of mulch is from the drip line out, not under the foliage, as there is a higher percentage of feeding roots beyond the canopy. This isn't always practical, but it is a good goal to aim for.

Fertilizing

To avoid additional fertilizer, choose your rootstock carefully. Most of the time (with the exception of when nutrient deficiencies appear), you will not need any additions. If the forest can do it, so can the home gardener. The forest has many ways to feed itself and promote vigor and new growth:

- *Nitrogen-fixing plants grab nitrogen gas from the air and make it available to nutrient cycles in the soil.*
- *Leaves drop to be recycled into loamy forest topsoil.*
- *Worms and millions of other critters digest and circulate decomposing organic matter and minerals and improve the pore structure of the soil.*
- *Entire trees fall and act as long-term "bank accounts" of slow-release nutrients.*

- *Animals, insects, and caterpillars browse on foliage and deposit their droppings.*
- *Even the sugars in the clear excrement of aphids help stimulate the growth of microorganisms in the soil below.*

One of the most important dynamics of tree growth often goes unnoticed by gardeners. There are beneficial fungi called vesicular-arbuscular mycorrhizae (or VAM) that colonize the roots of trees, promote tree growth, and literally link many of the forest's trees together in one big living tapestry. They live just below the surface of the leaf mold (in the decomposing duff) and in the topmost inches of soil.

The microscopic filaments (also called the mycelium) formed by the VAM either grow into the cells of the tree's root hairs or extend the root hairs. The mycelium forms a symbiotic (nonparasitic) relationship with the plants—a mycorrhizal association. The VAM provide trees and shrubs with phosphorous, as well as with some copper, potash, and zinc. In return, they receive carbohydrates. *Boletus* spp., *Amanita* spp., *Lactarius* spp., and some types of puffball mushrooms are indicators of VAM activity.

Undisturbed soils naturally have plenty of VAM. But removal of natural topsoil down to subsoil to build a house, any form of cultivation, elimination of the duff around and beneath trees, any form of compaction (even a gardener's feet), or too much phosphorous and nitrogen fertilizer injures or destroys the VAM. Of course, bags of sterile soil mixes lack these helpful fungi. Adding VAM to sterile potting soil can be impressive: Jack pine (*Pinus banksiana*) seedlings increased their weight by 28 times, and citrus trees (*Citrus* spp.) in containers grew 1600 percent larger in one study.

The solutions for the yard are fairly simple: Keep vegetable gardens and flower beds far from trees to leave the VAM undisturbed. To help prevent compaction due to frequent foot traffic, use as many permanent pathways as possible, and locate them far away from trees. Place deep mulches where you occasionally walk. Always renew the layer of duff.

If you must purchase topsoil for your garden and you want to guarantee the presence of VAM, you can purchase some of the new VAM inoculates available (see Resources on pp. 180-181). Or, just scoop up some duff from under a tree where you've spotted VAM mush-rooms and sprinkle it on the topsoil.

CHAPTER TWELVE

Pruning Trees & Shrubs

PRUNING IS MUCH LIKE GETTING A HAIRCUT—no pain is felt, and the trimming helps improve the overall presentation. Pruning may not be required for a well-shaped plant carefully selected at the nursery, but some shaping of a hedge, shrub, or tree can help direct the major structure of the trunk and main limbs early in its life. Judicious pruning helps form a sturdier and healthier plant for its entire life. Moderate pruning throughout the plant's life may actually promote more dramatic blooming and fruiting. Hedges and some living screens require ongoing

153

periodic pruning to maintain density and form.

However, severe pruning of a tree or shrub can ultimately harm the plant if rot proceeds from the pruning cuts into the core of the tree to destroy its heartwood, which acts as a ballast for strength and normally helps defend the tree from rot. The key to healthy pruning in a young tree or shrub, or restorative pruning of a mature plant, is making each cut properly.

The Anatomy of a Proper Cut

In the forest, nature doesn't often make nice clean cuts in just the right places. Storms snap branches at bad places, even splintering the wood. However, woody plants have special plant tissues that protect the heartwood from rot-specific zones of rot-resistant tissues or cells. Any rot that tries to enter the plant can be effectively cordoned off by these special cells—a process called compartmentalization.

The goal of pruning is to remove unwanted growth without causing rot inside the attached shoot, branch, or limb. This does not mean cutting flush against the trunk. A flush cut exposes a portion of the protective layer of heartwood, increasing the chances of disease entering the heartwood.

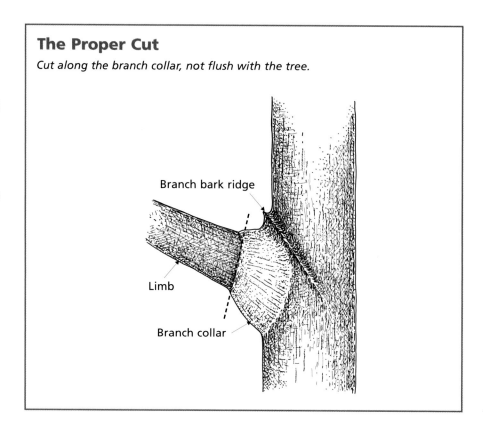

The Proper Cut

Cut along the branch collar, not flush with the tree.

Branch bark ridge

Limb

Branch collar

Prudent pruning requires you to identify two parts of the attachment you're cutting: the branch collar and the branch bark ridge. The slightly swollen, shoulder-shaped lump where each shoot, branch, or limb is attached is the branch collar. In the forest, after the branch or limb has fallen off, the branch collar becomes covered with a callus—made of cells from the cambium (the layer that also produces the cells for the sapwood) to heal a pruning cut or wound.

The branch bark ridge is usually identified by a dark, diagonal ridge of tissue that originates from the crotch formed between the two attached parts. A healthy branch bark ridge often has a slight outward puckering.

Prune any size stem, branch, or limb along the line of the outside edge of the branch collar, leaving the protective zone of cells intact. When a shoot is small, the proper cut will look, at first glance, like a flush cut because the branch collar is so small. Older limbs have more noticeable branch collars. Furthermore, the size of the collar varies from tree to tree: Some majestic, old oaks have branch collars protruding 12 in. to 18 in. from the trunk.

Some trees or shrubs don't have a noticeable branch collar, but they still have the same zone of protective cells within the heartwood. This zone of root compartmentalization must remain intact to protect the core of the plant. Don't guess about where to cut and don't merely leave a long stubby piece of the shoot, lateral, or branch. The stub can be colonized by diseases and fungi, which may subsequently enter the heart of the branch or trunk. Instead, use the branch bark ridge to determine the best angle for the cut.

When a branch or limb is too large to cut with a pruning lopper, special steps should be taken to protect the tree or shrub while pruning. Use a hand-held pruning saw for larger-diameter wood. Cut halfway through the underside of the limb about 12 in. or so past the branch collar. Then, 6 in. or so beyond this first cut, cut through the entire limb. If any bark begins to strip back toward the trunk, the first cut will stop the damage. Finally, cut the remaining 12 in. or so off at the line defined by the branch bark collar.

If the pruning job calls for something bigger than a hand-held

Cutting along the Branch Bark Ridge

Imagine a line traced over the branch bark ridge from point A to point C, and an imaginary plumb (vertical) line from point A to point B. Note the angle from C to A to B. This angle should approximately equal the angle from B to A to D, where the line between A and D indicate the cut you should make.

Equal angles

Cut here.

Branch bark ridge

Imaginary plumb line

C   B   D

A

pruning saw, you should consider the services of a professional arborist. Using a chainsaw is dangerous enough on the ground but *very* risky up in a tree. Look in the telephone directory under tree service. Call only arborists that display their certification symbol and number from the International Society of Arboriculture (an ISA symbol in many ads) or its regional chapter.

Contact a number of arborists to get referrals and estimates.

When the cut is made correctly, nature takes over to slowly form a healthy callus to seal over the wound. Pruning paints and tars are a waste of time and money, and they can do nothing to rectify bad cuts made flush to the trunk or in any other improper fashion.

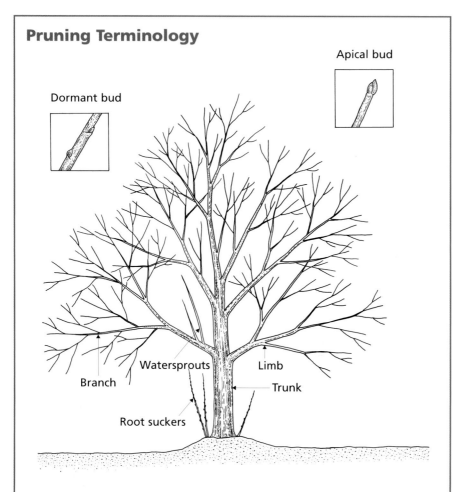

Pruning Terminology

Dormant bud

Apical bud

Branch

Watersprouts

Limb

Trunk

Root suckers

Many horticulturists define a shoot or lateral as unbranched growth 1 year old. A branch is growth that is 2 to 4 years old and branched. A limb is older than 4 years, it is well branched, and it often remains for the life of the tree. The trunk forms the bulk of the core of the tree and contains heartwood—often a different color from that of the active layers of sapwood (used for food and water transport) just under the bark.

How Pruning Works

The bud at the tip of each shoot is called the apical bud. It produces two important hormones that control shoot, branch, and limb growth. One chemical encourages the shoot to grow vertically. The first or highest apical bud to begin growing usually grows faster, more vertically, and taller than the next lower bud. The tallest apical bud on a tree usually grows more vertically and faster than any other apical bud on the tree. The apical buds below the highest buds compete for growth based on their relative position to every other bud on the tree. The lowest or most horizontal apical buds put on the least amount of new growth and have less vertical height.

The apical, or tip, bud on top of a vertical shoot that is becoming the main trunk of the tree is called the leader, the central leader, or an excurrent tree. If more than one apical bud shares the rounded top of a tree with more than one main trunk tip, it's called a decurrent tree. A decurrent tree has many nearly vertical shoots sharing the top position on the tree, called codominant (shared) apical buds.

The second hormone generated by the apical bud travels down the shoot to stifle much of the competition from buds and shoots below. This phenomenon is called apical dominance. During the summer, you can find a tiny bud between the base of each leaf's stem and the shoot. This immature bud is called a dormant bud because it hasn't become either a shoot or a flower bud. Apical dominance suppresses the growth of dormant buds into side shoots, which don't appear often on tall vertical shoots.

Pruning Cuts

Before you prune, you need to know about the two main pruning cuts—thinning and heading cuts. Shearing cuts, a third type, are almost a combination of the first two, used to maintain the form of trees and shrubs.

Thinning cuts are meant to reduce the amount of wood, foliage, and fruiting area. Heading cuts are designed to stimulate more side shoots to provide more places for fruiting or flowering, or a denser foliage. The natural progression is to use heading cuts when a tree or shrub is young to fashion its main branching pattern and to fill in the form. Thinning cuts are reserved to remove unwanted wood from trees or shrubs of any age, and to control crowded and vertical growth on older trees.

Thinning cuts

Thinning cuts are used to reduce the height of a tree and control its growth. They are used to remove

Pruning Cuts

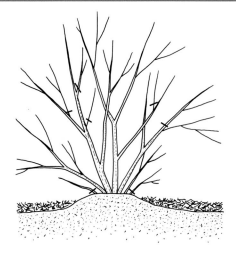

THINNING
Cutting to the base of a season's growth is a thinning cut. Such cuts are often used to remove unwanted shoots, branches, or limbs.

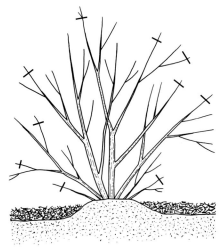

HEADING
A heading cut removes wood back to a dormant bud or to a side shoot during winter or early spring pruning. Such cuts often force lower dormant buds to sprout.

unwanted growth by cutting it to its base, where it originated as a shoot, branch, or limb. They are also used to open up the canopy to more sunlight (for better-colored and better-flavored fruit) and better air circulation (to mitigate diseases).

Thinning cuts are made anywhere throughout the canopy where these benefits are desired.

When restoring abandoned trees or shrubs, cutting undesired branches to their bases can thin out older growth. A cluster of noticeable wrinkles and a change in bark color or texture identify the start of each year's growth. It is often possible to locate the beginning of each season's growth for four or more years by locating these rings of wrinkles. However, the more you thin older growth back to its original starting point, the more likely you are to stimulate unwanted shoots elsewhere in the tree or shrub. The restoration process must be done gradually over a number of years to prevent an imbalance of unwanted new growth.

Heading cuts

Unlike a thinning cut, a heading cut is the *partial* removal of the previous year's shoot, either to a dormant bud or to a smaller branching shoot. Heading cuts allow the gardener to stimulate new shoots where they are needed along the previous season's growth—or even older growth.

Heading cuts also involve removing the apical bud, which is the most reliable way to force laterals where you want them. The chemical signal made by the apical buds— which normally keeps the dormant buds on the branch from sprouting into shoots—is no longer available to suppress lower buds from sprouting into shoot growth. The lack of apical dominance combines with the "extra" stored food energy, and the plant makes two, three, five, or more

shoots. The number of shoots depends on the vitality of each plant. A strong, vigorous tree or shrub may make five or six new shoots below each cut, while a poorly growing plant may produce only two shoots. Practice will help you anticipate each plant's vigor and how many shoots to expect after each cut.

Usually, the dormant bud just below the heading cut is the first to grow. This bud grows taller and faster than any other bud below it—apical dominance at work again. The more severely you prune back a branch while it's dormant, the more new shoots you're likely to stimulate. Thus, a tree or shrub that has been severely pruned in early spring, especially across the top of its crown, often produces a riot of vertical growth.

The goal of most heading cuts is to help fill up open spots or voids in the tree's crown with new growth. If one portion of your tree or shrub is lacking a well-branched structure, heading back existing growth will help force more side shoots. (Heading cuts don't involve the branch collar, since they are cuts made to an existing side shoot or dormant bud.)

Shearing cuts

Hedge shearing involves pruning the shrub or tree to a particular shape. When you shear a hedge, you are actually using both thinning and head-

ing cuts. As you use the hedge shears, you will randomly cut some of last season's or the current season's growth back to its base—a thinning cut.

But since you are pruning for the shape of the hedge, very few of the cuts will be true thinning cuts. Instead, most cuts will be along the length of the shoots, between dormant buds—that is, heading cuts. Thus, when a hedge is sheared, a number of the dormant buds below each cut will sprout to make the foliage bushier and denser. Remember to shape the hedge so that the sunlight easily reaches the lower foliage—the top should be at least slightly narrower than the bottom (see the drawing on the facing page).

When to Cut

There are two primary seasons of pruning. Dormant-season pruning begins before spring growth commences and while deciduous trees are leafless. Pruning during the growing season, or summer pruning, occurs when deciduous trees are in leaf and evergreens are making new growth. Dormant-season pruning encourages new growth and promotes fuller foliage. Summer pruning slightly reduces the tree's vigor and is good for removing unwanted growth.

In general, the more you prune a tree throughout these two seasons, the

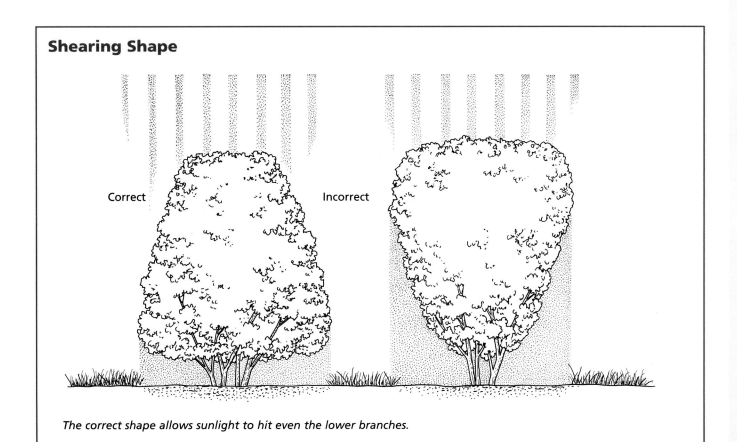

Shearing Shape

Correct

Incorrect

The correct shape allows sunlight to hit even the lower branches.

more control you can have on so-called watersprouts (tall, vertical shoots with strong apical dominance), wayward limbs or branches, and overly vigorous growth. Hedges can be sheared on an as-needed basis in the summer to constrain wayward or vigorous growth. (If the leaves are large, use hand shears to avoid partially cut and disfigured foliage. Otherwise, use hedge shears to shape hedges.)

Thinning cuts in the winter

The dormant season is not the most opportune time to use thinning cuts, because it encourages rapid vertical growth early in the summer that can overpower the normal growth of the tree or shrub and encourage so-called watersprouts (not due only to extra water).

After a limb or branch is thinned out, the apical and dormant buds left nearby on other shoots, limbs, or branches will begin to grow with more or less vigor (depending on their position above the ground or to surrounding buds). These new shoots grow because the former apical bud is gone and can no longer assert its chemical control. Each new shoot has an apical bud, so the race is on to see which one grows the tallest and becomes the dominant apical bud.

Furthermore, the accumulated food energy from the previous summer, which has been stored in the lower portions of the tree over the winter, returns to the upper portion of the tree each spring. This food energy is redistributed to the remaining dormant buds, which are now beginning to grow because there is less apical dominance. At the same time, many dormant buds have sprouted. The effect is that thinning cuts made when the tree is dormant generate a thicket of new shoots. Any unwanted sprouts can be prevented if you rub young shoots out with your fingers as soon as you spot them. The wiser approach is to make thinning cuts in the late summer.

Heading cuts in the winter and early spring

Heading cuts can be made at any time of the year but are often most appropriate for the dormant pruning season. Below each cut, a number of dormant buds are stimulated to form side shoots, which grow to fill in spaces in the canopy. Heading back single branches on a young fruiting or ornamental flowering tree produces side shoots that provide more places in the canopy for flower and fruit formation. Heading cuts in the spring, after the deciduous trees have leafed out, have much the same effect as cuts made in the dormant season.

Dormant-season pruning of deciduous hedges—and in mild winter climates, evergreen hedges—is a perfect example of a good use of heading cuts. With these cuts, many more shoots sprout and the hedge is fuller and denser. Evergreen plants also benefit from early spring heading cuts by producing more luxurious growth.

Summer pruning

Fortunately, there is a very effective way to minimize the excessive vegetative growth stimulated by winter pruning—summer pruning. Contrary to the assumptions of many gardeners, summer pruning will *not* cause trees and shrubs to "bleed" to death. While some trees and shrubs will ooze some sap after a summer clipping, the healing callus begins to form quickly to seal the wound. In fact, cuts made during the early spring are left exposed to water, pests, and disease longer because the tree isn't making callus tissue while it's dormant.

The nineteenth century European tradition was to control the size of trees, especially espaliered trees, by pruning *only* in summer, but this doesn't stand up to modern research. However, summer pruning is *part* of the solution, simply because a single dormant pruning won't *shape* the tree or shrub. If a tree or shrub is not very vigorous and somewhat small to begin with, then one pruning a year in the summer might be enough to limit its height or vigor. When trying to restrain a tree or shrub with abundant growth, pruning is best done several times in the late spring and throughout the summer. Some pruning all season long is best for controlling overgrown trees and shrubs.

Summer pruning offers gardeners many advantages:

- *It's easier to spot diseased, damaged, or dead growth when the plant is in full leaf.*
- *It helps control unwanted suckers coming from the rootstock (be sure to remove them from where they originate on the roots).*
- *You can remove tall, spindly vegetative shoots, called watersprouts.*
- *By spreading the pruning work over more time, it more easily fits into your busy schedule.*
- *You can enjoy a prolific bloom—with mid-summer blooming plants—and then control the size of the tree or shrub.*
- *You can see how your pruning affects sun and shadow patterns.*
- *Summer pruning affects the balance of nitrogen and reduces the suppleness of the plant's growth. The result is that new growth is more resistant to some diseases.*
- *Perhaps the best reason is that you can wait to prune on a warm, sunny day in comfortable summer clothing.*

Summer pruning is done when you want to limit the plant's shoots and foliage, *not* when you want to awaken new shoots or laterals. Thinning cuts slightly control rampant, out-of-control growth best when done during the growing season. These cuts can be made from spring through early fall, depending on the climate. Waiting until later in the summer to use thinning cuts usually means more control over unwanted growth from each cut.

Pruning in May has almost none of the advantages of summer pruning and acts like dormant pruning by forcing more buds to sprout. June pruning may *feel* more like summer in some parts of the country, but pruning in June can also cause excessive growth. On the other hand, if you prune too late in the summer, any succulent, new growth is vulnerable to early hard frosts and winter's deep freezes.

For the best effect from only one round of summer pruning, wait until growth has naturally slowed down due to the weather and reduced water, in August or September (depending on where you live). Summer pruning can be done one or more times after the flush of spring growth. The timing will change from year to year depending on the temperature and rainfall of the season.

Using heading cuts in the late summer to stimulate growth is likely to be less effective, as growth may have slowed down—especially in the arid West. Yet, late summer rains in much of the country can cause heading cuts to produce some side shoots. Pruning too late in the summer or in the fall leaves the new tender shoots vulnerable to freeze damage. Where winters come early in the fall and are frigid, don't use heading cuts after August, to give the new shoots time to toughen up.

Pruning and Plant Diseases

A program of summer pruning can help avoid some dreaded diseases. Bacterial gummosis (caused by *Pseudomonas syringae*) attacks lilac bushes, mulberry trees, olive trees, and stone fruit trees. Bacterial canker (*Pseudomonas mors-prunorum*) infects citrus trees, lilac shrubs, pear trees, stone fruit trees, many woody plants, and sometimes apple trees. These two common diseases can enter via pruning cuts, especially those made in late winter through early summer while it's raining.

Cytospora spp. canker disease (perennial canker) enters pruning cuts made in late winter on almond, apple, cherry, nectarine, peach, pear, plum, poplar, maple, spruce, and willow trees. It's much safer to prune these trees in the summer where this disease is known to be a problem. Cut back to clean, healthy wood. This is often 12 in. to 18 in. below the point of visible damage. If you spot discolored wood in the cross section of your cut, the prudent approach is to cut farther down on the shoot, branch, or limb. Be sure to disinfect the clipper's blade after each cut with a 10 percent solution of chlorine bleach, with isopropyl (rubbing) alcohol, or with Lysol brand disinfectant.

Powdery mildew infects apple, pear, plum, and prune trees, and rose bushes. Where this disease is a problem, avoid spring pruning altogether. Summer pruning is more effective for avoiding this disease because it doesn't force succulent growth. (Still, fungicides are usually more effective than selective pruning.)

Cherry trees are prone to bacterial blight. Spraying with copper sulfate before bloom each spring and then pruning after the harvesting helps to control this disease.

Some diseases, such as the fungus *Anthracnose* spp., which causes cankers, begin during the first rains of fall in the West and may be spread by late summer pruning. Check with your local nurseries, the cooperative extension service, the Master Gardener program, or an arborist for other diseases specific to your area.

CHAPTER THIRTEEN

Curbing Pests
& Diseases

SOMETIMES CONTROLLING PESTS and diseases feels like waging a war. Both begin by identifying the enemy, accumulating as much information as possible about the enemy, and anticipating and attempting to prevent conflicts. When the problem escalates, an attack is launched with the lowest-cost and least-harmful ammunition, and an attempt is made to avoid unnecessary damage. Back-up plans are in place for gradually escalating the attack, if required. And the key is to know when to stop fighting.

There are, of course, some specific ways this war translates into steps for pest and disease control. First, identify the pests and diseases that are common to your locality, and try to plant varieties that might avoid the anticipated problem(s).

If there is already an infestation, determine how big it is and learn about the life cycle of the pest or disease before taking action. When action can no longer be avoided, launch your attack with the least toxic strategy or substance, and use more toxic compounds only if absolutely necessary. Try to avoid damaging the myriad good insects, molds, fungi, and other life-sustaining organisms surrounding the plants under attack. And stop the treatment as soon as you notice it's been effective.

This approach to pest and disease management—known as integrated pest management (IPM), or the common-sense approach—calls for a certain level of careful observation coupled with "inspired laziness" (not acting unless absolutely required). Unlike war, proper pest and disease management means never really winning, but rather striking a natural, healthy balance.

Pests

A plethora of pests, literally hundreds of them, are waiting to launch an assault on your prized shrubs and trees. The enemies range from aphids, which lurk just below the soil line and suck on the juices of trees, to borers mining their way through the bark and trunk, to frightfully hungry caterpillars devouring huge masses of foliage. The worst-case scenario is not a pretty picture.

Fortunately, nature's seasonal ebb and flow doesn't bring every pestilence to bear on every garden. And the well-educated gardener has an extensive arsenal of strategies, gadgets, and sprays available for action when some new problem arises. Here are a few of the more common pests of trees and shrubs, and the IPM approaches to managing them.

Aphids

Perhaps no pest is more prevalent, and more misunderstood, than aphids. Their presence often indicates a lack of balance—usually too much water or too much nitrogen.

The primary problem with aphids is that they feed on the sap of plants, taking away some valuable nutrients and sugars. If they move from plant to plant, they can also bring undesirable viruses, which may disfigure plants or reduce the yields of fruiting shrubs and trees.

Second, they excrete honeydew, a sweet liquid that falls onto lower

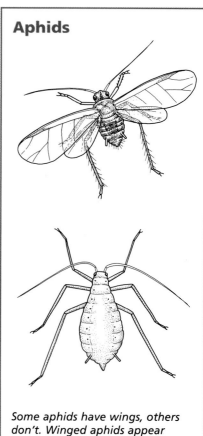

Aphids

Some aphids have wings, others don't. Winged aphids appear when the population of the aphid colony becomes high, or when the nitrogen level in the leaves is reduced. The winged aphids float on the wind to other host plants.

leaves, buildings, and cars. A disfiguring dark, sooty mold then grows on it, which can cover enough of the foliage to significantly reduce photosynthesis.

There are more than 4,000 species of aphids, in myriad colors and

slightly different sizes (most are ⅛ in. or less). Some species are specific for certain types of plants, and others are general feeders that eat many plants.

The appearance of an aphid doesn't change much throughout its life cycle. They all have small, almost pointed heads with two tiny antennae and a pointy, beaklike mouth. They have large, rotund abdomens and six small legs. Overall, they are soft bodied and pear shaped. They are usually found in mass groupings and are more likely to be found on new, succulent growth than on older leaves or stems. Some are wingless and others have clear wings pointing up over the body. Winged aphids don't really fly: They are wafted on the wind (primitive hang-gliders?) to other plants—sometimes 100 miles away!

Resistant plant varieties Almost every plant is vulnerable to aphids.

Life cycle Most garden aphids are females that produce live daughter nymphs for the entire summer without males or mating. These nymphs, the larval stage of the insect, shed their skin (molt) many times as they grow. At the end of the summer, some males are born in the colonies of females. When the males mature, mating

occurs, and the results of the matings are not nymphs but eggs. The aphids secrete the eggs under bark and buds, and in cracks and crevices, where they remain over the winter. In the spring, females hatch from the eggs with minute immature nymphs already formed inside their bodies. There are some aphids whose life cycle entails reproduction by eggs only.

Plan of attack Spring normally brings enough succulent growth to attract aphids to the readily available sap flow, but you can help by not forcing your plants to grow so fast that they produce weak leaves and stems. Additional nitrogen can boost growth, or extend it further into the summer, making your plants a welcome feeding ground for aphids.

You can also prune out young shoots covered with masses of aphids, but pruning may not reduce enough of the succulent spring growth to deter the pests completely.

Don't panic when you see just a few aphids in the early spring. It may take a few days for the many beneficial insects to find the new colony and consume enough aphids to create a balance. Exercise restraint while you watch their population carefully.

Parasitizing Wasps

Tiny beneficial wasps (some from the Chalcidoidea *family) insert one egg into each aphid.*

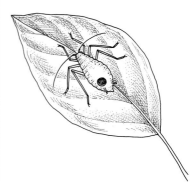

You know a beneficial wasp has been there if you see bloated bodies of parasitized aphids— called mummies. Once the wasp larva has devoured the interior of the aphid, it cuts a little doorway and crawls out the hole.

A good indicator that the good guys are doing the work for you is the appearance of the bronze-colored (sometimes black, tan, cream, or brown), bloated body of a parasitized aphid, called a mummy. Tiny parasitic wasps lay one egg in each aphid (see the drawing on the facing page). A larva hatches from the wasp egg and devours the inside of the aphid. It then cuts a little hinged doorway on the back of the parasitized aphid, crawls out, and stings other aphids to insert more eggs.

The hinged openings are a telltale sign, and counting them (a magnifying glass may be helpful) reveals how many wasps are hatching. Once you've spotted a number of swollen aphids or the door hatches from emerging wasps, wait to see if the number of aphids goes down before taking action yourself.

You should also learn how to recognize the following the good insects and their predacious larvae: convergent ladybug beetles (the ugly larval stage does the most damage, but the adult ladybug is beneficial), lacewings, syrphid fly larvae, and members of the paper wasp family. All these predators are visible with the naked eye. Watch the interaction between the predators and the aphids and see if the tide is turning in favor of the beneficial insects before progressing to some form of response. You can purchase beneficial insects from organic gardening supply companies for release in your garden.

Aphid Enemies

Female adult parasitic wasp

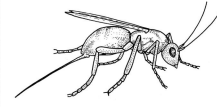

Parasites of aphids include the small parasitic wasps (Aphelinus, Ahidius, Ephedrus, Praon, and Trioxys species); green and brown lacewings (Chrysoperla spp.); the larvae of syrphid flies (Syrphidae spp.); and convergent ladybug beetles (Hippodamia convergens; the larval stage does more damage than the lovable adult ladybug).

Lacewing adult

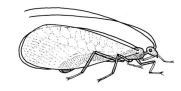

Lacewing larva

Adult ladybug beetle

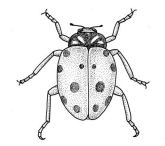

Ladybug beetle larva

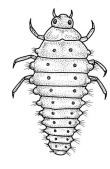

Syrphid fly adult

Syrphid fly larva

While many insects are helpful, ants actually increase the aphid problem. They "herd" aphids up into trees and shrubs to "milk" the honeydew as a food resource. To control this problem, apply a 2-in.- to 4-in.-wide band of sticky goo around the base of susceptible plants. (There are several products made to last a long time exposed to weather.) Unless the label says otherwise, don't place the sticky band directly on the bark of young trees; instead, tie a layer of plastic tightly to the trunk and put the sticky trap on top of the plastic. Make sure the foliage on the trees you're treating doesn't touch another plant (or a structure), or the ants will return by that route.

If these measures don't work, the next step is to use various sprays. The safest spray is a strong blast of water from a hose: Try to knock as many aphids off the trees and shrubs as you can. Unfortunately, most herbal, homemade concoctions have not been shown to be very effective.

Neem is an oil extract of a tropical tree (*Azadirachta indica*) that repels over 150 so-called pests. It acts generally as a repellent, inhibiting insects from feeding. It is also an insecticide that affects each portion of an aphid's life cycle. Neem sprays do harm some beneficial insects (such as ladybug beetles), and they are toxic to honey bees. The spray lasts for 1 to 2 weeks, or until rain or new growth negates its impact. Spray early in the morning.

All other sprays kill a broad spectrum of insects—good and bad. The next more toxic insecticide, with a greater impact on beneficial insects, is insecticidal soap. These are liquid sprays made with extracts of the most caustic compounds of ordinary soap, so they are more useful than the old-fashioned soapy sprays of the 1970s.

Other so-called natural sprays have been successfully used, but they also kill beneficial insects. Other options include summer-applied horticultural oil, diatomaceous earth, and pyrethrin, pyrethrum, and pyrethroids. Many chemical insecticides list aphids as one of the many insects they will kill. However, for aphids on trees and shrubs, try to avoid all botanical and chemical insecticides, as time or natural predators usually control the problem. (When aphids attack favorite annual flowers, vegetable plants, and herbaceous perennials, more drastic action may be required.)

The eastern and western tent caterpillars

Caterpillars can do plenty of damage to trees and shrubs; they practically defoliate some plants if left unchecked, or in a "bad" year. Caterpillars belong to the Lepidoptera order of insects, and they metamorphose into moths or butterflies. Caterpillars are not grubs, which turn into beetles. They're not slugs. They shouldn't be called worms; they don't wriggle through the soil to eat.

The eastern tent caterpillar (*Malacosoma americanum*) is a good example of a difficult-to-manage caterpillar. It is considered to be one of the two most prevalent and destructive caterpillars from the East to the Rocky Mountain states (the other is the gypsy moth). Other species of *Malacosoma* and other types of tent caterpillars (*Hyphantria cunea*) occur throughout the country.

Adult tent caterpillars are about 1 in. to 2 in. long and have short, fuzzy bodies. They may be reddish brown (the western tent caterpillar) or have blue spots alongside rows of brown and yellow lines (the eastern variety). The most noticeable signs of their presence are their silky, webbed tents in the forks of deciduous tree branches. As they grow, the caterpillars build new tents in larger forks.

Resistant plant varieties Conifers aren't attacked. Other than that, it's easier to list what they like to eat so you know what to avoid. The eastern caterpillar prefers the following:
- *apples* (Malus *spp.*)
- *ashes* (Fraxinus *spp.*)

The Life Cycle of Tent Caterpillars

The eggs are shiny masses wrapped around stems in the East, or long or encircling dull gray masses in the West.

Tent caterpillars are 1 in. to 2 in. long, with fuzzy hairs.

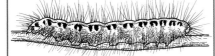

They form silky, webbed tents in the forks of deciduous tree branches.

- *birches* (Betula *spp.*)
- *crabapples* (Malus *spp.*)
- *maples* (Acer *spp.*)
- *oaks* (Quercus *spp.*)
- *plums* (Prunus *spp.*)
- *poplars* (Populus *spp.*)
- *wild cherries* (Prunus *spp.*)

The western version consumes the foliage of many of the trees just listed as well as the following:

- *madrone* (Arbutus menziesii)
- *redbud* (Cercis occidentalis)
- *toyon* (Heteromeles arbutifolia)
- *willows* (Salix *spp.*)

Resistant cultivars for these susceptible trees have not been developed or selected. Use the same basic treatment for both the eastern and western tent caterpillars.

Life cycle The eastern version eats foliage within the silky tent and also migrates outside the tent to eat, whereas many of the western varieties forage only on leaves outside the tent. Both usually return to the tent at dusk. When they are mature, the caterpillars crawl into a leaf, under bark, or into the litter below the tree to pupate inside a cocoon in mid or late summer. The adult moths hatch in summer to lay eggs, which winter over.

The eastern moth is reddish-brown with yellow and brown striping on the upper wings; the western moths are either dull yellow, gray, or brown. The adults lay eggs in shiny masses wrapped around stems in the East, and in long or encircling dull-gray masses in the West. The eggs hatch early in the spring, often when ornamental or wild plum trees just begin to leaf out or when sugar maples (*Acer saccharum*) bloom in the East, or in the mid summer. Tents are soon visible.

Plan of attack Many gardeners can't tolerate even one tent of ravenous caterpillars. Most trees can tolerate some partial defoliation, but the tents look messy, and repeated, extensive defoliation may kill some trees or shrubs.

The best defense is to watch for the egg masses while pruning in the dormant season. Destroy them by smashing the eggs with your fingers, disposing of them in the garbage can, or burning them.

In the early spring, clip small shoots with early signs of tents. The trick is to go out at night, on cloudy or rainy days, or before sun warms the tent in the morning to remove the tents, because that is when most of the caterpillars are inside. Destroy the prunings by burning them in a metal

pail. The typical healthy tree will easily grow new leaves after partial defoliation.

You may handpick caterpillars found outside the nest during the day; drop them into a bucket of soapy water to kill them. Insecticidal soaps that list tent caterpillars on the label may also be effective. Spray directly on exposed caterpillars, not the tent. Watch for leaf burn from concentrated soap sprays.

An important spray is the naturally occurring *Bacillus thuringiensis* (BT), more accurately called *Bacillus thuringiensis* var. *kurstaki* (BTK) when used specifically to kill caterpillars. (There are many products that contain this valuable biological control; read the labels carefully.) The bacterium is a stomach poison for all members of the *Lepidoptera* order. Spray it on both sides of the leaves early in the day when it's not sunny or hot. Once the caterpillar eats a bit of the foliage, it stops feeding, but it may not die for 2 days or more. The spray works best on young caterpillars.

Carefully target the caterpillars you want to spray. Leave any with white cocoons on their backs alone, because this is a sign that there are already natural parasites using the tent caterpillar as a host. Soon, these parasites will hatch and fly in search of other tent caterpillars to "terrorize."

The next step up in toxicity is either organic or synthetic insecticides. Organic pesticides, such as pyrethrum (made from the flowers of *Chrysanthemum cinerariaefolium*), or synthetic insecticides, such as Acephate, Malathion, or Carbaryl, are broad-spectrum insecticides that also kill beneficial insects. Pyrethrum is slightly toxic to mammals. Acephate is a systemic insecticide that is absorbed by the plant's tissue and kills for up to 3 weeks—not the wisest choice for fruit and nut trees. Carbaryl is highly poisonous to mammals and insects, including honey bees.

Bagworms

Bagworms (*Thyridopteryx ephemeraeformis*) are caterpillars that eat conifers as well as deciduous tree foliage—feeding on over 125 plant species. They're a problem in the eastern half of the United States and Canada. Bagworms can partially defoliate and weaken trees and shrubs, leaving them unsightly and sometimes even killing them. They are more likely to defoliate arborvitae (*Thuja* spp.) or cedars (*Cedrus* spp.) enough to cause death than other plants. Most deciduous trees are harmed but not killed.

This caterpillar is the "bag lady" of caterpillars. It forms a spindle-shaped cocoon around itself made from bits of the plant's foliage. This helps camouflage the caterpillar and protects it from predators. It also makes it harder to kill with contact insecticides. The bags resemble 1-in. to 2-in., tapered Christmas tree ornaments. The size of the bag increases as the caterpillar grows.

Resistant plant varieties There are no selections for resistant cultivars, but you can try plants that aren't bagworm favorites. Their favorites include the following:

- *arborvitae (*Thuja *spp.)
- *buckeyes (*Aesculus *spp.)
- *cedars (*Cedrus *spp.)
- *firs (*Abies *spp.)
- *ginkgo (*Ginkgo biloba)
- *hemlocks (*Tsuga *spp.)
- *honey locust (*Gleditsia triacanthos*)
- *juneberries (*Amelanchier *spp.)
- *junipers (*Juniperus *spp.)
- *larches (*Larix *spp.)
- *locusts (*Robinia *spp.)
- *maples (*Acer *spp.)
- *oaks (*Quercus *spp.)
- *persimmons (*Diospyros *spp.)
- *poplars (*Populus *spp.)
- *pines (*Pinus *spp.)
- *red cedar (*Juniperus virginiana*)
- *spruces (*Picea *spp.)
- *sweet gum (*Liquidambar styraciflua*)

Bagworms

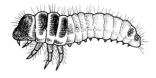

Bagworm caterpillar without its protective cocoon.

A bagworm forms a spindle-shaped cocoon around itself made from bits of the plant's foliage. The bag resembles 1-in.- to 2-in.-long tapered Christmas tree ornaments.

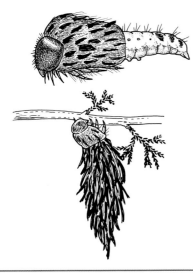

As the caterpillar feeds on foliage, the hanging cocoon moves along the branch.

The adult males have black, furry bodies, feathery antennae, and nearly transparent wings about 1 in. wide. The female adults have no wings and remain in the cocoon.

The males have black, furry bodies, feathery antennae, and 1-in., nearly transparent wings. The females have no wings and remain in the cocoon, where mating occurs. Each female lays between 500 and 1,000 eggs within the cocoon and then dies. The eggs hatch any time the following May or June.

In the Midwest, you can precisely time the emergence of the caterpillars by when the catalpa tree (*Catalpa speciosa*) is in full bloom—which varies depending on the weather. The young caterpillars crawl out of the cocoon and begin feeding immediately. Very soon after emerging, each caterpillar produces its own protective bag with its head and legs free so it can move around to feed.

Plan of attack While birds and predacious insects may help to control the problem, most people react when they see noticeable infestations because populations are likely to increase each year if left completely alone.

On short shrubs, start by handpicking and destroying the bags. You can use BTK to kill bagworms, following the instructions outlined for tent caterpillars. The BTK will be more effective if used as soon as you spot the young caterpillars. You may

- *sycamores* (Platanus *spp.*)
- *willows* (Salix *spp.*)

Life cycle As they eat, the caterpillars drag their bags along. If a plant becomes defoliated, the caterpillars crawl off with their bags to look for fresh foliage. In late summer, the bags are attached firmly to a shoot, the openings are closed, and pupae are formed. In a few days, the winged male moths emerge.

have to repeat spraying every 10 days for a while.

Pheromones are synthetic chemicals that mimic the sexual attractant odor of a particular insect. A trap coated with a sticky substance and containing a capsule of the female bagworm pheromone will lure some male bagworm moths as soon as they emerge. When the trap starts catching moths, it's time to watch for the first eggs to hatch; spray BTK while the larvae are tiny and without their defensive bags. Set the traps out in late March to be ready for the first flying males.

All contact insecticides are difficult to use because the larvae's bags act as armor.

The more toxic options include chemically manufactured insecticides such as Acephate, Malathion, and Diazinon. These are broad-spectrum pesticides that also kill beneficial insects. This can lead to a serious imbalance between naturally occurring parasitic wasps and the bagworms, causing a larger outbreak of bagworms in the following season.

Japanese beetles

The first Japanese beetle (*Popillia japonica*) in North America was noticed in New Jersey in 1916. From there it has spread to New England and the eastern seaboard, into much of the Midwest, and, in periodic

Japanese Beetles

The young grubs can be found in the soil.

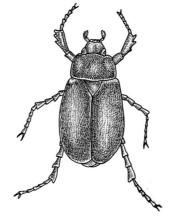

Japanese beetles are up to ½ in. long and have a hard shell that is metallic green or blue with coppery or bronze wing covers.

outbreaks, to the West Coast. These pests will no doubt continue to expand their range.

This hard-shelled, metallic green or blue insect with coppery or bronze wing covers is beautiful. On the abdomen, there are two distinct patches of white hair. At the most it's ½ in. long, and it's a prolific breeder.

The beetles are most active during the heat of the day, preferring full sun. They hang from leaves, flowers, or fruit in clusters of 100 or more. They may completely consume petals, ripening fruit, and young, tender leaves. They may skeletonize tree and shrub leaves so only the veins remain.

Resistant plant varieties
Unfortunately, the adults feed on almost 300 species of plants, including fruiting and ornamental shrubs and trees. However, some trees and shrubs are rarely fodder for these ravenous beetles:

- *American arborvitae (*Thuja occidentalis*)
- *ashes (*Fraxinus *spp.)
- *black oak (*Quercus velutina*)
- *box elder (*Acer negundo*)
- *dogwood (*Cornus *spp.)
- *firs (*Abies *spp.)
- *forsythia (*Forsythia *spp.)
- *ginkgo (*Ginkgo biloba*)
- *hemlocks (*Tsuga *spp.)

- *holly trees and shrubs* (Ilex *spp.*)
- *honeysuckle shrubs* (Lonicera *spp.*)
- *hydrangeas* (Hydrangea *spp.*)
- *juniper trees and shrubs* (Juniperus *spp.*)
- *lilacs* (Syringa *spp.*)
- *locusts* (Robinia *spp.*)
- *magnolia trees and shrubs* (Magnolia *spp.*)
- *mulberries* (Morus *spp.*)
- *pine trees and shrubs* (Pinus *spp.*)
- *post oak* (Quercus stellata)
- *privets* (Ligustrum *spp.*)
- *rebuds* (Cercis *spp.*)
- *red maple* (Acer rubrum)
- *rhododendrons and azaleas* (Rhododendron *spp.*)
- *scarlet oak* (Quercus coccinea)
- *snowberry shrubs* (Symphoricarpos *spp.*)
- *spruces* (Picea *spp.*)
- *sweet gum trees* (Liquidambar styraciflua)
- *white oak* (Quercus alba)

Life cycle The beetles feed first on low-growing plants and later fly up into shrubs and trees. Each beetle lives 30 to 45 days. After mating, a female lays 40 to 60 eggs in the soil under lawns. The eggs hatch 2 weeks later, and the young grubs feed on small grass roots until winter weather forces them below the frost line (where winters are cold enough to freeze the soil). The grubs resume feeding on grass roots in the spring and then pupate near the soil's surface. The beetles emerge between May and July, depending on the location.

Plan of attack While established woody plants can tolerate much defoliation, most gardeners can't tolerate skeletonized leaves on their favorite plants. The first step is to watch the ballet of prey and predator. Birds, moles, shrews, skunks, and toads are known to eat Japanese beetles and grubs.

Trap crops may work, but they are difficult to utilize. The idea is to plant the beetle's favorite food, and when the beetles begin to fly, you'll see them massed on it. If you wait until hordes of beetles gather on the trap crop, you can destroy the plants and beetles in a mass execution. Possible trap crops are borage (*Borago officinalis*), evening primroses (*Oenothera* spp.), white geraniums (*Pelargonium* spp.), grape vines (*Vitis* spp.), and zinnias (*Zinnia* spp.).

Handpicking the beetles is an option, but only for those with plenty of time and short shrubbery. Do away with harvested beetles in a tub of soapy water. While you're handpicking, use pheromone traps to attract and trap the beetles in a sack. Place the traps 25 ft. to 50 ft. from the vulnerable plants, preferably upwind from them. Many mail-order gardening catalogs and garden centers sell traps; some suggest one trap for every 100 sq. ft., others, one per acre. Trapping enough adults to "control" the problem is difficult. Neither hand picking nor trapping alone will solve the problem, but using both methods will help reduce the population.

In the grub stage, Japanese beetles are at their weakest, especially near the soil's surface. Milky spore disease (*Bacillus popilliae*) infects and kills the Japanese beetle larvae. This disease doesn't hurt earthworms, other soil flora, or parasitic wasps (*Tiphia* spp.), which attack the grub on the East Coast. There are various products available. Apply one to the lawn as a dusty powder as soon as you notice grubs in the spring (following the label's instructions). After dusting the lawn, water lightly to soak the spores into the thatch and upper soil. It will take repeated applications over several years for long-term effectiveness.

A more recent approach is the use of two parasitic nematodes: *Heterorhabditis heliothidis* and *Steinernema carpocapsae*. These beneficial nematodes, which attack only certain insects, not plants, are purchased, applied to the soil, and watered in with as much as ¼ in. to ½ in. of water. The nematodes enter the cuticles of the grubs, kill the grubs, and create an environment

favorable to the development of more nematodes. The nematodes may go through several life cycles within the grub. The last generation of nematodes to populate the grub leaves the cadaver to seek out other grubs.

Neem oil products repel Japanese beetles or suppress their urge to feed. You'll need to spray every 7 to 10 days and after each rain.

The next more toxic approach is to use botanical insecticides on the adult stage—but only if necessary. One option is pyrethrum applied in two applications, 3 to 4 days apart. A 5 percent dust of rotenone can also be used. These are easy to use for spot treatments. The problem is that beneficial insects will also die when sprayed.

Diseases

As if pests weren't enough to give a gardener white hairs from worry, fear, and vigilance, there are dozens of insidious and virulent diseases in nature's mixed bag of delights and turmoils. Some diseases creep into the plant via the roots. Others float silently on the wind or arrive in the rain. Some splash up from puddled mud during irrigation. The effects range from frosty white mildews disfiguring foliage, to brown splotches of fungus-infected leaves, to

partial or complete death of the plant. Again, the flexible gardener remains calm, observes, and acts only when necessary.

Phytophthora (root rot)

Perhaps more trees and shrubs die undiagnosed from root rots (*Phytophthora* spp.) than from any other disease. The problem can go undetected for a long time between the development of symptoms and actual damage and the plant's death.

Often, the leaves at first seem drought stressed, sometimes turning dull green, yellow, red, or even purple. Then they all dramatically wilt at the same time, turning darkish brown prematurely and dropping from the plant. Infected trees may survive a few years before dying, or they may suddenly perish.

Around the soil line, the bark may appear darkened—but this is often missed. The only sure way to analyze the problem is to cut away some bark. Instead of the normal green and whitish layers of tissue beneath the bark, you will find red-brown or dark brown streaks of discoloration in the wood under the bark. Sadly, if the knife test is positive, you have determined the cause—but it's too late to save the shrub or tree. *Phytophthora*-infected roots are brittle and firm, while roots that have

merely rotted from excessive water are soft.

Resistant plant varieties
Ornamental trees and shrubs with resistance to this disease include the following:
- *Alaska cypress (*Chamaecyparis nootkatensis*)
- *American arborvitae (*Thuja occidentalis*)
- *garland daphne or garland flower (*Daphne cneorum*)
- *hiryu azalea (*Rhododenderon obtusum*)
- *Meyer juniper (*Juniperus squamata 'Meyeri'*)
- *mugo pine (*Pinus mugo var.* mugo*)
- *Pfitzer's juniper (*Juniperus chinensis 'Pfitzerana'*)
- *sasanqua camellia (*Camellia sasanqua*)
- *savin juniper (*Juniperus sabina*)
- *sawara cypress (*Chamaecyparis pisifera 'Filifera'*)
- *white cedar (*Chamaecyparis thyoides*)

While no definitive study has been made with fruit trees, Asian pear roots (*Pyrus calleryana* and *P. ussuriensis*), European pear roots (*Pyrus communis*), apple roots (*Malus* spp.), and plum and prune roots (*Prunus* spp.), in descending order, have good resistance to *Phytophthora*.

With apple trees, fruiting varieties on the standard-size rootstock are generally more resistant (except the Alnarp 2 standard rootstock) to this disease than most semi- or dwarf rootstock.

Life cycle Some species of *Phytophthora* (such as the predominant species in California) require a warm soil to proliferate, and others prefer a cool soil. All require a moist soil to spread and do damage. Soil saturated or flooded for 6 to 8 hours is especially susceptible to the spread of *Phytophthora*. The fungi can infect the crown of the root system, major roots, or the entire root system. The worst damage usually occurs when *Phytophthora* encircles the active layer of transport of the entire trunk or stem near the soil's surface, preventing any movement of water and nutrients to the upper portion of the plant.

In places where rain comes only in the cool winter, irrigating around the trunks of trees and shrubs once the dry summer soil is warm creates a disaster. That's the reason why mixing many plants with lawns and planting trees and shrubs in low spots is difficult. Where summer rains occur periodically, many ornamental and fruiting trees are just as vulnerable.

The fungal fruiting bodies are not visible, and contaminated soils always remain infected with the fungi. The fungi can be spread through contaminated soil on shoes and garden tools and by rains and wind.

Plan of attack Protecting all plants is important. Losing even one favorite tree or shrub to *Phytophthora* is probably intolerable. Ask local nursery personnel, Master Gardeners, or the cooperative exten-

---

Evidence of Dieback

Phytophthora *makes leaves look drought stressed, and they sometimes turn dull green, yellow, red, or even purple. Then all the leaves wilt dramatically at the same time, turn darkish brown, and drop from the limbs.*

sion office if your area is prone to *Phytophthora*.

One indication of this disease is finding a portion of the canopy of shrubs and trees dead, although many other diseases and pests can do this. Each climate has some special indicator plants. In the arid West with mild winters, rosemary (*Rosmarinus* spp.) is one of the first plants to develop dieback after a late spring rain or summer irrigation. Use the knife test described previously to see if *Phytophthora* was the culprit. If so, then next time you plant in that area, be sure to increase the drainage.

The best solution is to prevent the problem by planting resistant varieties. If a tree dies from *Phytophthora*, plant a resistant variety in its place. Another important preventative is to plant all trees and shrubs, resistant or not, on high planting mounds to provide good drainage around the upper 12 in. to 18 in. of the crown of the root system (see the drawings on pp. 135 and 137 for details). Avoid overwatering, and irrigate outside the drip line.

There is no chemical cure for this fungus.

Anthracnose

Anthracnose, also called leaf, shoot, bud, and twig blight, is actually a group of many related fungal diseases that infect shade trees. The genus and species of fungus may differ from tree to tree (for example, maple anthracnose and oak anthracnose are caused by fungi of different genera). The symptoms may differ or be quite similar, but in general, infected plants may look sun scorched and have sunken red ovals containing fungal spores on infected twigs.

Sycamores (*Platanus* spp.) and maples (*Acer* spp.) are often infected by this fungus. The typical symptoms for these trees are lesions around the leaf veins, curled and distorted leaves, death of portions of the leaf (resembling frost damage), and premature drop of the leaves. Symptoms occur from May through August, especially after humid weather.

Oaks (*Quercus* spp.) and walnuts (*Juglans* spp.) exhibit tarlike, black, tan, or brown spots on infected leaves. The disease generally infects the leaf veins, killing the vein and surrounding tissue. The area of dead tissue appears more irregular in ashes

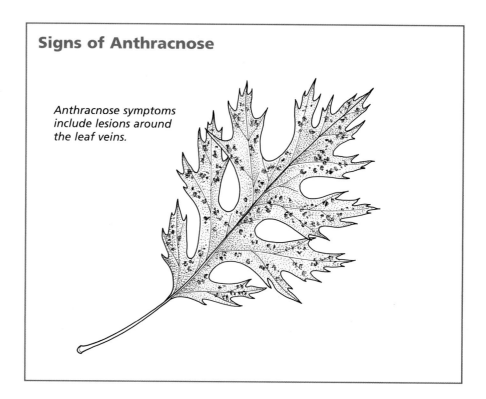

Signs of Anthracnose

Anthracnose symptoms include lesions around the leaf veins.

(*Fraxinus* spp.), birches (*Betula* spp.), redbuds (*Cercis* spp.), and elms (*Ulmus* spp.).

Sycamores (*Platanus* spp.), oaks (*Quercus* spp.), elms (*Ulmus* spp.), and ashes (*Fraxinus* spp.) often exhibit shoot or branch dieback due to cankers that encircle the growing stems. Cankers are dead areas of tissue without noticeable callusing. Growth from below the cankers often is gnarled and crooked.

This disease is difficult to distinguish from other fungal diseases, mildew, and bacterial diseases on trees. Take samples to local nurseries, the cooperative extension office, or a Master Gardener group for exact identification.

Resistant plant varieties Some selection for resistant varieties has been done for this disease. These have been given cultivar names and are grafted so as to maintain the desired resistance. Resistant cultivars include the following:

- *Ash (Fraxinus spp.) cultivars 'Moraine' and 'Raywood'*
- *Bloodgood plane (Platanus racemosa 'Bloodgood')*
- *Drake Chinese elm (Ulmus parvifolia 'Drake')*
- *Privet (Ligustrum spp.) cultivars 'Amur', 'Iobota', and 'Regal'*

Ask you local nursery about recent introductions.

Life cycle The fungus overwinters on fallen leaves, shoots, and branches infected the previous year. The infection then shows up again the following spring and summer, appearing on young leaves when they are moist with rain, humidity, or irrigation spray, and when the weather is cool. Infection is often most harsh on the lower third of the tree, where the humidity is usually highest. Control measures for all anthracnose diseases are comparable.

Plan of attack Plant resistant varieties. Trees can survive considerable foliage damage and still continue to grow each year. If the infection is particularly severe, several years of repeated infection will allow the disease to move into the branches. Damage is usually not serious unless there is repeated serious defoliation or extensive canker development. Aesthetic tolerance is up to each gardener.

Collect and destroy fallen infected leaves. Prune out all dead shoots or branches, being sure to disinfect the pruning shears after each cut. During normal summer pruning, thin out excessive growth to promote better air circulation within the canopy. Be

sure trees are growing well, but don't force growth with too much water, fertilizer, or dormant-season pruning.

Fungicide sprays are most befitting younger, newly transplanted trees that may not withstand defoliation. All fungicides are for prevention and will not cure the problem once it's visible. Fungicides must be applied before any spotting occurs, when leaves are beginning to emerge from the buds. Spray with a copper sulfate fungicide, and reapply every 7 to 10 days for two or three more applications. Copper sulfate sprays can injure or kill leaves if misused, so be sure to read the label thoroughly. They can also irritate the eyes and skin, so wear long-sleeved shirts, pants, gloves, and protective eyewear.

The next level of toxicity includes the many chemical fungicides on the market, but simple copper sulfate sprays are usually all that's required. Use the micronized (finely ground) copper sulfate sprays to get an even, thin covering over the entire bark, bud, and leaf surface.

APPENDIX 1: USDA Zone Map

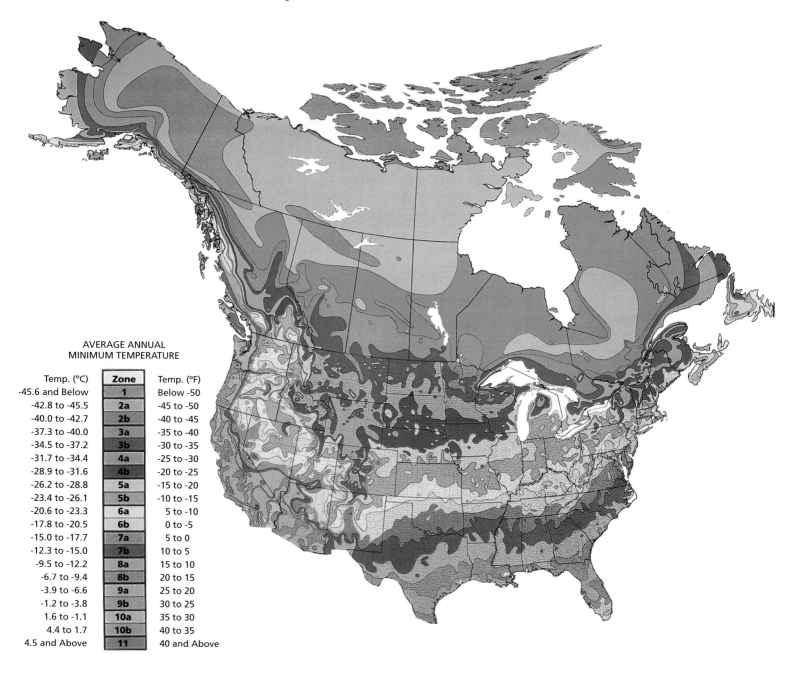

AVERAGE ANNUAL
MINIMUM TEMPERATURE

Temp. (°C)	Zone	Temp. (°F)
-45.6 and Below	1	Below -50
-42.8 to -45.5	2a	-45 to -50
-40.0 to -42.7	2b	-40 to -45
-37.3 to -40.0	3a	-35 to -40
-34.5 to -37.2	3b	-30 to -35
-31.7 to -34.4	4a	-25 to -30
-28.9 to -31.6	4b	-20 to -25
-26.2 to -28.8	5a	-15 to -20
-23.4 to -26.1	5b	-10 to -15
-20.6 to -23.3	6a	5 to -10
-17.8 to -20.5	6b	0 to -5
-15.0 to -17.7	7a	5 to 0
-12.3 to -15.0	7b	10 to 5
-9.5 to -12.2	8a	15 to 10
-6.7 to -9.4	8b	20 to 15
-3.9 to -6.6	9a	25 to 20
-1.2 to -3.8	9b	30 to 25
1.6 to -1.1	10a	35 to 30
4.4 to 1.7	10b	40 to 35
4.5 and Above	11	40 and Above

APPENDIX 2: Trees and the Law

As property liability laws change, property owners need more information about their responsibility for trees growing on their land. If legal action should arise, they need to know whom they can turn to for qualified legal assistance.

Attorney Victor D. Merullo, who co-wrote the 1992 book *Arboriculture and the Law* (published by the International Society of Arboriculture), offers some advice on the frequently changing world of trees and the law. Trends indicate that as the risk of harm increases (for example, from general population growth, or more traffic on tree-lined roads), the duty of the homeowner to inspect trees increases, and liability increases.

Fortunately there are guidelines you can follow based on past court decisions. Remember, the particulars of the guidelines change with location and vary as new cases set new precedents.

- *The homeowner shall maintain trees in such a way as to prevent injury to a neighbor and his property.*
- *In rural areas where populations are not dense, homeowners whose natural trees overhang a property line and cause damage or death cannot be held liable; the homeowner is held liable only for damages or death caused by those trees he planted and maintains. In urban areas, though, the homeowner has a responsibility to inspect every tree on his property.*
- *If a tree on private property falls on public property (the right of way) and causes damage or death, the homeowner is liable. More and more municipalities are passing ordinances that allow public agencies to enter private property for the purpose of inspecting trees to see if they present a potential hazard with regard to falling into the public right of way.*
- *Trees planted and maintained by a municipality (an incorporated city or a homeowners' association) between the curb and the sidewalk may be the liability of the municipality (but this varies with the municipality).*
- *Heaved sidewalks are often the liability of the city. In some cases, the liability is determined by whether the damage was done by municipally owned or privately owned trees. Some cities are passing ordinances that divide the maintenance and liability of the sidewalk between the city and adjacent property owners. Check with your local office of planning or the city attorney's office.*
- *The common law of the United States does not guarantee the homeowner an unobstructed view—a view easement. Two adjacent homeowners can write up a view easement and enter it into the deed of grant, where homeowner A allows homeowner B to trim the trees on A's property, so that B can maintain a view. And some municipalities have passed ordinances to require unobstructed views.*

To protect yourself in a legal dispute, hire a certified arborist from the International Society of Arboriculture (ISA) to determine the extent or cause of the damage. You can find certified arborists in the commercial listing of the phone book under tree services, where they will display the ISA symbol and sometimes list their certification number. Be sure to double-check the certification number when they arrive for a consultation.

If a trial occurs, Merullo suggests getting an expert witness from the American Society of Consulting Arborists. You will need one of these experts to work with an attorney knowledgeable in personal injury and damage cases.

APPENDIX 3: Glossary

Acidic soil A soil with a low pH (below 7.0). Below 6.0, iron begins to become more available.

Alkaline soil A soil with a high pH (above 7.0). Soils with a pH higher than 9.0 are strongly alkaline and often have harmful amounts of sodium.

Allelopathy Process by which chemical compounds exuded from one plant into the soil inhibit the growth of another.

Amendment Any material added to the soil to adjust or improve it. Examples include lime for acidity, sulfur for alkalinity, fertilizers, and compost.

Anthracnose A large group of related fungal diseases that result in similar symptoms: curled or distorted leaves, lesions, and even the death of portions of leaves, buds, shoots, or fruit.

Apical dominance The suppression of the sprouting of dormant buds below the apical (tip) bud on a lengthening shoot. The more vertical the shoot, the stronger the dominance, which results in fewer buds sprouting into shoots or flower buds.

Balled-and-burlap (B-and-B) A technique whereby a deciduous or evergreen tree or shrub is dug up with its roots in the native soil and covered with a protective wrapping (formerly of burlap, but now synthetic materials are often used).

Bare root Deciduous trees dug while still fully dormant and sold with no soil around the roots.

Branch attachment The physical union of a lateral shoot to a stem (see also Crotch).

Branch bark ridge The darkened and enlarged diagonal line of tissue on the upper side of a stem, branch, or limb where it attaches to another part of the tree or the trunk.

Branch collar The enlarged mass of bark tissue where the branch meets the limb or trunk. This collar is very prominent on some trees, such as oaks, but almost negligible on others, such as conifers. Leave the branch collar intact when pruning to keep rot from advancing into the core of the tree.

Caliper The diameter of the trunk. If a trunk is less than 4 in. in diameter, measure the caliper 6 in. above the soil. For diameters greater than 4 in., measure 12 in. above the ground. When mature trees are measured, the caliper is taken at breast height (see DBH)—54 in. above the ground.

Callus Tissue produced in response to wounding or pruning. With proper pruning, the callus will eventually evenly cover the entire cut.

Cambium The area of cells that gives rise to both the phloem and xylem. When grafting, the goal is to form a uniform callus between the cambium of the rootstock and that of the scion.

Canker Fungi or bacteria can cause the localized death of the tissue of a branch or stem. Usually noticed as a sunken, oozing tissue.

Canopy The branches and foliage above the top of the trunk.

Carbon dioxide One of the harmful by-products of the soil's bacteria and microbes.

Chlorosis A condition resulting from a shortage of chlorophyll. Affected leaves turn pale to bright yellow. The shortage of chlorophyll may be caused by a shortage of either iron (because the soil is a neutral or alkaline pH) or nitrogen.

Compost A mixture of raw organic wastes that undergo biological decomposition into a more stable material with a high organic matter content.

Conifers Evergreen trees and shrubs with needlelike leaves that bear seeds within a cone. One exception is the ginkgo tree *(Gingko biloba)*, which is related to conifers but has deciduous leaves.

Crotch Where two branches meet to form an angle. The angle of attachment is often determined by the genetics of the tree or shrub.

Crown All parts of the tree or shrub above the ground: shoots, stems, branches, limbs, and trunk.

Cultivar A selection cultivated from vegetative cuttings or cloning that resembles the species but has slightly different or unique traits. Denoted by a set of single quotation marks: In *Lavandula angustifolia* 'Munstead', 'Munstead' is a cultivar of English lavender.

DBH Diameter of a tree at breast height, measured at 54 in. (4½ ft.) above the ground.

Deciduous Describes trees or shrubs that lose their leaves each fall or at one time each year.

Dormant bud A single bud at the base of a leaf's stem that has not yet developed into a flower or a shoot.

Drip line The width of the foliage or the crown (see Crown).

Duff The layer of undecomposed litter on top of the soil; most of the raw ingredients (such as leaves, stems, twigs, blades of dry grass) are still recognizable.

Evapotranspiration rate The amount of moisture a plant uses via transpiration from the leaves plus that lost by evaporation from the soil. Often measured in total inches of water used per month.

Evergreen A plant whose foliage is visible throughout the year. On evergreens, the leaves or needles (on conifers) fall at different times of the year. But the plant is never leafless and the leaves or needles are constantly replaced.

Fibrous roots Many-branched roots with lots of lateral, horizontal roots. Fibrous roots have sinker roots but no predominant main root or taproot (see Sinker roots).

Focal point An element (such as a sculpture or a special plant) that captures one's attention in the landscape, seducing the eye away from nearby plants or structures.

Glaucous There are three definitions: a pale yellow-green color; foliage with a powdery or waxy coating and a smoky appearance, which tends to rub off; and a light bluish gray or bluish white color. The last definition is the most commonly used in referring to foliage color. Many drought-resistant plants display one or both of the last two definitions.

Included bark Found where the branch bark ridge folds inward instead of outward, creating an invagination. Usually indicates a weaker angle of attachment.

Also called embedded or invaginated bark.

Mistletoe A parasitic plant seen as a tuft or thicket of olive-green shoots radiating from a branch. Cut at least 18 in. below all visible mistletoe growth to remove the rootlike attachment inside the limb or branch.

Mycorrhizae The beneficial fungi that help most trees and shrubs thrive by assisting with absorption of phosphorous and micronutrients in exchange for some carbohydrates. A cooperative, nonparasitic relationship.

Nitrogen A major gas of the atmosphere that can be "captured" by certain beneficial bacteria and microbes and made into a soluble form that plant root hairs can absorb.

pH The measure of the soil's chemical reaction, expressed as acidic, neutral, and alkaline. On a scale of 4 to 9, 7.0 is neutral. Soil below pH 7.0 is acidic, and above 7.0 it is alkaline. The greatest range of nutrient exchange and soil flora occurs in a pH range of 6.0 to 7.5, except for iron and manganese, which are made available in acidic soils.

Pore space The tiny channels within soil that allow water to percolate down and drain the soil. The same channels help exude harmful gasses generated by the soil life, and they "inhale" beneficial air.

Root hairs The tiniest, yet most prolific, part of a root system. The emerging cells at the tip of the fine root hairs absorb most of the water and nutrients for the plant.

Shade Formed when mixing any color with black to darken it.

Sinker roots These vertical roots descend from various places along the horizontal roots of a tree or shrub.

Taproot The root of a seedling that descends vertically beneath the stem or trunk. It withers away with time on most trees and shrubs, to be replaced by a fibrous root system with horizontal roots and sinker roots (see Fibrous roots, Sinker roots).

Thatch The undecayed and decomposing leaves of grass and the living roots and stolons that lie above the soil in a lawn or meadow. Too much undecayed organic matter can inhibit the exchange of gases between the soil and the atmosphere.

Tint Formed when mixing white with a color.

Tone Derived when mixing a color with variable percentages of white, black, or gray.

Turf Another word for lawn.

Witch's broom A noticeably dense thicket of smaller, weaker shoots surrounding a branch. The leaves may be discolored. The weakness and discoloration may be caused by insect damage, disease, or mistletoe (see Mistletoe). Usually not harmful. If visually undesirable, merely cut out the section with the tufted growth.

APPENDIX 4: Resources

Tree and Shrub Resources

A. M. Leonard, Inc.
241 Fox Dr.
Piqua, OH 45356-0816
(800) 543-8955
(800) 433-0633 fax
www.amleo.com
My favorite mail-order catalog for the widest range of sturdy, no-nonsense tools and horticultural supplies. They carry three sizes of tree/shrub B-in-B carriers with two handles. They sell a wide range of cultivating and weeding tools.

American Nursery and Landscape Association (ANLA)
1250 I St. NW, Suite 500
Washington, DC 20005
(202) 789-2900
www.anla.org
For information on the nursery trade's guidelines for ratios of B-in-B and container stock diameters to tree and shrub heights, call the ANLA or visit the publications catalog section of their web site.

Cornflower Farms
Wildland/Agricultural Catalog
P.O. Box 896
Elk Grove, CA 95759
(916) 689-1015
(916) 689-1968 fax
Excellent choice of shrubs and trees that attract hummingbirds, butterflies, and beneficial insects. The emphasis is on California native plants. The plants are available in various small-size containers.

Drip Works
190 Sanhedrin Cl.
Willits, CA 95490
(800) 522-3747
(800) 616-8321 (catalog requests)
(707) 459-6323 (tech assistance)
(707) 459-9645 fax
dripwrks@pacific.net
www.dripworksusa.com
A large selection of drip irrigation systems for home gardeners. Also, a wide range of parts and tubing for commercial or large-scale plantings.

Gardener's Supply Company
128 Intervale Rd.
Burlington, VT 05401-2850
(800) 863-1700 (orders)
info@gardeners.com
www.gardeners.com
Sells a basic number of drip irrigation components, including the Netafim in-line emitter tubing. Offers a range of alternative irrigation devices.

Gardens Alive!
5100 Schenley Place
Lawrenceburg, IN 47025
812-537-8651
812-537-5108 fax
gardenhelp@gardens-alive.com
www.gardens-alive.com
A good resource for beneficial insects, pest-control devices, and mycorrhizal fungi.

Great Lakes IPM
10220 Church Rd. NE
Vestaburg, MI 48891
(517) 268-5693, (517) 268-5911
(517) 268-5311 fax
glipm@nethawk.com
A great source of many types of monitoring devices, lures, and traps for a wide range of insect and some mammalian pests.

Harmony Farm Supply and Nursery
3244 Gravenstein Hwy. N.
Sebastopol, CA 95472
(707) 823-9125
(707) 823-1734 fax
www.harmonyfarm.com
Sells ready-to-use rubber tree straps to attach to temporary tree stakes.Extensive listing of drip irrigation hardware and in-line emitter irrigation parts. The catalog is filled with numerous irrigation options, gardening and small farm tools, and organic gardening supplies.

Itasca Greenhouse
P.O. Box 273
Cohasset, MN 55721
(800) 538-TREE, (218) 328-6261
igtrees@northernnet.com
www.pconline.com/~itascagh
Sells both native and exotic species of trees and shrubs via the mail in various small containers. Also lists a good set of supplies to promote growth, including mycorrhizal inoculants.

Musser Forests, Inc.
P.O. Box 340, Route 119 N.
Indiana, PA 15701
(800) 643-8319, (724) 465-5685
(724) 465-9893 fax
info@musserforests.com
www.musserforests.com
Offers a huge selection of 2-, 3-, and 4-year-old seedlings of native and exotic trees and shrubs. Shipped bare-root. Catalog includes some supplies for planting and establishing the plants.

Out 'n' About Treehouse Institute and Treesort
300 Page Creek Rd.
Cave Junction, OR 97523
(541) 592-2208, (800) 200-5484
www.treehouses.com
They rent a number of different styles of treehouses for vacations. Their web site provides links to other treehouse associations.

Peaceful Valley Farm Supply
P.O. Box 2209
Grass Valley, CA 95945
(530) 272-4769
(888) 784-1722 (orders)
(530) 272-4794 fax
www.groworganic.com
Sells ready-to-use flexible plastic chain links to attach to temporary tree stakes. Sells all the tubes and tube racks you need to grow your own tree and shrub seedlings.

Plants of the Wild
P.O. Box 866
Tekoa, WA 99033
(509) 284-2848
(509) 284-6464 fax
kathy@plantsofthewild.com
www.plantsofthewild.com
Offers a wide selection of trees and shrubs native to the U.S.

Rincon-Vitova Insectaries, Inc.
P.O. Box 1555
Ventura, CA 93002-1555
(800) 248-2847, (805) 643-5407
(805) 643-6267 fax
bugnet@rinconvitova.com
www. rinconvitova.com
One of the oldest and most diverse suppliers of beneficial insects. Also sells seed mixtures to establish plantings to attract beneficial insects.

Regional Experts

Tim Boland, Curator of Horticulture Collections
Doris Taylor, Plant Information Specialist
Dr. Gary W. Watson, Root System Research Biologist
The Morton Arboretum
Route 53
Lisle, IL 60532
(630) 968-0074
(630) 719-2433 fax

Ron Brightman, Horticulturist
9004 184th SW
Edmonds, WA 98117
(425) 774-1413

Barrie Coate, Consulting Horticulturist
Barrie Coate and Associates
23535 Summit Rd.
Los Altos, CA 95033-9307
(408) 353-1052
(408) 353-1238 fax

Donald R. Hodel, Landscape Advisor
University of California Cooperative Extension
2 Coral Circle
Montery Park, CA 91755-7425
(323) 838-4531
(323) 838-7408 fax
drhodel@ucdavis.edu

Mary Irish
Desert Botanical Garden
1201 N. Galvin Pkwy.
Phoenix, AZ 85008
(480) 941-1225
(480) 481-8139 fax

Mike Ruggiero
New York Botanical Garden
Bronx, NY 10458-5126
(718) 817-8189
(718) 817-8041 fax

Dr. Ken Tilt
Department of Agriculture
Auburn University
Auburn, AL 36849-5601
(334) 844-4862
(334) 844-3131 fax

Chip Tynan
Missouri Botanical Garden
P.O. Box 299
St. Louis, MO 63166-0299
(314) 577-9447
(314) 577-9465 fax

Books

Brickell, Christopher, ed. *The American Horticultural Society Encyclopedia of Garden Plants.* New York: Macmillan, 1992.

Dirr, Michael A. *Dirr's Hardy Trees and Shrubs: An Illustrated Encyclopedia.* Portland, OR: Timber Press, 1997.

Hobhouse, Penelope. *Color in Your Garden.* Boston: Little, Brown, 1985.

Nelson, Peter (with Gerry Hadden, contributor). *Home Tree Home: Principles of Treehouse Construction and Other Tall Tales.* New York: Penguin, 1997.

Olkowski, William, Sheila Darr, and Helga Olkowski. *Common-Sense Pest Control.* Newtown, CT: Taunton Press, 1991.

Perry, Bob. *Landscape Plants for Western Regions: An Illustrated Guide to Plants for Water Conservation.* Claremont, CA: Land Design, 1992.

Stiles, David R. and Jeanie Stiles. *Tree Houses You Can Actually Build.* New York: Houghton Mifflin, 1998.

Photo Credits

Front cover: Robert Kourik (top left, top right, bottom left); Howard Rice/Garden Picture Library (top center); David Cavagnaro (center top left); © Derek Fell (center right); T. A. Allan/Out 'n' About Treehouse Institute & Treesort (center bottom left); Brigette Thomas/Garden Picture Library (bottom center); © Ken Druse (bottom right)

Front flap: Melabee Miller/Envision

Back cover: © Bart Barlow/Envision (center left); Michael A. Dirr (center); Richard Shiell (center right); David Henderson/A-Z Botanical Collection Ltd. (top right); J. Paul Moore (bottom left); Delilah Smittle, © The Taunton Press, Inc.

Back flap: Neil Holmes/Garden Picture Library

p. vi: © Ken Druse (top); Richard Shiell (bottom left and bottom right); Gene Ahrens/Bruce Coleman Inc. (bottom center)
p. 1: © Ken Druse (left and center right); Delilah Smittle, © The Taunton Press, Inc. (center right); © 2000 Janet Loughrey Photography (right)
p. 2: Robert Kourik
p. 3: Susan A. Roth
p. 4: © Derek Fell
p. 5: © 2000 Michael S. Thompson
p. 8: © 2000 Michael S. Thompson

Chapter 1
p. 10: © Ken Druse
p. 11: © 2000 Michael S. Thompson (top); Susan A. Roth (bottom)
p. 12: David Cavagnaro (left); Robert Kourik (right)
p. 13: Michael A. Dirr
p. 20: Robert Kourik (left); Michael A. Dirr (right)
p. 22: Maggie Oster
p. 24: © 2000 Michael S. Thompson
p. 26: Robert Kourik

Chapter 2
p. 27: © Ken Druse
p. 28: Gene Ahrens/Bruce Coleman Inc.

p. 29: Stuart Craig/Bruce Coleman Inc.
p. 31: Robert Kourik (top); Norman Owen Tomalin/Bruce Coleman Inc. (bottom)
p. 33: Michael A. Dirr (top); © Derek Fell (bottom)
p. 36: © Derek Fell
p. 39: © Bart Barlow/Envision
p. 41: Michael A. Dirr

Chapter 3
p. 44: Delilah Smittle, © The Taunton Press, Inc.
p. 49: J. S. Sira/Garden Picture Library
p. 50: © Derek Fell
p. 51: Werner Stay/Bruce Coleman Inc. (top); Robert Kourik (bottom)
p. 52: © 2000 Michael S. Thompson
p. 54: Delilah Smittle, © The Taunton Press, Inc. (left); © Derek Fell (right)

Chapter 4
p. 56: © Ken Druse
p. 57: Richard Shiell (left); © Michael S. Thompson (center); Geoff Kidd/A-Z Botanical Collection Ltd. (right)
p. 59: Steve Silk, © The Taunton Press, Inc.
p. 60: Robert Kourik (top); Lee Anne White, © The Taunton Press, Inc. (bottom)
p. 63: Robert Kourik
p. 64: Delilah Smittle, © The Taunton Press, Inc. (top and bottom right); Robert Kourik (bottom left)
p. 66: © Ken Druse (top); © Derek Fell (bottom left); John Glover/Garden Picture Library (bottom right)
p. 68: J. Paul Moore/Garden Picture Library
p. 70: Howard Rice/Garden Picture Library (top); © Ken Druse (bottom)
p. 72: David Cavagnaro (top); © Michael S. Thompson (bottom)
p. 73: Mayer/Le Scanff/Garden Picture Library (top); John Glover/Garden Picture Library (bottom)
p. 74: Robert Kourik

Chapter 5
p. 75: © 2000 Janet Loughrey Photography
p. 76: Howard Rice/Garden Picture Library (left); Charles Mann (right)
p. 80: © Harry Haralambou (top left);Neil

Holmes/Garden Picture Library (top right); © Derek Fell (bottom left); Michael A. Dirr (bottom right)
p. 84: Neil Holmes/Garden Picture Library (top left); David Henderson/A-Z Botanical Collection Ltd. (top right); © 2000 Michael S. Thompson (bottom left); Robert Kourik (bottom right)
p. 85: Howard Rice/Garden Picture Library (left); J. Paul Moore (right)
p. 88: Densey Clyne/The Garden Picture Library

Chapter 6
p. 89: Richard Shiell
p. 91: Steve Silk, © The Taunton Press, Inc.
p. 93: Jerry Pavia (left); © 2000 Janet Loughrey Photography (right)
p. 94: Laura Riley/Bruce Coleman Inc.
p. 95:Robert Kourik (top); David Cavagnaro (bottom left and bottom right)
p. 97: Michael A. Dirr

Chapter 7
p. 98: Gene Ahrens/Bruce Coleman Inc.
p. 99: T. A. Allan/Out 'n' About Treehouse Institute & Treesort
p. 100: Susan A. Roth
p. 101: Andrew Ackerley/A-Z Botanical Collection Ltd. (top); © Derek Fell (bottom)
p. 103: Robert Kourik (left); © Derek Fell (right)

Chapter 8:
p. 107: Richard Shiell
p. 111: Melabee Miller/Envision
p. 112: Michael A. Dirr
p. 113: Robert Kourik
p. 115: David Cavagnaro (left); Robert Kourik (right)
p. 116: Neil Holmes/Garden Picture Library (top); Brian Carter/Garden Picture Library (bottom)
p. 117: Richard Shiell (top); Michael A. Dirr (bottom)
p. 118: Brigette Thomas/Garden Picture Library
p. 119: Malcolm Richards/A-Z Botanical Collection Ltd. (top); Richard Shiell (bottom)

Index

Note: References in bold indicate photos; references in italic indicate illustrations.